The Rise and Fall and Rise of Modern Dance

The Rise and Fall and Rise of Modern Dance

Don McDonagh

Dance Books
Cecil Court   London

This edition published in 1990 by arrangement with *a cappella books*
by Dance Books Ltd., 9 Cecil Court, London WC2N 4EZ.

British Library Cataloguing-in-Publication
Data available

Cover Photograph: *Imago,* choreographed by Alwin Nikolais
　　　　　　　　Performed by the Nikolais Dance Theater
　　　　　　　　Photograph by Tom Caravaglia
　　　　　　　　Courtesy Nikolais-Louis Dance Theater

Cover design: Fran Lee
Interior design/Editorial direction: Richard Carlin

ISBN 1 85273 020 X

Contents

I would like to thank all of those who generously gave of their time and skills to help me achieve a completed manuscript. In particular, I acknowledge the patience and insightful suggestions of my wife, Jenny. Thanks also to Arlene Croce for editorial assistance with the Robert Dunn interview. Janet Fennell and Jennifer Dunning always managed to find time to type yet another section of what probably seemed an endless stream of fragmentary pages and I thank them for their patient understanding.

Introduction

When I wrote this book, I was driven to do so out of a sense of fury. At the time it was a very polemical text. Today, it's history. The cozy world of modern dance in the early 1950's consisted of a handful of major companies. They performed in a limited number of acceptable performing venues. In general, modern dance enjoyed a sympathetic press in New York, its de facto home. The majors all had established studios and increasingly numbers of their students started performing careers or entered developing dance departments at the university level.

The "big four" of the 1930's founding generation were still at the helm of the major companies. Martha Graham was in full command of her creative powers that were undiminished until a decade later. During this exceptional period she brought out her first evening-long work, the powerful *Clytemnestra*. Her collaboration with sculptor Isamu Noguchi crested with *Seraphic Dialogue*, twenty years after they had begun to work together. In this time they evolved the finest scenic and performing arts collaboration in American theatrical history.

Doris Humphrey, who had been forced to retire from active performing in the middle 1940's because of an arthritic hip, was artistic advisor to the José Limón Company that carried on the tradition that she and Charles Weidman had established. Weidman continued to work on his own. Limón had begun to study with both in 1929 when he came to New York. Now, with his own company, he pushed forward creatively, and demonstrated his commitment to those humanistic concerns for an equitably ordered society that had marked much of the repertory of the Humphrey-Weidman company.

Hanya Holm had opened her own summer school of dance at Colorado College in Colorado Springs in 1941. Two years previously she had presented the first telecast dance in the United States, her *Metropolitan Daily*. In addition to her concert work she was much in demand as a choreographer on Broadway, including such musicals as *Kiss Me Kate*, *My Fair Lady*, and *Camelot*.

The critical establishment, led by daily critics John Martin of the *New York*

Times and Walter Terry of the *New York Herald Tribune*, were strongly committed to the narrative orientation of the modern-dance founders. Louis Horst, publisher of modern dance's house organ *Dance Observer*, was similarly oriented. A major concern of the field was respectability. It did not have a 300-year tradition as did ballet and so certain externals were deemed important. One of them was suitable (i.e. dignified/conventional) performing spaces. In Manhattan, it was commonly held that a Broadway Theater or the YM & YWHA at 92nd Street and Lexington Avenue were most suitable venues. The time for concerts in one's own studio, gymnasiums, or high-school auditoriums was over. Reviewers did not cover concerts in the outer boroughs or outside of the preferred venues.

Merce Cunningham, who had studied and performed with Graham in the 1940's, established his own company and scheduled its first New York season in 1953 at the Theater de Lys in Greenwich Village. Not a single program of the weeklong season was reviewed by the major dailies. A decade later in his *Book of the Dance,* John Martin saw fit to include a single small photograph of Cunningham with a caption that identified him as having "defected" from the Graham company. There was not one word about his work in the text.

The "big four" companies had tripled by the late 1950's in the geometric manner that modern dance has tended to develop. The aspiration of these younger choreographers was to have a yearly recital at the "Y" because a season on Broadway was financially out of reach. The "Y" instituted an audition process to select those lucky choreographers from among all who applied. Paul Taylor was welcomed and in 1957 did an "unacceptable" program and was informed that he would never be invited to appear in the house again. That was akin to expulsion from the "family."

There simply were not a sufficient number of "respectable" theaters to accommodate those young choreographers who needed to show their work. The churches came to the rescue. The first, and most notable, was Judson Memorial Church on Washington Square South. The choreographers who showed their work there were unbound by narrative or almost anything else that had been previously considered obligatory—certainly not "respectability."

I found their work provocative, humorous, and above all intelligent. It was unconventional by the standards of the time but it made sense to its small but growing audiences. The critical establishment at first reacted with indifference followed quickly by hostility. It was in reaction to this hostility to work which I respected that I decided to write about the young choreographers and their aesthetic concerns. Nothing in the reprinted text has been revised. It is what it was—a contemporary account unmediated by hindsight.

Don McDonagh
1990

Preface

Modern dance, the only form of serious, indigenous, theatrical dance developed entirely outside the tradition of classic ballet, reached a pinnacle of acclaim in the 1930's. It had been created out of the American experience in the same improvisational manner in which jazz had been created—as a method of dealing with artistic concerns removed from those of the formal schools. And it combined within itself the individual movement concerns of a handful of prodigiously talented choreographers, each of whom had channeled out a private dance approach.

What began around the turn-of-the-century as a revolt from the music hall and classic ballet had expanded by the late 1940's into accredited academic courses in the fine-arts departments of universities and colleges. The increasing acceptance of this once rebel art, however, also served to yoke the energies of the choreographers who followed modern dance's historic generation of the 30's. The frustration experienced by younger choreographers intensified toward the end of the 1950's. At that time, Connecticut College, modern dance's Bayreuth in New London, had become the summer home of the American Dance Festival (previously housed at Bennington College) and promulgated the fixed concerns of the earlier generation. A symbol of the fixity was the attitude of Louis Horst, whose career as composer, accompanist, friend, and theorist had spanned the modern dance years from 1915 to 1964, and who thundered against the newer developments in choreography. His once fervid enthusiasm for modern dance had turned into a series of cavils against the creative efforts of the younger generation. His creative composition course, which was the product of his understanding of the ideological currents of the 1930's, had fallen upon sterile days. He was totally out of sympathy with those whose dances did not fit into the categories of "primitive," "archaic," and "medieval," the touchstones of his diagnostic method. Horst's string of assistants—Anna Sokolow, Welland Lathrop, Nina Fonaroff, and Jack Moore—became the cushion between the curmudgeony old man and the students who still attended his course. (One of the pupils who had taken the course

twice was candid enough to remark that Lathrop had given it more imaginatively, on the West Coast, than Horst himself did in New York.)

When Paul Taylor, a brilliant dancer with the Martha Graham company
and a promising young choreographer, gave a program of "Seven New
Works" in 1957 at the Kaufmann Concert Hall of the YM & YWHA (New
York), Horst greeted him with a quarter column of blank space as a review
in *Dance Observer*. It was severe criticism, especially from the magazine that
was the advocate journal of modern dance and had been established by
Horst in 1934 to reflect the creative importance of the then fledgling art.

The ultimate blow against Taylor came from John Martin, the doyen of
dance critics, who had furthered modern dance tirelessly in the pages of the
New York Times (and had taught a course in critical writing at Bennington).
He chose not to review the concert at all. The works, his silence seemed to
imply, were beyond the scope of extant criticism and, worse, beyond the
realm of serious consideration.

John Martin, John MARTIN, JOHN MARTIN. It is difficult to convey
exactly what his endorsement meant to a dancer in the early days of
modern dance. It was more than just critical attention, it was a certification
of a special sort. There were other secondary critics whom a dancer could
cite, but John Martin's approval was something special.

A smile from Martin was enough to give a dancer courage to continue. A
favorable notice meant that it would be easier to tour, since dancers would
want to work with you. The universities after dutifully reading the pages of
the *New York Times* would want to have a company that was praised by John
Martin. John Martin had once gotten on a lecture platform with Martha
Graham during a course at The New School for Social Research and told
Michael Fokine, the great exemplar of the traditional Russian ballet, that he
was out of order. Martin said that "ballet had its chance too of saying what
it had to say during three centuries, so the modern dance has a right to talk
for three weeks." John Martin in effect looked at the tradition of the Russian
ballet and declared that it had had its chance, that it was time for another
form of dance to take over the center of the stage. He looked at the inheritor
of "Swan Lake" and "Sleeping Beauty," the man who had created the first
important plotless ballet, "Les Sylphides," who choreographed "The Dying Swan" for Pavlova, and who had collaborated with Stravinsky on
"Petrouchka" and told him that modern dance wanted a chance to make its
message known to the world. He told the product of centuries of ballet
training that there was a new approach to movement rampant and that this
new approach was going to carry the day.

John Martin, during his active newspaper career from 1927 to 1962, spoke
for a generation of dancers as no critic before or since had spoken. He stared
at traditional theatrical dance and relegated it to the position of "spectacle."
He was not impressed by its pedigree, by the fact that it had been nurtured
in the houses of kings and that royalty had given its vocabulary and its

Part One

Fall and Recovery

just dance—that the country had ever seen. Eventually even famous actresses came to study dance movement in order to move across the stage most effectively. Drama had come to dance for tutelage. The revolution had succeeded. Dance was accepted as one of the serious theater arts. Colleges granted degrees in dance, serious composers wrote scores for dancers, important fine artists devoted their talents to providing decors for dancers.

But then in the 1950's and 1960's the partisan John Martin, who had cradled modern dance in his understanding prose, ignored, as had Louis Horst, a new generation of dancers who followed in the footsteps of the pioneers he had championed. The distance between the generations was made completely visible in Martin's *Book of the Dance*, published in 1963, which ignored the presence of the brilliant Merce Cunningham, except for the inclusion of one small picture. There was indeed a generation gap.

The following pages will attempt to illuminate the current position of modern dance after the historic generation and the concerns of those contemporary choreographers who are steadily expanding their own creative ideas.

I have attempted to trace what appears to me to be the dominant concerns that link the work of the most exciting of the younger modern dance choreographers during the decade of the 1960's. (Some of the individuals included for discussion began their major work in the 1950's.) In order to place the work of the contemporary choreographer in context, a small sketch of modem dance history has been included. It does not claim to be exhaustive, although it does attempt to outline the major artistic concerns of each successive wave of choreographers. Because of space limitations, many of the current choreographers who would merit fuller consideration in a larger book have been clustered in anthology chapters. Though this does not allow for fully adequate examination of their individual contributions, it does at least serve the purpose of acknowledging them.

Modern dance as the term is popularly understood has an unnecessarily restrictive application. The term usually evokes only one phase (the 1930's) in the choreographic genealogy of serious theatrical dance outside of the ballet tradition. But in its broadest sense, the term properly connotes the works of both pioneer Isadora Duncan and contemporary Yvonne Rainer. Throughout the text I have used the term "historic" modern dance to identify the work of major choreographers of the 1930's and have retained the term modern dance for broader application. The name has never been completely satisfactory, but it serves to characterize creative dance activity that is not easily definable in terms of one special technique, such as ballet.

All of the dancers to whom an individual chapter is devoted have been interviewed at some length, and much of the personal historical information included in the profiles emerged in the course of these conversations.

prestige to ballet. He spoke on behalf of a doctor's daughter who had not seen a dance until she was thirteen, a girl from the lower East Side with a name adopted from mythology, and on behalf of a generation which wanted to say in movement those things which it was not able to express in any other way.

John Martin was more than a critic, he was an advocate, a friend, a champion; he understood, and even when he had to chastise in an unfavorable review, he did so with understanding. Often he took the recipient of a bad notice to lunch the next day. He was the patriarch of a family, a boisterous and sometimes quarrelsome one nonetheless united by interior blood ties and a special feeling that made it close ranks against any who wished to place it at a disadvantage by talking about technique at the expense of content. Hardnosed Agnes de Mille, who is eloquent in front of congressional committees, lost her voice for a week (she herself reports) when John Martin said a few kind words about her work.

Martin was the first full-time dance critic on any major newspaper in the country. It is to his undying credit that he saw the importance of the dance form that was struggling to be noticed in its formative years. A one-time actor turned journalist, Martin recognized that in the absence of a traditional dance discipline such as ballet, American dancers were trying to express in movement terms the concerns which were part of their lives and which they thought should be part of the theatrical life of the country. In 1926, he applied for the job as reviewer with the *New York Times* and a year later was allowed to assume the full-time position of dance critic.

The very title was a triumph. When Diaghilev's company was in the United States, through the sponsorship of opera buff Otto Kahn, its appearances were covered by one of the music reviewers. Through sheer chance Carl Van Vechten, who was the music critic assigned to the task, had an enormous sympathy for dance and wrote some of the most perceptive criticism on dance that the country has ever seen. But it was chance at best. The rule was ill-informed music or drama critics who were assigned to do dance performances in other parts of the country and could barely hide their boredom at what they considered a less than desirable assignment. It was commonly assumed that dance was meant to be seen and not thought about, that it did not deserve the critical attention, say, that one brought to the most recent touring Broadway show. Dance was, after all, simply dumb show or high kicking, and everyone knew that words were the most important thing in the theater, that dancing, to be effective, should be kept decoratively in the background.

Against a popular attitude of such monumental disdain, Martin pitted the courage of his convictions and his career. It really would have been safer to remain an actor than to risk exposure for itinerant dancers of no fixed abode. Martin took the chance and the dancers delivered that which he had foreseen they would. They created the most exciting form of theater—not

A Brief History of Modern Dance

The Pioneers

Modern dance began on the east and west coasts of the United States in the 1890's when Isadora Duncan, Loie Fuller, and Ruth St. Denis each came to practice a dance form for which there had been no descriptive category. Ballet, although at a low level of competence among American students, was a recognized discipline. In addition to ballet, the only other form with which the public had any familiarity was show dancing. This mode comprised an exceptionally varied range of movements, for minstrel and vaudeville show dancers had adopted material everywhere, from black dancing observed in the South to semi-balletic specialties. In the case of both styles—ballet and show dancing—the intent of the dancers was to reach for and touch the spectator in a light, non-demanding way. They were there to entertain, not to inform or to stimulate.

It was the desire to inform that became the driving motivation that created the modern dance movement. The three first-generation pioneers—Duncan, Fuller, St. Denis—each created an individual approach to dancing and never saw any reason to modify it in accordance with what anyone else had done. They each formed a movement style tailor-made for their own choreographic intentions. This expression of individuality became one of the hardest held tenets of modern dancers. It was the source of much of its strength as well as its organizational difficulties.

Isadora Duncan was born in San Francisco in 1878, where she received some early ballet training and was continually exposed to concert-level music through her music-teacher mother. Duncan recounts how she interpreted music even as a small child and showed a precocious self-reliance before her teens. Having decided that she did not like ballet, she then proceeded to examine her own movements to discover exactly where movement originated. Since she thought that ballet dancers moved like mechanical people, she had to discover the source of her own movement. She decided that it came from the solar plexus and flowed outward. The

3

combination of this outward flow and her own deep understanding of music eventually made Duncan the international force that she was.

She headed for the New York stage and attempted to make a career in dance there. She found that the producers of theatrical spectacle were not interested in dancing with a message but only in a well-turned leg shown prominently to the audience. Dancers were not supposed to have thoughts. Whenever Duncan expressed some of her aspirations to producers, they would explain exactly what they wanted, and she found herself high-kicking to Sousa's "The Washington Post March" or performing mime or small dance interludes in Shakespeare. She left the regular theater and went to the period's equivalent of off-Broadway in an attempt to escape from commercialism. The only off-Broadway theater which then existed was in the salons of society ladies who invited poets to read, dancers to dance, and musicians to play. It was a system modeled on that of continental salons. It was precious and inbred, but became the means of earning a livelihood for Duncan. She danced in many of the homes of New York ladies and was invited to Newport to perform during the season. It was a meager existence but enabled her to survive outside of the commercial theater.

Inevitably she found that she wanted to have broader horizons, and looked to Europe. The immediate attraction in Europe was London, and she managed to get herself and her family, including her mother, there in 1899 by charitable contributions from society ladies. In London, she danced in salons as she had done in New York, with about as much success. It was a trip to Paris a year later, and the salon performances there, that was the turning point—it was a triumph for her. She received the type of critical attention that she had not been able to attract in New York or London. She was seen and admired by writers, musicians, and sculptors.

Her career for the remainder of her life remained oriented toward Europe and European taste. She was not to return to the United States again until 1909. She came again periodically afterward to tour but remained firmly based in Europe. There she was received with respect, something which had eluded her in her native United States.

Western Europe at the time of Duncan's arrival was languishing in terms of dance. Ballet was definitely pallid and did not revive until 1909, when the first season of the Diaghilev Ballets Russes took place. Previously various types of exotic dancers had come to appear in Europe from the East, Middle East, and finally from the United States and were all received with varying interest.

The American dancers made a spectacular impression. Loie Fuller was the first to appear in Paris, followed by Duncan in 1900, and by St. Denis a few years later in 1906. All were hailed as messengers of a better and profounder world of dance experience than had been seen for a long time.

Loie Fuller, who had had a spectacular European commercial success prior to Duncan's and artistic acclaim as well, invited Duncan to come with her on a tour of Germany. The result of the tour was that Duncan was engaged to appear for a month in Budapest. It was the longest engagement that she had ever had and the broadest public that she had ever played to. After Budapest she began a steady routine of touring which brought her across Europe and Russia. Critical acclaim was hers, and wherever she went she tried to set up a school to teach children the rudiments of her art and to rear them in a school system which would not crush their creative instincts. The schools were established in Berlin, New York, Paris, and Moscow but none of them proved satisfactory in the end. Her "technique" was not one which was easily transmitted except in her own enthusiastic presence, for it was not so much a technique as a mental attitude in approaching movement.

Duncan believed in the total importance of music, whether it was the music produced through reading poetry or that of serious composers. She felt that carefully listening to music would produce within one those sensations which were naturally translated into movement. Once one had heard the inner life of music, then one would begin to move in a perfectly balanced and artistic manner. Toward the end of her life she lamented that others who thought that they were doing Duncan movement were in effect destroying her theories. She was particularly annoyed about schools of "plastique" dance or music interpretation which had sprung up in imitation of her own pioneering in this field. The melting of one static pose into another was not dancing to her mind. She strove for an abstract idealization of the music in movement rather than a mirror of it, and it was this abstracting principle of her work which she and she alone seemed able to convey to pupils. Even she was unable to do this, or provide any method of achieving such harmonious and spontaneous movement, except by example. There are various schools which carry on in the tradition of Duncan but none which produced any talent comparable with hers.

Her contribution to modern dance was not destined to come from direct imitation of her methods or the application of her theories but from an appreciation of her seriousness. She did believe that dancing was the basis of all theatrical art and that it came before drama. It was the fundamental performing discipline and was one which was not to be relegated to an inconsequential place in the theater. Her insistence on the point was such that it continually overrode conventional common sense in her personal life. Early in her career she even refused to appear at a time when she was desperately in need of money because the booking agent wanted to advertise her as "the first barefoot dancer." She was not going to be presented as a freak or a music hall curiosity. She was a serious dancer and would win the respect to which that status entitled her.

As a serious artist, she danced using the music of serious composers and not facile spinners of melodic webs. Even in Russia where ballet was accorded an honored position in the theater, music was not highly regarded in relation to dance. Being appointed to the official post of musician in the Imperial Ballet Theater system was much like being made the poet laureate in Great Britain. The post demanded suitable "pièces d'occasion" but not inspiration. Occasionally something good would come of the arrangement but more often not.

Into the mildly contemptuous atmosphere of soothing aural blandness, Duncan introduced Wagner, Beethoven, and Chopin. Working with first-rank composers was one of the most important factors in her pursuit of dance seriousness. After Duncan died, concert-caliber music had been claimed for dance, but most importantly, dance was exerting a serious theatrical presence.

Loie Fuller, who was sixteen years Duncan's senior, was equally serious about dancing but conceived of it as a combination of light and motion effects, representational in nature, rather than as an emotional conceptualization. She entered the theater in 1864 at an early age, two and a half by her own reckoning, reciting inspirational religious verses. She developed into a bit player in comedy and had some success as a minor comedienne. At no point in her career does it appear that she had ever had any serious dance training. She was set on her dancing career by chance. Appearing in a play, she improvised a scene in which she was to be hypnotized. The impact of the swirls and floating lightness of her silk dress achieved a great success and she began to appear independently as a dancer. The effects that she was able to achieve with her use of flowing light-weight materials and imaginative lighting were unique on the stage at the time and she was in considerable demand.

She was the first of the pioneer trio to visit Europe. Her initial tour was in Germany and then she traveled to France in 1892. She secured a job at the Folies Bergère and rapidly became known for a program of four dances—"The Serpentine," "The Violet," "The Butterfly," and "The White Dance"—which took about forty-five minutes to perform. As she conceived of dance, it was the natural reflex of the body to ideas. Her ideas tended to be highly pictorial and illustrational. They consisted for the most part of imitating natural phenomena such as flowers or the movement of flame or of insects such as the butterfly. The dances were not so much an abstraction of phenomena as a representation of them. Duncan, whose wrath was later aroused by such visual realization of music, had nothing but praise for Fuller's art. Her testimony and that of other contemporaries reveals that there were a considerable number of imitators of Fuller but that none of them was able to hold the attention as well as did the originator of the form. In this, Fuller was like Duncan—she could be copied but not successfully imitated.

Fuller's body was far from the shape of the dancer of today. She was bulky, and her dances were mainly levered from the torso and relied upon the exceptional sensitivity of her arm movements, often encased in yards of cloth. She did not attempt nor did she need the elevation that would come from a jump. Through the deft use of supports inside of her draperies she could extend her effective control over a large area of the stage. These sticks enabled her to create movement patterns that radiated out from herself in the manner that a butterfly's wings articulate from a small core. She was passionately devoted to the use of light and it was the combination of light and large areas of cloth that enabled her to create her special kind of visualizations. She explored the possibilities of stage lighting and properties as an expressive medium in a way that was not seen in the dance theater until the mature work of Alwin Nikolais. Fuller never appeared without her team of electricians. She was secretive about this aspect of her art to such a degree that it probably was the significant factor that made her presentations so different from those of her imitators. There probably were any number of imitators who had equal facility in the manipulation of light-weight materials but none were able to combine the shapes so formed with the dramatic lighting that Fuller employed.

Like Duncan after her, she was appreciated seriously in Europe to a degree that was not matched in the United States, although she did have successful engagements in her native land. Writers in particular were attracted to Fuller. Yeats mentioned her in "1919," Alexander Dumas encouraged her to write her memoirs, and Anatole France contributed an appreciation to her completed book.

Unlike Duncan, who hated the commercial theater, Fuller reveled in it and its technical effects. By the time that she had finished her active career, she had demonstrated that cloth animated by the human form moving through space could create plastic shapes having an impermanent but powerful effect. It was a revelation of dancing that had nothing to do with physical technique except of a very modest order, but one that could have great theatrical impact. In some ways, it was an even more fundamental break from the idea of dancing then current than was Duncan's physical expressiveness. Despite the fact that Duncan did not appear conventionally corseted or in shod feet, she was a person. Fuller was like a moth in a beam of light. She abjured personality and contented herself with becoming a radiant entity. A complete child of the theater, she had extended its expressive range through dance.

Overt mysticism entered the blood stream of modern dance when Ruth St. Denis decided upon her career. Like Duncan and Fuller, St. Denis began her career in the theater. She eventually abandoned it in the early 1930's to devote her time more fully to realizing that blend of spirituality and physical movement that had always been her primary interest in dancing. If Duncan was the wayward heart of modern dance and Fuller the technical head, then St. Denis would be the spiritualized longing that inspired so many to enter dancing as a career.

St. Denis was born Ruth Dennis in 1877. As a child she was put through a system of popular rhythmic exercises by her mother and later permitted to take lessons from a local dancing teacher. She was reared in a religiously aware home and was sent to a denominational school from which she was expelled over a dispute concerning school theatricals. She decided to pursue her dancing career seriously and even attempted ballet class but did not find it at all to her liking. She eventually began to appear in modest dance entertainments and tried out for Broadway plays as a dancer. She was successful in a small way and at one point attracted the attention of David Belasco, the producer who was somewhat disappointed at her prim deportment and nicknamed her "Saint" Dennis. Abbreviating the first name and dropping an "n" from her family name, she evolved her stage name. An exceptionally attractive young woman, she was to draw the attention of Stanford White, the architect of Judson Church (destined to be the cradle of the 1960's dance revolution), who adopted the avuncular role of protector. He helped her with small sums of money and encouragement, evidently for the satisfaction of seeing her career develop.

When White first saw her, she was struggling along doing catch-as-catch-can jobs that brought in enough money to sustain her but little out of which one could project a career. She made her formal decision to change from a standard show dancer and become an innovator in Buffalo, New York, while on tour with a musical. Although she had been impressed with Loie Fuller a few years previously, she had not made any final career determinations until the epiphany produced by the sight of a cigarette poster. She and a friend were sitting in a drug store when St. Denis became inordinately attracted to a poster of the Egyptian goddess Isis on a pack of Egyptian Deities cigarettes. She asked her friend to buy the poster no matter how much it cost and bring it back to their room afterward. St. Denis studied the figure as another might study a textbook. She was thoroughly enchanted with the quiet power of the deity and began to evolve ways to duplicate it. By the time that the company had reached San Francisco on its tour, she had created a costume imitative of the figure and posed in it for a photographer. The dance ideas which had been germinating finally evolved into a series of pieces that she performed in a solo recital in 1906. Dancing still was of little consequence in the East Coast cultural community and the matinee performances had to be sponsored by society women. It had to be a matinee because female dance soloists were not considered serious enough fare for evening performances. (Three years later, in 1909, St. Denis was to break down this barrier.) The proceeds from the matinee series gave her enough money to go to Europe, where she had a spectacular success. She followed in the footsteps of Fuller and Duncan and was well received in Paris. (She even duplicated an awkward experience of Duncan's. Individually and years apart, each had been invited to the studio of Auguste Rodin to pose for the venerable sculptor. Both were taken aback by the amorous interest of the elderly artist and both fled from his studio.)

St. Denis went on to Germany, where she found herself caught up in a circle of writers and musicians. Enthusiasm for her work in Germany was so high that she was offered an extensive contract and a theater to be constructed according to her own specifications if she would remain there. Her decision was to return to the United States and around 1910 begin a series of cross-country performances.

Her dances up until this time were solos—"Incense," "Radha," "The Cobras," and "Nautch"—for which she drew heavily on Near and Far Eastern thematic material. There was a definitely exotic appearance to these dances which St. Denis sustained with skillful costuming and flowing body movements. Her special talent lay in the area of the upper torso, with a special sinuousness flowing across the chest and into the arms. These were of unusual suppleness, so much so that doctors in Germany asked if they could examine her arms to determine whether they were anatomically different from those ordinarily encountered. Nothing unusual was found in the structure—only in performance. Shortly after her return to the United States, she choreographed and performed the lead role in a full evening dance-drama "Egypta." The work was not particularly successful and when her backer died in the sinking of the *Titanic,* she returned to vaudeville to support herself.

Several years later, in 1914, she decided that she would form a small company which would feature herself and a male partner to do social dancing such as Irene and Vernon Castle were then doing with popular success. She chose Ted Shawn for her partner, and they were married shortly afterward.

The Denishawn company developed out of their union, and during the 1920's was the chief dance force in the United States. It blended a seriousness of purpose with a show-business intelligence that had not been seen in the American theater up until that time. Denishawn schools were established across the country and the company toured in the United States and abroad.

Almost from the beginning of the company in 1919, Louis Horst had been its musical director. As a composer, he insured that the company's musical standard was constantly infused with the advanced music of the day. As a result, Shawn once created a dance to the "Gnossienne, Number 1" of Erik Satie, who at the time was almost unknown in the United States. Later, again with Horst's aid, he was to use music of Honegger for one of his first all-male dances, "Pacific 231."

St. Denis had been a ringing success as a solo star. She was to go on to greater commercial and historical success with Shawn as her partner. Alone among the trio of pioneer women dancers, St. Denis could look upon

Ruth St. Denis in a characteristic pose. (Courtesy of Robert Williams, Friends of Terpsichore)

succeeding generations of dancers who had sprung from her successful partnership with Shawn in the Denishawn venture. The other pioneers, Fuller and Duncan, while they possessed theatrical magic in their own persons, were unable to produce any line of succession to themselves. All they could engender were imitators of lesser competence. It was through her progeny that St. Denis was to become the first lady of American dance. Her special brand of inspirational encouragement was a vital force in the growth of the modern dance.

Ted Shawn's most outstanding characteristic has been zeal, an enormous thirst for and belief in activity. He was the motivating force behind the entire Denishawn operation of touring companies and schools. He set up the curricula of these schools so that all sorts of dance instruction were given, from classical ballet right through to as much ethnic dance as a pupil had time to absorb. At the same time he continually busied himself with plans for new productions, new tours, and arranging for new places in the United States or abroad to which the Denishawn troupes could go. At one point in 1924 to 1925 he put together twenty-eight weeks of touring during one season, which was unheard of in the United States for a dance company of any description. His final coup for Denishawn was a fifteen-month tour of the Orient starting in 1925. It was the flower of his efforts on behalf of the company.

The relentless one-night stands of the company created an audience for dancing that had not existed before. Other dance troupes and extravaganzas had remained the memory of a single night or week, but Denishawn established schools and repeated their tours. They were part of the theatrical life of the country in a way that no other dance troupes had managed to be, no matter how successful an individual appearance might have been. Denishawn meant theatrical dancing.

In 1931, Shawn and Denis separated to pursue their own individual careers. St. Denis devoted her time to working with the combination of religious ritual and dance expression that had been so vital a part of her life. During this period she performed in churches and at her studio in New York. Later St. Denis and Shawn reunited for performances at the Museum of Natural History and subsequently at Jacob's Pillow in Becket, Massachusetts, where Shawn had established his summer home and the first festival devoted solely to dance in the United States.

After separating from St. Denis, Shawn created a group of male dancers with whom he toured up until 1940. He was determined to prove that dancing was a profession that men could take up and not have to apologize for. The numbers of male pupils in various dance schools is a tribute to his efforts. Without the balancing presence of a male, modern dance would have remained unbalanced in terms of development. It would have stayed in the special realm of a society lady's divertissement. Shawn was the arch-evangelist with a message to sell and that message was dance. He was at times indiscriminate in his advocacy of dance, but his basic enthusiasm for people who could move came through everything that he did or wrote.

The Jacob's Pillow Dance Festival each summer has emerged as his final contribution to dancing. He always insists upon balanced programs of ethnic, ballet, and modern dance, and has pioneered in the effort to bring foreign touring companies to the United States. He was the first to ask the Ballet Rambert, the Western Theater Ballet, stars of the Royal Danish Ballet, and many others to this country. Shawn's contribution to dance has been that of an inspired advocate and performer rather than that of an inspired choreographer.

As a company, Denishawn had the tendrils of art nouveau wrapped around it, still glowed with the iridescence of Tiffany stained-and-swirled glass; it swathed itself in the atmosphere of the exotic. Its approach to dance was personal and at times even gnostic, drawing on the glamour of the remote or the mysterious for its interest. It was not an approach that could be used to conceptualize the immediacy of people struggling to reconstitute the formal order. It was private and not public in its concern with order. It attempted to define an area of epicurean artistic sensibility that isolated a portion of life from mundane concern. It did not attempt to change its milieu but only to permit elevated breathing space within it. It did, however, spawn major choreographic talents who did want to change the social and intellectual order. The young choreographers—Martha Graham, Doris Humphrey, and Charles Weidman—who were to grow out of Denishawn, repudiated its "dancing gods and goddesses" approach and attempted to express in dance movement the changed ideology of the contentious years between two world wars. This second wave of theatrical dance, created outside of the ballet tradition, distinguished its "concrete" aims from those of the founder generation's by perjoratively labeling the achievement of the latter "romantic" dance.

The Historic Generation

Martha Graham, Doris Humphrey, and Charles Weidman all left Denishawn within five years of one another (1923–1928), and in the subsequent two decades forged the sensibility of that special blend of serious theatrical dance that has traditionally meant "modern dance." Graham was the first to leave and was the first to give her own solo recital outside of the nest of Denishawn. After she left, she initially secured a job in the Greenwich Village Follies, where she achieved a popular success. As she herself recalled, "I could have stayed there and done sexy little things." However, she decided that it was not the sort of dancing for which she had left Denishawn. Entertainment was for the less dedicated who might choose to remain at the Greenwich Village Follies, art was for those who chose to dance outside that to which the popular taste had become accustomed.

Inevitably the first few recitals that Graham gave were strongly touched with the exotic, which she had absorbed from Denishawn. Leonide Massine engaged her to dance the "Chosen" in his production of "Rite of Spring," but she did not begin to establish her true voice until 1929 with the creation of "Heretic" and "Sketches for the People," which were studies for mass movements. They combined both a concern with form that had not been part of her Denishawn training and a clear social message. "Heretic," which was constructed on a central group from which dancers broke away and returned only to break away again in a different timing and phrasing, was particularly successful. In the following year, she tried and then abandoned her only attempt at producing a dance without a musical accompaniment, "Project in Movement for a Divine Comedy." From this point onward, she would work with scores, and as she developed further in her career, only with scores which she herself had commissioned.

Although her work slipped back and forth between the narrative and the abstract as her descriptive and poetical titles indicated, she tended to favor the dramatic side of her talent rather than the strictly abstract. Occasionally there would be an exquisite fusion of the two in dances such as "Primitive Mysteries" (1931) or "Frontier" (1935), but the basis of her work had a secure emotive foundation. She was not often drawn into social themes of such explicitness that they could only have meaning to an audience experiencing the political or social rigors of the time, although the Spanish Civil War caused her to choreograph "Immediate Tragedy" (1937). Most often she was able to keep a balance between the artistic and the political. The absence of such balance resulted in many other choreographers creating dances that have become as shopworn as outdated news.

Graham's specific reaction to the lush Oriental sinuosity that had characterized her experience in Denishawn was at first to emphasize a percussive spareness in her work that left much to the viewer to fill out in terms of movement. She would sharply accent a gesture and then, for example, rather than perform a full circular arm movement, would only sketch out an arc for the viewer to complete. She evolved a naturalistic approach to movement based on the in-and-out rhythm of breathing, which became codified as the contraction and release of tension. She constantly strove to idealize the particular and not to become enmeshed in authenticated time and place in her early work. The line of development which resulted from an early trip to New Mexico produced works like "Two Primitive Canticles," "Incantation," "Dolorosa" (all 1931), and "Ceremonials" (1932), in which she distilled a pre-Christian religious sentiment into generally applicable terms.

She later began to develop a line of choreography which dealt with the specifically American mythic heritage. The first of these works was "Frontier." It was also the first time that she had used decor, and it inaugurated her long-time association with Isamu Noguchi, who was to provide her with the finest sustained collaboration on decor that has been developed in the American theater.

"Frontier" revealed a softness hitherto absent from her work. It combined nostalgia and warmth with formal precision. It was a solo of enormous power in which a single woman staked out an area of control in the center of an infinite plain through a sequence of carefully controlled movements. It combined the adventurousness of the pioneer with the vulnerability that accompanies such resolute colonizing efforts in a strange land.

The American experience was to provide Graham with one of the richest veins of source material for her dances. She had always been interested in myth, whether couched in universal non-differentiated terms such as "Primitive Mysteries" and the later "Dark Meadow" (1946) or as expressed through the national consciousness of individual peoples. After her American phase, she was to explore the sagas of classical antiquity in Greek and Hebrew myth. The peak of her development of these themes was reached in the full-evening work "Clytemnestra" (1958), which recounted the unhappy plight of the Grecian queen. Her most recent work has been in the form of reflective exercises covering ground that she had previously charted. Her development of a technique of movement designed to present her dances with their full emotional impact has been one of her most outstanding achievements.

It was an achievement with mixed blessings. Totally responsive to her own creative desires, it was not always a suitable vocabulary for dancers from her own company who wished to choreograph works themselves. It became apparent that only those who strongly modified the Graham technique for their own creative purposes were able to create a body of dances which revealed their special concerns rather than a watered-down reflection of Graham. Merce Cunningham and Erick Hawkins, who had danced with the company and who had also had strong ballet training, were able to forge technical instruments to suit themselves. The choreographic efforts of Helen McGehee, Bertram Ross, Ethel Winter, and Yuriko, to name only the most famous of the Graham dancers, never have quite emerged from the shadow cast by Graham's accomplishment. The vocabulary which had been such a supple instrument in the powerful imagination of Graham became less forceful in the hands of others.

Graham's concerns were with mythic material as it existed in an almost Jungian sense as part of a universal mental deposit of mankind. Although she used specific national stories for most of her works, the themes which they were concerned with did not have only a local application. As a twentieth-century American, she appropriated the classical mythology

Marthia Graham and Erick Hawkins in "Puritan Love Duet" from *American Document*, 1938. Photo © Barbara Morgan, 1980

with the same quest for structure as great dramatists had. The stories were concerned with human experience and provided a framework within which another time could pour its own experience. There was room enough for a contemporary dancer to express in movement that which the common experience of another people had cherished in dramatic form.

That Graham was not entirely bound by stories is shown by the number of abstract works she created throughout her career. She did, however, bring to all her work a unifying conception that was linear in development. Random things rarely occurred in any Graham composition. They occurred neither in the music she commissioned, nor in the costuming and decors which clothed her works, nor in the movement that gave them their impetus. Her long-time musical director, Louis Horst (who had left Denishawn to study composition in Vienna and then joined Graham), encouraged her thematic conceptions of dance and encouraged her to work with music of a suitable nature. His own stated conviction regarding music was that it was a useful frame for dance. He compared its function to what an actual frame could do for a picture. It was a modest statement for one who had created some of Graham's most interesting scores but betrayed a mental set that was no more able to conceive of a painting without a frame than of dance without similarly structured limits. The idea was of a dance being an entity of clear and unambiguous import, neatly existing within the discipline of the stage framework—of dance that, like an easel picture, would not venture outside of its frame.

One of the things that directed the course of modern dance powerfully, and that was encouraged by Horst, was the drive for intellectual respectability. The one-night stands in one-horse towns did not have sufficient status for the second generation of dancers. They were serious and gravitated toward the universities for support and encouragement. They did not dance to entertain, they danced to uplift, instruct, or disturb. Unlike a previous generation, they wanted to accredit dance scholastically as a fine art like painting or music. Showman Shawn later snapped that he was glad that he hadn't "turned morbid." It was the reaction of many who could not readily accustom themselves to the "ugliness" of modern dance. The second generation were heedless and prepared their assault on the American consciousness.

One interesting sidelight about their desire for respectability was that it led them to rent Broadway houses whenever they wanted to put together a season. It was a lesson that had been learned from the Denishawn experience. Major houses were a form of respectability.

Doris Humphrey, who had been at the Denishawn school and in the Denishawn troupe at the same time as Graham and Horst, decided at the end of the Denishawn Oriental tour in 1927 that changes were needed in the direction of the company. When these changes were not forthcoming, she and Charles Weidman both chose not to appear at the Ziegfeld Follies with Shawn and St. Denis but to take charge of the Denishawn school in New York instead. A year later they set up their own school. (Graham had already had her first season of dances and had been joined by Louis Horst on his return from Vienna.)

Charles Weidman and Doris Humphrey's first season in New York was a success. The two complemented each other. Humphrey, who was the more theoretically inclined of the two, set about to create a new dance language in much the way that Graham was doing with her conception of contraction and release of tension. Humphrey's discovery lay in the conception of dancing as an activity that lay between the two polar extremes of balance and unbalance, fall and recovery. This rigorously intellectual approach to dance, coupled with her early intimation that natural phenomena were properly the subject matter of dance, produced dances like "Water Study" and "The Life of the Bee" (1928). Weidman, who was not so rigorously inclined to recreate universal dance movement out of a basic exploration of the motivational centers of activity, provided pantomimic studies like "Japanese Actor" and "Singhalese Drum Dancer" (1928) to complement Humphrey's architectural ordering of space. It was a combination that worked well together and Humphrey-Weidman concerts followed this basic pattern until the pair split in 1945.

Humphrey was attracted by the logical and Weidman was attracted by the illogical, and both demonstrated a skill for abstracting the essential elements of a situation. With Humphrey it came to the fore in the structuring of "The Shakers" in 1931, and even more clearly later in 1931 to 1932 in "Two Ecstatic Themes: Circular Descent, Pointed Ascent." Weidman's dissecting sensibility was more subtle but equally operative. It consisted of drawing a movement from commonplace incident and using it as a dance unit removed from the emotionally charged situation in which it had originally occurred. The peak of this line of development in his craft was reached in "Kinetic Pantomime," which was premiered in 1934. It was a collection of gestural pantomime joined by abstract dance movement in which a motion would begin as one thing and then change into another, much in the way that an object in a surrealist painting would be a cliff and then metamorphose into a face.

Weidman is a brilliant mime, and despite some of the formal explorations that he made in such dances as "Two Preludes" and "Dance Profane," his basic imitative and comic skill is what determined the tonality of his work. He has created a number of dances employing his humorously sharp observations of social and personal characteristics, such as "And Daddy Was a Fireman" and "Flickers" (1936), and the realization of selected James Thurber fables in "Fables for Our Time" (1948). Most recently he has been performing in a loft studio in a series in which he collaborates with the graphic artist Mikhail Santaro. The output of recent years has not been distinguished. Abstract dance works that he has created have not shown a

Doris Humphrey and Charles Weidman in *Square Dance*, 1938. Photo © Barbara

great deal of vigor. But his eloquent hands can still frame characterization vignettes, many of which have been of those personages with whom he has been connected in the past.

Humphrey on the other hand moved more and more toward a heroic ideal. With the creation of "New Dance" in 1935–36, the first really long piece she had attempted with her new vocabulary, the methodology she had adopted was greatly extended. In the three sections of the work— "Theater Piece," "With My Red Fires," and "New Dance"—individuals were cast as types and the unifying theme of the work was the harmonious development of people within a society. The somewhat simplistic distillation of individual human experience suggested the unreal aspect of allegory but had the monumentality that was congenial to modern dance forms at the time.

Two years later, Humphrey overstepped the ideological mark of the period with her dance "Passacaglia in C Minor" (1938) to Bach's score. It was criticized in strong terms as being formalist and without social content and was compared most unkindly to Massine's symphonic ballets. The comparison was a revelation of how profoundly disappointed the modern dance audience was in the turn that Humphrey's work had taken, for to this audience ballet was the enemy. It is difficult to convey the depth of feeling that the second generation of modern dancers and their partisans felt about classic ballet. It was consistently characterized as being "outmoded," and Diaghilev, the catalyst of modern ballet, was referred to derogatorily as a "promoter." When Vakhtang Chaboukiani, one of the great Soviet dancers and one of the legendary figures of Russian ballet, appeared in New York, it was suggested by *Dance Observer* that he would be better seen in the equivalent of Radio City Music Hall than at Carnegie Hall.

The reaction to her "Passacaglia" was a blow to Humphrey and she never again wandered as far in her abstracting approach to dance. Her work took the direction of expressing social commentary in generalized thematic terms, generally displaying a concern for economic inequities or political imbalances. She continued working throughout the Second World War, became a founder member of the dance faculty of the Juilliard School of Music, and died in 1958.

The choreographers who had appeared out of the companies of Graham, Humphrey, and Weidman continued for the most part to explore thematic material that reflected social anxiety, but with diminished incisiveness. Something was seriously wrong. The modern dance world had struggled for recognition through the thirties and forties and had achieved what it set out to do, but there was no one in sight who seemed capable of significantly extending the body of work that had been created. The wars for academic and performing respectability had been won, but institutionalizing modern dance also had stultified its choreographic spontaneity.

Universities offered dance as a credit-carrying major and would grant a degree to dance candidates. However, the Bennington Summer Festival, which in 1934 had been the meeting point of all of the early creators, decided in 1940 that the festival should be broadened to include all of theater arts and should not concentrate just on dance. It was a blow for modern dancers who had regarded Bennington as their private haven. After the Second World War, in 1948, Connecticut College began to function much as Bennington had done earlier, as an institutionalized meeting place and workshop for modern dance. It encouraged choreographic explorations, but according to the established formula. Musicians, choreographers, and designers gathered for a six-week summer course which provided substantial support for many upon which they could establish an economically stable year of performance and teaching. Dance concert bookings, normally thin in summer, were bridged by the college.

In New York, the Kaufmann Concert Hall of the Young Men's and Young Women's Hebrew Association on 92nd Street and Lexington Avenue had been one of the early bastions of modern dance. Under the direction of William Kolodney, who was the head of the Educational Department, dance in the 1930's became an important part of the cultural life of the institution. In the middle 1940's, a system of new choreographers' concerts was set up to provide a showplace for developing talent. Under the system a jury would select promising young choreographers who would present a program of works. Normally four or five choreographers would appear together. Soon it was expected that the more talented would go on to present half a program in subsequent years and then finally a concert composed entirely of their own works. It was like being a matriculated student. The selection committee relied heavily on the standards of modern dance of the 1930's to make their selections. The number of dancers wishing to give concerts at the "Y" increased steadily, until in 1954 a requirement was made for an audition of completed work for any unknown choreographer, after which the jury then decided whether or not to allow the choreographer to rent the hall. It was the start of an increasingly tight contraction, which forced young performers to seek elsewhere for an opportunity to display their works. What was, on the part of the "Y," a regulating necessity became in fact a choking collar for many young choreographers. It was a form of means test to which many were unwilling to submit.

However, there were not that many other places to perform in New York. Henry Street Playhouse was one. Dance Associates, guided by James Waring, found another in the Master Institute (310 Riverside Drive, New York). But the difficulties felt by younger choreographers were not clearly seen, because many of those who had succeeded Graham, Humphrey, and Weidman were achieving a popular success. Strangely enough, it was in the area of the commercial Broadway theater that a number of dancers—Anna Sokolow (of the Graham company), Hanya Holm, and Valerie Bettis—danced or choreographed. The commercial theater previously had been considered a seductive temptation and it was disturbing for the audience to find modern dance energy being expended outside of the concert hall.

There was one choreographer, however, who inherited the dedication and adherence to the dance ideals of the second generation and avoided Broadway, and that was José Limón. He became the lion of the ever-hopeful Connecticut College directors. Limón had come to the United States from his native Mexico in the late 1930's and became a member of the Humphrey-Weidman troupe. He was a powerful dancer and a choreographer of some promise. After his military service in World War Two, he returned to the concert dance field with a small company and progressed to the point where he had a substantial performing ensemble. He was in sympathy with the socially oriented and narrative ideas of Doris Humphrey, who assisted him as artistic director of his company, and he produced a string of works that showed thematic cleanness and systematic development. Most notable among them were "La Malinche" (1947) and "The Moor's Pavane" (1949). Each was a playlet, the latter being drawn from Shakespeare's tragedy *Othello* and the former from Mexican folk sources, and each told its story in unambiguous and inventive terms.

The four character dancers in "Moor's Pavane" consisted of the Moor and his bride and two malevolent "friends" who destroyed the happiness of the couple in the movements of a formal dance that kept passions carefully channeled until the murderous explosion. "La Malinche," with similar formal control, again displayed the disruption of a relationship, this time between a native boy and his woman after the appearance of a foreign conqueror. The dance begins as if the dancers were a group of strolling players recreating a story. The three personages enter gaily and then actually begin a serious dance conflict. When the native boy and girl are successfully reunited, the three gather together again and exit as they had entered, not as dancers in a drama but performers in an entertainment.

For the larger ensemble which he began to work with, Limón created "There Is a Time" (1954), a beautiful dance based on the cyclical order laid down in a scriptural passage from Ecclesiastes. After this, Limón began to create even larger-scaled works that retained his choreographic fluency but tended to be less substantive. He began to draw more heavy-handedly on social themes, which had a power of their own, creating dances in which the dance element became subordinate to the thematic crisis. "Missa Brevis" (1958) detailed the attempts of citizens of a bomb-ravaged city to build their lives again. "Psalm" (1967) was based on the inhumanity of the concentration camp, and "Legend" (1968), on the inequities of the system of nineteenth-century slavery as practiced in the United States. Parts of these works had choreographic interest, especially in the solos he created for his leading dancers, but increasingly they were removed from the movement concerns of the succeeding generation, which did not have a specific interest in stories and their development and whose members wished to explore the possibilities of personal non-literal dance development. Limón, however, continued to be the cornerstone of the Connecticut College seasons and was seen by *Dance Observer* as the major direct connecting link with the past.

The core problem for historical modern dance, from its own perspective, was advocacy for something outside of the self. It courted causes and found abstracted personal movement generally unsuited to express dramatic conflicts. It sought thematic material in universal mythology or in the energetic struggle of the civil arena. The individual played out his role as a representative of a vast shadowy epic. His personal sexual concerns—of some interest to this generation—became blended into the universal pageant of the Freudian conception of the unconscious, and his social concerns into the structured sweep of mythic models or contemporary philosophies. But the battering of contending ideologies, which had forced the individual to seek emotional or social shelter in organizations larger than himself, was beginning to wane. And an emergent generation simply wished to be rather than to be for something; choreographers seriously began to think more about themselves.

The Changing Emphasis

As early as 1942 there had been indications that all was not totally well in the course of modern dance—and also that a radical solution to the difficulties was possible. Sybil Shearer, who had performed with the Humphrey-Weidman company, indicated a possible new direction in her own first solo recital. It was exciting but somewhat self-indulgent. There were no stories told, and on the contrary, there seemed to be an excessive concentration on the sheer physical and very personal act of moving. A further disturbing element was her disregard of linear development in her dances. She gave a solo program that consisted of impressions of trees, love, clouds, play, death. It was a program full of fantasy and had been created without the strong intellectual formulations that had been the principle underpinning of modern dance up until that time. However (the general response went), "mood" pieces which were lyric in quality did not really need a story line, and Shearer, after all, was only an individual who did not seem to be anything more than an idiosyncratic element in the dance world.

Shearer was an exceptional dancer who chose to display technique at the expense of other elements of dance. There had always been dancers of this sort, with special performing skills, such as Helen Tamiris, whose early cycle on spirituals was especially effective but whose work had then lapsed from that high standard, although she had always retained her fluid grace in performing. (Tamiris left the concert field and had had a very successful career choreographing Broadway musicals. She was a performer of special distinction, and although her choreography tended to the over-literal, there was always a special pleasure in her own person.) Shearer, despite her divergence from the dance perspectives of the time, was actually given a dance award by John Martin as the most promising solo choreographer in her inaugural year—honored by the establishment she was to dissent from. Yet she was the first of an increasing group who dissented from the values of the second generation of modern dance and began to break out of the established conventions of "dos and don'ts," though the profundity of the shift in focus away from institutional to internal themes was not to be felt fully for another twenty years.

After the 1942 season, Shearer did a most surprising thing. She took her award and left New York for Winnetka, Illinois, just outside of Chicago, with the announcement that New York was a "marketplace" for dance and no place in which to develop dance as an art. She has remained in Winnetka ever since, with side trips to other places, including for a while—though no longer—New York. Her behavior was not typical of dancers, who have always clustered around New York, which provided them with a receptive audience.

In any case, her subsequent visits to New York were not entirely satisfactory. She began to be regarded as a slightly dotty favorite aunt, with a formidable technique, who was liable to do anything on stage. She was odd and unpredictable and was held in baffled affection. She stopped using stage makeup, and Helen Morrison, who created her lighting designs, used lights to chop up the stage area in new and intriguing ways. Shearer then took to letting her hair hang loose during performances to remove any feeling of artificiality in the presentation of her person. She still maintained the custom of costume changes but decided that a full evening of dance was a seamless whole and not to be interrupted by intermissions. During one New York concert in 1949, the management of the theater insisted that there be an intermission and stopped the performance in the middle. Shearer was furious.

She also had the disturbing habit of changing programs if she did not feel that the audience was in sympathy with what she was doing. She performed in out-of-the-way places, and if she was scheduled at a hall which she did not like, she would search the neighborhood looking for the right one. On one such occasion her audience, which was trailing behind her, became lost, arrived only after she had started and insisted on being seated. Shearer was furious.

She chose not to appear if she did not feel that the conditions were right. She became more wayward, and at the same time insisted on using the most incredibly old-fashioned mishmash of music, ranging from Rachmaninoff to Scarlatti on the same evening, in rapid succession. At times she

seemed to be a throwback to the earlier Duncan-Fuller-St. Denis generation. In a way she is.

No one has ever had anything but the highest praise for Shearer's
technical ability, her method of deliberate understatement, and her gift for
improvisation. At the same time, no one has been able to trace a straight
line of choreographic development in her work (partly because few have
seen enough of it to judge, and those who have seen it find that it changes
considerably from performance to performance). She is somewhat of an
earth mystic who relies on direct integration of her feelings into a dance
phrase. Her comic talent has a broken phrasing which is reminiscent of
Charles Weidman, and probably owes something to the years she spent
with the Humphrey-Weidman company. Shearer remains an outsider who
prefers to work with a small, intimate group and not for a large, impersonal
audience. The design of her performance is for direct communication on an
almost conversational level. When she left New York to escape the commercial theater, she had decided to work on a closer basis with her audiences.
To this end, she converted the Winnetka Community Theater into a dance
theater and performs mainly there. The National College of Education
nearby has given her a life-time appointment to their staff as artist in
residence and she also performs there.

The individuals, like Shearer, who began to explore other possibilities of
dance development outside of literary or musical domination tended to
examine personal gesture or one aspect of dance dynamics, such as flow.
Though not linked in any organic way, dancers like Merle Marsicano, Midi
Garth, Erick Hawkins, Katherine Litz, and Jack Moore found imposed
elements of stories or conventional musical time increasingly irrelevent to
their own personal concerns. Hawkins had been a lead dancer with Graham from 1938 to 1950 and before that had had extensive ballet training. He
had been a member first of the American Ballet Company during 1935 to
1937 and then of Ballet Caravan. When he left Graham in 1951, he began a
concert career that continues to this day.

Hawkins has from the start of this career worked closely with the
composer Lucia Dlugozewski and sculptor Ralph Dorazio. Dorazio, in
addition to his formal work of costuming and setting Hawkins' dances, has
also prepared a series of percussion instruments for Dlugozewski. Some of
these consist of lozenge-shaped drums, lengths of flexible plastic which
give off a distinctive sound when shaken, and various instruments pat-
terned on xylophone principles. The effect of these instruments is as
pleasing to the eye as the semi-Oriental haze of sound that is created from
them is to the ear. They have a decorative appearance and remind one of
the practice common in Far Eastern countries of having the musician on
stage with performers.

Hawkins' theater is a combination of ritual and soft rhythm. He presents
an entirely personal ceremony of dance to the viewer. It is saturated in

obscurity, and little attempt is made to form the direct transitional links that would elucidate the intent of his dances. He removed narrative from his dances in favor of presenting associated movement episodes. He relies on poetic juxtaposition from which an impressionistic concept is created. His dances are not aimed at producing a spectacular effect through contrasts of phrasing or dynamics but seek to cumulate their effect slowly and evenly over a period of time. In works such as "Eight Clear Places" (1960), he presents a succession of tableaux featuring his dancers holding poses for long periods of time and flowing easily to another pose, then exiting. Masks, floor-length robes, and highly stylized props complete the mixture of Oriental tone and Western dance dynamics. Hawkins has created his own personal blend of dance theater out of a concentration of the physical dynamics of flowing movement and a mental discipline that is able to accommodate endless reiteration of material to draw attention to its import. Hawkins' pacing is measured in units that have more in common with Eastern conceptions of time than Western.

Katherine Litz, who danced with the Humphrey-Weidman company, came into contact with Sybil Shearer when touring with a Chicago production of *Oklahoma!* She found a sympathetic presence in Shearer and later moved further in the direction that Shearer had taken. Litz has a skilled sense of comic pantomime that is reminiscent of that shown by Weidman, and is also attracted by standard theatrical forms such as melodrama. She created a dance based on the Bram Stoker Gothic chiller, "Dracula" (1959), in which she unsuccessfully attempted to fuse the humorous and horrible. The work alternately polarized into one or the other mood. She has managed to convey more clearly in abstract dance pantomime that which eluded her in a work like "Dracula." "The Glyph" (1952) is probably her most fully realized work, synthesizing as it does humor and striking sculptural images. In this dance she is completely encased in a tubular sheath of elastic jersey cloth, which she stretches into odd configurations in a semi-hopeless struggle for deliverance.

At her finest, Litz portrays a slightly distracted tragedienne for whom the ultimate horror lies not in the unnamed, unhappy fate but in her inability to focus her attention on it sufficiently to accomplish it as a cathartic act. She begins time and time again to develop a line of gesture only to have it slip off almost uncontrollably into something else. At the moment when she should be portraying a powerful emotion in theatrical terms, she becomes aware that in order to do so she has had to assume a posture or attitude of body that in and of itself has little to do with the emotion being framed. Thus, bent over backwards with grief, she follows the logic of the gesture and collapses in a heap. All thoughts of grief are dispelled and one has to deal with a young lady in a somewhat inelegant pile on the floor. She operates at a balance point where theatrical reality and physical reality collide. Looked at strictly from the theatrical side, the gesture would retain its emotive content, but if, for a moment, one does not suspend disbelief, then it begins to have a life of its own outside of the dance. Litz possesses a double vision in the best of her work, allowing her this twofold aspect of commenting on what she is doing while she is doing it. It is a choreographic form of having one's cake and eating it too.

Litz has stated that she saw no reason not to compose a dance about the relation of a straight line to a curved line. She has believed that the dancer ought to have the freedom to say anything, as long as it was done in an interesting way by a skilled dancer. Yet, despite the fact that she disputed the dicta that dance had to be about a specific subject and be clear and unambiguous, she still clung firmly to the idea, soon to be dismissed by an emerging group of younger choreographers, that dancers ought to be highly trained people who could do things physically with their bodies that others, who had not received dance training, could not do.

Litz is a gifted performer whose sense of timing contributes much to the humor of her work. In a duet she prepared for herself and Paul Taylor, who shambled around in a gorilla suit, she was dressed in the flowing costume that would typify a dancer at a time when the assiduous cultivation of woodland ecstasy was at its height. She was experiencing the delights of flowers and the small movements of leaves in the breeze, only to find herself seized at the waist by a creature unthinkable in such a locale. Fluttering away in honest transport, she baffled the poor beast, who never quite understood what type of person he had stumbled upon, or what exactly was happening. The feigned shock, which alternated with rapturous enchantment, followed at intuitively calculated intervals with great effect.

Litz continues to mine the vein of dada and surrealist reality that originally attracted her. At times she will place a trained gymnast working on a trampoline in the context of a sketched-in family scene. She uses whatever sound sources she finds congenial to her purposes, whether it be conventional music or something picked up from the sounds that a crowd might make. She is fascinated by the deceptiveness of appearances, as she demonstrated in a short work in 1969 in which a man and a woman sat at a café table and watched a girl do a belly dance—except that the "girl" doing the dance was a man and the "man" in the derby hat who followed the dancing girl out was Litz herself. In finding her own creative voice, she has moved toward the unconscious area of experience which travels along the winding paths of the associational and allusive rather than the straight line of conscious, sequential logic.

Also fleeing from the logical strictures of cause and effect—and narrative story—were dancers Merle Marsicano and Midi Garth, both of whom had studied composition with Louis Horst before beginning to work in the special movement vocabulary which each had developed for herself. Horst, whose composition course had traditionally divided dancing into three main types—the primitive, the archaic, and the medieval—found that these former pupils and others did not fit easily into such categories, and so he invented the category of the "impressionistic." This was, in fact, a catch-all designation which included all of the dancers whose work had ceased to be concerned with the socially conscious choreography of second-generation modern dance. It was a stopgap term and like most such expedients did not give full recognition to the variety of individual dancers' qualities and creative expressions. It was, however, useful for categorizing a tendency toward inward individual mood as opposed to the logical structures of the typical 1930's choreographer.

Merle Marsicano, who was alertly aware of current trends in music, painting, and sculpture, found in these areas sources of formal exploration that had not been part of her schooling in dance. Thus it was, when she began her career as a choreographer, that she chose to work in the fragmented manner in which pictorial artists were at the time handling their material. In addition, she chose scores from advanced musicians like John Cage and Morton Feldman and Stephan Wolpe. The music tended to be spare and so did the movement vocabulary with which Marsicano chose to accompany it, in dances like "Fragment for a Greek Tragedy" or "Figure of a Memory" (1954). It was obvious that she was a choreographer of great conviction and individual talent, but it was and has been difficult to follow the developing line of her work. She did not employ jumps or leaps to any great extent but developed her dances from the torso and arms. In later works, such as "Images in the Open," she chose to choreograph totally in silence. This latter work appeared to have a life all its own outside of the stage context. It did not peak and develop but simply followed its own internal developmental logic and then trailed off without the climax of a definite ending. Despite the somewhat veiled motivation of her pieces, she has worked within the confines of a proscenium stage and has tended to have her dances frontally positioned in the conventional manner and, while her choice of music at first met with some criticism, the impact of her own dancing was always praised.

Midi Garth also presented a private theatrical dance world which had a recognizable impact on its audience but which also avoided literary specifics. It was not exactly mood dancing, in the sense that the term had been used about movement studies in the Duncan manner, but it was definitely lyric in feeling although elusive in meaning. Garth displayed an improvisational expertness that managed to keep the wisps of her choreography aligned in an evocative manner. Once again, as with Litz and Marsicano, it was the personal skill of the choreographer that gave the work its effectiveness and was difficult to transmit to other dancers. Skimming as close as it did to the edge of formlessness, Garth's choreography has always run the danger of simply degenerating into meandering postures without any vital linkage. In works in which her discipline was tight, as in "Anonymous," the mysterious allure of her private vision worked well. The economy of gesture in Garth's dances required that each move had to add a precise deposit of emotional weight to the structure. Tentativeness or a moment's vague hesitancy was sufficient to destroy the fragile skeleton of the dance. In many of her later works, such as "Day and Night" and "Impressions of Our Time," an uncertainness of approach has worked heavily against the realization of her concept.

While not inhabiting the intensely interior world explored by Garth and Marsicano, Jack Moore shares a similar dissatisfaction with the A-B-A compositional development of literary ideas in dance form, although his career is a model of how the historic modern dance establishment attempted to educate young choreographers.

Originally an art major in college, his only dance experience had been as a child in Indiana, where he had taken neighborhood school jazz and tap, with baton twirling thrown in. After service in World War Two, he entered college and began to do some amateur theatrical work. While pursuing his major in art at the University of Iowa, he found increasing pleasure in actual stage performance. The interest developed so far that he was offered a dance scholarship for a summer course at Colorado College, where Hanya Holm, a central European expressionist dancer, had taught for many years. He accepted the scholarship. It was the deciding factor in his career, and he elected to go to New York in 1949 and try for a career in dance instead of going for a graduate degree in fine arts.

After further study and a period as Louis Horst's assistant, he performed with the Martha Graham company for a season in 1953 and then decided that he wanted to do something else. Anna Sokolow spotted him in 1954 and he worked with her in a variety of things, ranging from concert programs to the Broadway play *Red Roses for Me*.

Moore began his own choreographic career with a number of solos prepared for himself. The first of these were seen in 1957 at the 92nd Street "Y" as part of a program put on by Contemporary Dance Productions. Moore's solos were "The Act," a burlesque homage to an old circus performer, and "Somewhere to Nowhere." These were mood studies, as were many of his early works, such as "The Geek," which was premiered the next summer in 1958 at Connecticut College's American Dance Festival. "The Geek" delved into the world of the circus and extracted a rather repulsive type for examination—the side-show artist who eats live snakes and bites the heads off chickens. For the festival he also created another solo, "The Cry of the Phoenix," which was a symbolized portrayal of the mythical bird. These pieces were performed at a special young choreographers' Monday night program which the festival had inaugurated. Since the weekend performances were regularly given over to the Graham or Limón companies, the young choreographers' night was anticlimactic but it was an opportunity to work and to learn.

Jack Moore in *Songs Remembered*, American Dance Festival, 1960. Photo by Diana Mitchell (Courtesy of Bob Van Cleave)

By this time, Moore had firmly committed himself to the career path which had been forged out of the experience of the second generation of modern dancers. He had been Horst's assistant in his composition course and had studied in Doris Humphrey's course. He had appeared at Connecticut College and had had the opportunity to see and work with the people who were running modern dance. When he wanted to begin his own choreographic career, one of the first things that he had done was to try out at the open auditions that were part of the Dance Audition Program at the "Y."

He had found Horst a marvelous coach for those whose talent was visible but something less than an inspired teacher, since the older man didn't seem particularly sensitive or well equipped to bring out pupils' potential. In any case, Moore found the academic route congenial. He was a model example of how the system should work, the formularized system that was to encourage and nourish young choreographic talent and provide for the future of modern dance, which itself had emerged in defiance of any system. John Martin had entitled "Days of Divine Indiscipline" a short study of some of the pioneers, but orderly development was designed to be the method for succeeding generations. Moore had successfully passed each of the system's academic and social hurdles as he had come to them, and he continued to do so.

While teaching at Juilliard, he had the opportunity to create the first of his group works. The students complained that they did not have enough performing to do, so Moore promised each person who would attend rehearsals a part in a work that he would create for a 1:00 P.M. recital. "Intaglios" (1960) was the first of the pieces he prepared, and a few years later he prepared "Opticon" for a similar afternoon concert. Meanwhile, he found himself the first recipient of the Doris Humphrey Fellowship Awards, which were established to commemorate her work and afford young choreographers the opportunity to create dances of their own during a summer residency at Connecticut College. Moore also found that he had been promoted to the regular weekend schedule of performances at the college's festivals, a step up from the scarcely noticed Monday evening series. He offered two works, "Songs Remembered" and "Targets" (1961).

The first was a traditional duet for two people, in which vignettes of movement portrayed their emotional difficulties with one another. Despite the unsatisfactory nature of their adjustment to each other, there was some unseen force which compelled them to meet. "Targets" was a larger-scaled work for four dancers. It too was fragmented into sections and drew inspiration in part from Jasper Johns' series of target paintings. The work was in five sections, presented like five taut, succinct pictures. Three dancers march and salute, a girl works desperately and hopelessly at her makeup, another tries to convince a somewhat indifferent man of something unspecified, a couple tries a moment of recollection, and a trio gets impossibly entangled. The pictures succeeded one another without the connecting linkage of flowing movement. It was an auspicious pair of works that Moore produced that summer, touched as they were with a keen, restrained, and understated sense of malaise. Almost from the first of his works, he had shown a spare leanness in composition and "Targets" represented the logical development of his particular combination of character images and choreographic economy. It also became a turning point in his creative development.

Moore realized that there was no place further for him to go with the technique of characterization and thematic development that he had learned. "Targets" was a successful dead-end. He had, meanwhile, accepted a teaching post at Bennington College and began to work on new material there, to escape from the creative corner into which he had worked himself. One of the things that he learned during his work at Connecticut College was a method of composition that could be incorporated in regular class work. It was a device that he had picked up one summer after studying with Merce Cunningham, who often worked out new material in his classes. Moore had felt that modern dance classes were far too rigid and structured and thought that the structure of a ballet class was far more sensible, combining as it did barre and center-floor work. When he first came to New York, a generation of modern dancers brought up under the old methodology had been systematically and quietly going to the School of American Ballet for classes. Cunningham had even taught there. Now Moore was going to put the system to work for himself.

He began to develop a movement vocabulary that was not dependent on character or dramatic incident. He began this trial and analysis period with measured thoroughness, and over a period of three years (1963–1965) produced a group of nine short works to which he assigned the series title "Assays." These were fragments of movement, each one tried and tested for its abstract suitability and not for any naturalistic effect. They included solos as well as works for four and five dancers. They represented a development of the personal absurd. Structural logic was no longer sufficient to deal with the material that Moore was drawn toward and only gesture elaborated beyond any realistic implications could shape the menacing multiplicity of events that clamored for primacy of an individual's attention. Juxtaposition, inference, and noncompelling suggestion replaced the rigors of one-to-one logic. It was a particularly significant step for someone like Moore to have made. He was to all intents and purposes the inheritor of the pedagogical system which the previous generation had set up and should have found himself thoroughly in tune with the dictates of another age's solutions, but he was not; reality was far too insistent.

In 1964 he even stopped giving concerts at the "Y," the performing outpost of the establishment, and with Jeff Duncan collaborated in founding Dance Theater Workshop, which became a recognized tax-exempt entity the following year. It was housed in a loft that functioned as Duncan's studio and as a theater in which young performers and choreographers could have their works presented for a number of weekends and not just on a single evening. The possibility had to be created to afford them the chance to judge audience response to their work over a period of time and not just as a one-time occurrence. For Moore it was another step away from the system. The development had been slow but the drift away from inherited values was real. Like the jade which he collects, Moore always keeps cool and reserved, following his own star even when the logic of it leads away from the system. He continues to work in his spare, individual, and neo-dada manner, combining elements of absurd reality—such as real vegetation in "Five Scenes in the Shape of an Autopsy" and an automobile tire in one of his "Assays"—with severe, deft, and purposeful movement. A seemingly complete product of the system, he has grown to admire Merce Cunningham, ballet, and especially his own independence.

The assertion of the individual as the dominant focus of choreographic interest had reached a point which no one could ignore. The historic modern dance generation operated in a climate in which adherence could confidently be given to an externalized system. They subordinated idiosyncratic personal expression to the broader demands of formal order. They had found it necessary to reject the "romantic" personalism of the Duncan-Fuller-St. Denis pioneers who had operated, so the historic generation thought, within the framework of "outmoded" conventions. The generation that followed historic modern dance found it imperative to reestablish the individual amidst the welter of conflicting and mutually exclusive "isms." The dancers began to examine the basics of their craft in highly personal terms, perhaps because there were few outside premises that all could agree upon. At least at the personal level the confusion of intention and meaning could, it was hoped, be kept to a minimum. The dance could feel free to represent itself totally.

The first choreographer who completely proclaimed his independence in this way from previously hallowed wisdom was Merce Cunningham.

Merce Cunningham

New Concerns and New Forms

There was a time, which is now fast disappearing, in which the ordinary reaction to a dance concert by Merce Cunningham was shock. Cunningham was so vastly different from any other performer in his manner of presentation that it was difficult to concentrate on the specific works he had choreographed. He shocked a dance audience with his first solo recital in New York in 1944, then later with "Sixteen Dances for Soloist and Company of Three" in 1951, and over a decade later in 1964 with "Winterbranch." The historic modern dance devotee was thrown into a mild panic when he found that the usual handholds of story, character development, and musical cues were absent from Cunningham's work. The choreography became a sheer cliff face without any of the little nooks and crevices on which the dance audience could secure itself

To many followers of modern dance, Cunningham personifies the gadfly, intent, at best, on baffling the unwary, or more likely, deriving some personal satisfaction from practicing a unique audiovisual torture technique. The effect of his work for many was an assault upon their habits of viewing and upon their unspoken prejudices about how dancing should look. These latter were usually determined by previous dance experiences, either at modern dance concerts or at ballet performances. It is difficult now to estimate which audience found Cunningham more difficult to comprehend: the ballet audience, which was not that familiar with modern dance at all, or the family of partisans, who felt that they knew all about modern dance. Twenty-five years of steady performance and choreographing have demonstrated that Cunningham was speaking the language of his creative time almost before the time was aware that a new choreographic language was needed.

Cunningham addressed himself to the existential problems of the individual. It was a radical shift in creative orientation—the substitution of individual states of awareness for an external, "objective" logic. In Cunningham's approach, choreographic activity became concentrated on its own presence and not on any allegorical meaning that could be attached to it. Movement was freed from the necessity to accommodate its thrust to the demands of other disciplines. Cunningham created dance without reference to either story or special musical score. In actual performance, a score accompanied a dance and lasted the same time that the dance lasted. However, the dancers did not move in accord to its musical rhythm—they were not slaves to its commands—but merely within its overall time structure. Dance as both a time and spatial art thus had to be evaluated only in the use of its inherent dimensions. It no longer subordinated its temporal physicality to story or musical development; it had to be inventive within its own terms, the laws of motion and repose.

Cunningham began his career modestly and conventionally enough with neighborhood lessons in Centralia, Washington. He began studying at the age of twelve and his training included bits of everything including tap dancing, which he remains genuinely fond of to this day. One of his enthusiasms in the world of dance is Fred Astaire, a taste which he shares with George Balanchine of the New York City Ballet. "I am amazed at the way that he can change the entire phrasing of a routine with just the tiniest little adjustment. You have to watch very closely to see him do it."

Cunningham graduated from high school in 1937 and entered the Cornish School in Seattle. Two years later, in 1939, he attended the Bennington School of the Dance summer course, which was being held that particular summer on the Mills College campus in California. (Though the college had decided to broaden its summer program to include other theater arts the previous year, the administrators of the dance section remained the same.) The single summer at Mills College was long enough for Martha Graham to find Cunningham and invite him to become a member of her company. He danced with her for five years until 1945, when he left to begin his own concert career.

Beginning in 1943 he choreographed solos for himself, accompanied on the piano by John Cage, who has been his musical director since that time. During the time that Cunningham was with the Graham company and for about six years after he had left, the bulk of his work was the solo dance, which he performed himself, accompanied more often than not by Cage on a somewhat reconstructed piano. Curiously, the music of Cage and the variety of special effects which he was able to achieve by inserting bits of resonant and dampening material between the strings of a standard piano was more graciously received than Cunningham's choreography. In their collaboration it is a situation which has virtually reversed itself at present. Many who have come to appreciate Cunningham's choreography, with its special difficulties, are not able to adjust similarly to the current music of Cage.

In the early 1950's, Cunningham began to make more and more use of groups of dancers for his work. Cunningham dancers have had an independent self-awareness coupled with an elastic quality which permits them to combine in the most intricate assemblages and to disengage with equal rapidity for solo work. Basic to an appreciation of the Cunningham oeuvre is a recognition of the molecular individuality possessed by each of his dancers. They are not so much a performing ensemble as an association of soloists who come together under the benign and technically demanding rigors of Cunningham's choreography to perform a spiritually elevated exercise.

Dating from the early 1950's are such pieces as "Games" (1949) in which Paul Taylor first made his appearance with the Cunningham company in New York, and "Sixteen Dances for Soloist and Company of Three" (1951) in which the element of chance first entered into Cunningham's work. Chance, which can be used in a variety of ways, was at this time used sparingly as a means of determining the order that sections of the dance would follow. The individual sections were not choreographed by chance. This development would come slightly later in Cunningham's work. The culmination of this period came during a full week of performances at the Theater de Lys in 1953. It was the first attempt that Cunningham had made to hold an entire week of eight performances. It was, in its own way, as daring a risk as anyone in the modern dance world had taken until that time. With the exception of Graham, who always played in Broadway houses, modern dancers after World War Two, because of economics, found themselves increasingly confined to the Kaufmann Concert Hall of the Young Men's and Young Women's Hebrew Association on 92nd Street or to a weekend at the Hunter College Playhouse. Performances in these houses were regularly covered by the reviewers and enabled choreographers to receive a cross section of informed opinion unavailable anywhere else in the United States. By taking a theater off Broadway, Cunningham removed himself from the possibility of broad critical review. The season was ignored by the *New York Times,* which had not yet accustomed itself to the existence of off-Broadway theater. Cunningham had thought that after ten years of sustained choreographic work, he could be regarded seriously outside of a prestigious and ruinously expensive Broadway house. He was mistaken. (The prejudice for established showcases was a condition that was to persist until the early 1960's, when Rudolph Nureyev, who made his New York debut with the Chicago Opera Ballet at the Brooklyn Academy of Music, was equally ignored. After this oversight, the policy was changed.)

Cunningham did not attempt another sustained period of performances in New York for nearly a decade and a half subsequently. He worked and toured throughout the United States and abroad, confining his New York appearances to an occasional weekend. When in 1968 he appeared for a week in the spring at the Brooklyn Academy of Music, it was to popular acclaim. By that time his personal revolution had permeated the entire younger generation of the modern dance world.

The first thing that one is made conscious of in watching a Cunningham concert is the lack of strong central focus in the choreographic patterns. Unlike ballet, which is rigidly structured about a central position on the stage, with the lesser members of the company (such as those in the corps de ballet) spaced around the periphery, Cunningham assigns no such performing priority to the stage area. He allows his dancers a freedom to wander across the entire performing area without regard to rigid stratifications of space. At any time during the course of a Cunningham dance, one or another of the dancers will be the "first among equals." Their positioning on the stage is not what determines this factor but rather the inherent interest of the choreography.

There is always a variety of things to look at in a Cunningham dance, and attention is not compelled or directed to the same spot at all times. One of the clearest examples of this freedom of attention is to be found in "Place" (1966). In this dance, a man enters a totally deserted stage and dances a small solo of an inquiring nature, such as one might do in testing out the floor of a building that one was not entirely sure of—or the way a snake might sample alien air. No one else is visible. The inhabitants of the desolate place begin to appear one by one and rush about the stage. The girls are costumed in industrial-weight transparent plastic subtly tinted blue, pink, green, and yellow. The man dances with them at first but as their dance progresses he retires to the back of the stage and begins to draw a pair of small geodesic-shaped lamps across the stage. They are placed on a bit of carpet he pulls toward himself as he progresses backward. He lights one lamp and then the other, while the active dancing continues closer to the audience at the middle and the front of the stage. Interest, however, jumps back and forth between the quietly kneeling figure and the much more active group of dancers rushing about. Toward the end of the performance the man tending the lights performs another solo, half in and half out of a plastic bag, violently thrashing across the empty stage on his back. As the curtain comes down, he is still racked with convulsive movements. It is questionable whether he wishes to be engulfed by the bag or to escape from it. These are the major solos which he has in the work, and yet attention has been drawn to him and his quiet attentiveness to the lamps time and time again during the course of the modern dance.

The piece is also interesting in the manner in which it allows characterization to infuse the people in the dance. Cunningham, who does not ostentatiously make character studies and does not encourage his dancers to think in emotional terms, provides room within the movements of his dances for character development. This particular dance has also been shaped so that it faces entirely forward in much the same manner that traditional choreography has always used. Most of his works can be seen from almost any angle, since they are not frontally arranged, but "Place" consistently develops toward the audience. Cunningham, who broke loose from the rigidities of this format, is not averse to using it when it suits his purposes. But as can be seen, he uses it in his own distinctive manner.

Although the traditional plays an important part in his choreography, it has often been overlooked because of the basic changes he has made in the way that he constructs his dances. One of these differences concerns his use of music. When he was a performer with Graham, he was aware of the place that Louis Horst had played in her development. Horst was not only her musical director but also a composer who supplied her with some of her most interesting scores and an important confidant with whom she could discuss and refine her ideas. When Cunningham left to form his own company, he secured his own musical director, John Cage, whose theories have influenced much of modern music and, through Cunningham, the course of modern dance. Unlike Horst, though, who was committed to the idea that a dance developed in much the way that a traditional musical composition developed—that is to say, through theme and variations—Cage sought other forms of musical composition. What finally interested him the most was rhythmic development, rhythm being the relationships of sounds and silences. For Graham, music was a structural necessity commissioned to fit in with her ideas, which were sympathetic to thematic development. For Cunningham, music has been an aural entity which occupied a set time allotment, during which the dance occupied a neighboring space. Melodic line did not interest Cage any more than narrative development interested Cunningham.

For Cunningham, stories and all literary trappings were inhibiting the course of dance development. As he wrote, "The logic of one event coming as responsive to another seems inadequate now. We look at and listen to several at once. For dancing it was all those words about meaning that got in the way. Right now they are broken up; they do not quite fit, we have to shuffle and deal them out again."

When Cunningham separated movement from its dependence on narrative development in his first concert, he opened his horizons to a species of choreography springing from dance logic that flowed from the basic characteristics of dance instead of placing dance energy at the service of an "outside" non-dance element. What was discarded was the need for dancers to assume characterizations in the dramatic sense and to use gesture in a naturalistic manner. It was the most revolutionary thing that he did. By emphasizing movement he clearly demonstrated that dance was not a frustrated mate yearning to verbalization but a kinetic discipline capable of its own wordless truths.

In other ways, he retained the conventions of the theatrical world in which he was brought up. He did not dispense with stage makeup. He kept music as a companion discipline to his work. He lived for the most part within the limitations of the proscenium stage, although most of his dances were designed to be seen from almost any angle. He continued concert touring with his company as a previous generation had done and he stressed the importance of technique in his choreography. Although there are elements of non-dance movement to be found within his work, it is nearly impossible to imagine Cunningham working with a group of persons who did not have a high level of modern dance or balletic training. They simply would not be able to perform his choreography without it. Cunningham also retained the traditional desire of modern dancers to have a performing troupe under one's own direction for whom one could choreograph and with whom one could perform. In the light of his conventional feelings about the role of the theater in his work, it is surprising that he met with such resistance when he dispensed with stories.

A beautiful example of Cunningham's unusual use of non-dance, i.e., conventional gesture, occurs in "Variations V." This work is something of an electronic marvel and was first performed at Philharmonic Hall during the Salute to France Festival in July 1965. The dancers, in addition to performing the choreography which they are given, also function somewhat in the manner of musicians as they move. The stage is divided into transmitting areas by the placement of five electronically sensitive poles. The number varies according to the size of the stage. Each of these metal rods has a magnetic field which causes sound and sight changes when it is broken. As the dancers move through these invisible electromagnetic cobwebs, they automatically alter the environment in which they are dancing.

The dance has contrasted extremely slow, ordinary-paced gestures such as sitting and walking with dancing of headlong velocity. The dance opens with a simple diagonal walk across stage as Cunningham places a potted plant near the front of the stage. He exits the same way. A boy and girl enter. At first there are film projections of a dance studio and locomotives to provide a backdrop for the dancers. The girl stands on her head as the boy watches. Cunningham returns to do a solo in and among the metal wands. His partner enters to walk deliberately across the stage and place down a pot with newspapers in it next to the first pot. She then dances a duet with Cunningham. Three boys of the company do a series of solo variations, which overlap solos by three of the girls. Most of the solo work is done by three people at the same time. The film projections have reflected the bicycle motions of the boys and are now showing feet. Individuals of the company come and go off the stage with fast, bright alertness. The entire thrust of their dance is highly allegro. It is an all-stops-out pacing which contrasts strongly with the deliberately casual walking episodes. His partner reappears to smash the original pot and plant the flower in her own. After she has rearranged the plastic leaves, she exits. Shortly thereafter, Cunningham comes on to do a solo sequence of exercises on an electronic mat. The costumes of the dance change as it progresses. The girls appear from time to time wearing street clothes rather than the streamlined leotards of the dancer. The entire company and the movement of the dance accelerates to an even more rapid level in a series of running and leaping crossovers. Two men suddenly sit down in chairs to watch a pas de trois. The chairs are removed and the company unwinds a string and shapes it into a large zigzag form which they weave up and down. At the end of this variation, they all run off. Suddenly Cunningham appears riding an ordinary bicycle in and out among the magnetic wands, tooting the small air horn attached to the handlebars. He manages to break all of the magnetic fields, changing the sound and visual decor rapidly as the curtain comes down. Even the riding of a bicycle around the area which the dancers have enlivened is not done as quickly as their passage.

Cunningham is fond of introducing elements of ordinary life into his dances. He usually does it in an obvious way but derives the maximum shock value from them through the context in which they are introduced. Perhaps nothing currently in the Cunningham repertory is more startling than "Walkaround Time" (1968). This dance is broken into two halves by an intermission for the dancers. The houselights in the theater are taken up to half the illumination that they would ordinarily have in a "true," or audience, intermission and the dancers come out on stage in whatever clothes they care to wear. They are free to perform any actions which they wish to, including the practice of certain movements from the more formal part of the dance. At the conclusion of this "intermission," the second part begins with a solo by Cunningham in which he performs an "intermission" or off-stage act under performing conditions. He changes his costume with maximum fluidity while running in place. The costume he changes into is exactly the same as the one he has changed out of, and after he has completed this difficult technical feat, he simply walks off. It is a way of expressing the possible theatrical nature of almost any action, even one as simple as removing a sweater and tights.

Once Cunningham had determined that everyday experience was comprised of a score or more of impressions, all plucking at the sleeve of attention at any given time, it was logical to point out choreographically that linear stories were an exception to life as it is lived. Life is not completely harmonious in its parts, purposefully directed and without loose ends. It is, on the contrary, made up of arbitrary shifts of attention from one set of phenomena to another, and is the accumulation of a series of discrete experiential units, which are linked by the continuity of the individual existence rather than by thematic development. It is a method of composition which Cage has employed in his music and a means of choreographic expression that Cunningham has continually sought.

Cage has often observed that art must imitate life not in its effects but in its processes. Cunningham has been the choreographer who has most successfully translated this idea into dance. It was a revolutionary idea to a previous generation intent on ends and not means because of its implicit

Merce Cunningham (center) and company in *Walkaround Time*, 1968. Photo by James Klosty (Courtesy Cunningham Dance Foundation)

trust in the underlying order of materials and also in its restraint from the natural manipulative desire that one brings to raw materials.

Cunningham's own attitude toward his work is one step removed from that of his passionate advocates, who will defend anything Cunningham does, and a shade warmer in its concern that the audience have his pieces presented to them in an unambiguous manner. He has often complained about the indirectness of contemporary society and has attempted in all of his work to be direct. It was the primary impulse that made him disregard the persona that dancers put on when they are forced to assume a characterization which is not that of themselves. He is the total enemy of misrepresentation but has succeeded in creating a storm of doubt in the minds of many of his viewers as to what his true intentions in choreography have been. During his entire performing career he has been extremely reticent about explaining any of his work except in terms of task accomplishment or technical commentary. Echoing Robert Frost in replying to a question asking for an explanation of his work, Cunningham would rather not do less well in words what he already has done in movement.

One of his most joyous and accessible dances is "How To Pass Kick Fall and Run" (1965). The dance is made up of all of these title elements, although the passing is of one body in front of or behind another and not the transfer of an object from one person to another. The "music" which accompanies this group work is a series of stories selected from the writings of Cage and recited at the rate of one story per minute. The stories vary in length, so that some occupy just a few seconds of time and others require rapid reading to be compressed within the duration of sixty seconds. Cage has proven himself to be an exceptionally adept reader of his anecdotes and also a theatrical personage in his own right. He sits at the side of the stage well forward and out of the dancers' way and customarily opens a bottle of champagne and sips at a glass as he proceeds through the performance. At times the task of reading the stories is performed with the actor David Vaughan. Each reads a story, sometimes simultaneously, at other times not, and the juxtaposition of the varying thematic lines often results in a clashing and discontinuous humor. At other times, the mingled stories are nothing more than a discordant jumble.

Such hazards of daily life as the interrupted thought or attention flow were brought into the theater for the first time by Cunningham. Much has been made of the element of chance in Cunningham's work and little if any appreciative notice given the special order that applies in chance operations. Chance is not chaos, as Cunningham would be the first to acknowledge. For example, in dealing with chance operations the choreographer puts himself in the hands of the natural long-phrased rhythms which are ordinarily unseen but which are observable under the proper conditions. "Suite by Chance" (1953) is the first piece in which Cunningham introduced chance into the actual composition of a dance. He prepared a series of dance movement charts for a period of months and then tossed coins to determine which of the movements were to be strung together to make up the choreographic pattern of the dance. Two factors thus entered into the making of the work, and the first was not chance at all but the selective knowledge of an accomplished choreographer in making the charts, thereby preparing the ground upon which the chance operations could take place. If these charts had been made up by a person whose ability as a dancer was non-existent, then the resultant combinations would have been awkward and at times impossible to perform at all. Since they were the product of a dancer's imagination, they tended to have the logic of movement built into them from the start. It was only the order of the combinations that was determined by chance.

The selective nature of the dance steps to be employed is unquestionably the most important part of the operation. Inherent in the process of schooling a dancer (no matter what the particular dance discipline he is engaged in, whether ethnic, modern, or ballet) is a philosophy of movement and attitude toward people in space which is not necessarily made explicit but exists and influences the dancer in his own thinking. In Cunningham's case, because of his training, he would not unknowingly be lured into kinesthetic gaucherie. Further, once the charts were prepared, the chance method of composition was not a particularly difficult one since Cunningham has used the method as part of his instruction to aspiring choreographers. The charts are offered to a group of pupils and they are invited to toss coins for the particular movements that they are going to perform in their own dance. The choreography is their own but the vocabulary is Cunningham's. So it was with "Suite by Chance."

A more subtle and probably more important idea in the use of chance is the assumption that chance is an expression of order, although it is not an order that we are accustomed to deal with. For example, a hundred tosses of a coin will result in fifty "heads" and fifty "tails" without any special or conscious control. In human life, there are areas of experience which are manageable only by the laws derived from large numbers of observations, far exceeding those which would be encountered ordinarily by a single person. The most common demonstration of the order underlying chance is shown in the classroom exercises in which a hundred marbles are dropped one by one into a maze of evenly spaced pegs and allowed to bounce around freely until they come to rest at the bottom of the framework of pegs. When all of the marbles have been dropped, they will have formed a perfectly symmetrical bell-shaped mound. The confidence that there is such an implicit orderliness in the flow of phenomena is a necessary one and one which will allow a viewer to enjoy the flow of choreographic material which transpires in any Cunningham chance composition without the anxiety produced by apparent chaos. Chance as used by Cunningham is a discipline or a tool for composition that directs the choreographer's attention in a manner that it would not have followed easily of its own volition. It is not a surrender to anarchy but merely a use of natural process. For some reason, the presence of an element of chance has become for many a stumbling block in the enjoyment of all of Cunningham's work, although it is simply one of a variety of compositional methods that he uses. The vast bulk of Cunningham's work is not composed with the utilization of chance composition. Cunningham has more frequently used chance in the ordering of the sections of a dance than he has in assembling the combinations themselves. Once removed from the linear requirements of straight narrative, elements of a dance could move freely from one place to another inside the large framework of the piece. Cunningham, who regularly looks at dance as bursts of self-contained movement, thus finds it fresh and stimulating to have these sections occur in a variety of patterns.

A chronicle of the schedule Cunningham sets himself illustrates the seriousness of his work habits. He begins his day with a private session of exercise and choreographic exploration. As he himself observed, the dance often begins with a step. Then he plunges into work. During the preparation for a winter season in 1969 at the Brooklyn Academy, he had placed himself in the position of having to prepare four works, two completely new dances, the revival of an older one "Crises," and the completion of the final section of "Canfield." The two new works were "Tread" and "Second Hand"; both pieces were designed for the full company of ten. Because of a prior commitment to the Royal Swedish Ballet, he had to leave his rehearsals and go to Sweden in the early part of the fall, thus losing two weeks of rehearsal time for his own season. When he returned he had about six weeks in which to bring together all of the material needed for a new season.

"Second Hand" was to be based partially on an earlier work, "Idyllic Song," a solo choreographed to the music of Erik Satie which Cunningham had performed in 1944. As the piece developed, he first performed his own solo, then prepared a long duet for himself and Carolyn Brown, and then extended the development of the thematic material for his entire company. The dance evolved into a piece that was a lyrical study in the style of Graham group dances, without the psychological overtones and the stressed seriousness that characterize her work. It appeared to be a dance of a young choreographer who had just escaped from the powerful influence of an older, more established artist and who had blended elements of an original statement with much of the inherited vocabulary created by the older master.

"Tread," the second of the two new works, was unlike this piece in two respects. It did not draw on any extant material nor did it resemble the work of any choreographer other than Cunningham. In it, the dancers had the alert, poised, and ready-to-go-in-any-direction look that is characteristic of the Cunningham dancer.

"Tread," as it progressed toward its completion, emerged as a celebration of the special dance and acrobatic skills of Cunningham's company as then constituted. (Its members were: Carolyn Brown, Susanna Hayman-Chaffee, Valda Setterfield, Sandra Neels, Meg Harper, Mel Wong, Douglas Dunn, Jeff Slayton, and Chase Robinson.) Throughout the rehearsal period, Cunningham would watch his dancers extracting an attitude or carriage here or a quickness there—and then he incorporated these in the final fabric of the dance. Mel Wong, who has a high order of gymnastic skill, was suddenly asked to do a handstand in the middle of a sequence where such a gesture had not been included before. The handstand had to be held for several counts so that other members of the grouping could assume new positions. Since Wong was able to do it for the required time, the dance was set to include it.

The mood of the typical working rehearsal was low key with a great deal of mutual respect shown on the part of choreographer and dancers. The dance began to assume humorous shape as Cunningham invented more and more awkward situations for boys to meet girls. Three boys sitting on the ground would arch themselves upward and suddenly a girl fell across their upraised stomachs. A boy would walk in long strides across stage and find that a girl abruptly perched herself on his shoulder when he stopped. Another boy would be sitting alone in the center of the floor and Cunningham would balance a girl like a board across his shoulder and later assist her off. At one point in a fast sequence during which three boys would snap around and face forward at one-second intervals, a girl would present herself to each. The first boy would lift her vertically, the second would assist her in a leap, and the third would catch her in midair as she was parallel to the ground in a feet first dive.

The dance began to have the rapid pacing of a French bedroom farce. One choreographic door would open only to have another close at the opposite end of the stage. A third door would meanwhile have been partially closed, suddenly to burst asunder and spew forth a riotous gaggle of dancers veering and swerving to avoid one another.

During the entire time that the dance was being prepared, Cunningham worked without the aid of any musical accompaniment. There was a score that was to be used but it was not heard until the actual opening night at the Brooklyn Academy of Music. The decor that was to be prepared for the dance was also proceeding independently. At the start of the project, the members of the collaboration were told the emotional climate of the work in general terms but were not given specific details of choreography. The designer for the work, sculptor Bruce Nauman, did not in fact ever see the dance before it was performed and completed his design totally insulated from the particulars of the piece.

Nauman envisioned and worked with two basic energy currents, one sturdy and constant and the other fluctuating. He chose to characterize them with standing floor fans, ten in all. Five oscillated from side to side in much the way that the girls racketed around the pylons that the boys formed and the other five stood without any movement. The dance was at times momentarily masked by this fan decor, operating at the edge of the stage and blowing out on the audience. The dancers wore stylized versions of casual rehearsal clothes. The short tunic and leg warmers worn by the girls were particularly effective.

Almost from the beginning, Cunningham's company has been a breeding ground for choreographers. Among those who have danced with the company and who have demonstrated serious choreographic abilities have been Paul Taylor, Gus Solomons, Jr., Steve Paxton, Remy Charlip, Judith Dunn, Deborah Hay, Carolyn Brown, William Davis, Viola Farber, Jack Moore, Albert Reid, Job Sanders, Peter Saul, and Dan Wagoner. The Cunningham company, standing as it does at the crossroads of new ideas and experimentation, has characteristically been a congenial home for independent spirits. In the creative ambiance surrounding the company, many artists, among them Jasper Johns, Robert Rauschenberg, Alex Hay, Bruce Nauman, Frank Stella, and Andy Warhol, have found opportunity not only to assist in creating decors but, in the case of Rauschenberg and Hay, to create and perform their own dances. Among the musicians who have worked with the company are John Cage, David Tudor, Gordon Mumma, Earle Brown, and Morton Feldman. The confluence of talented designers and composers who are allowed to exercise their skill with a maximum of artistic freedom has created a tradition unmatched by any other modern dance company. It is a tribute to Cunningham, whose conception of dance as an entity freely responsive to its own internal energies created a double revolution.

The first of these revolutions was in the styles of movement. Cunningham introduced fresh, lyrical, almost hedonist elements into the stern discipline that was historic modern dance. He chose to include in his work elements of play, sport, even a stroll in the street. Anything natural, that is any movement meaningful to the dancer, became matter for a dance. The second revolution was an accompaniment to the first. Dance liberated as Cunningham had liberated it allowed in its setting and presentation for the fanciful deployment of technical theatrical resources that had been kept in relative check by the demands of naturalism.

A subsequent generation was to make further imaginative uses of all the new possibilities set free by Cunningham's double revolution.

Robert Dunn

Educating for the Future

Robert Dunn is a composer who, during the years 1960–1964, assisted by his wife Judith Dunn, gave a series of dance courses at the Merce Cunningham studio on 14th Street and later at Judith Dunn's studio. These courses were attended by dancers and choreographers who were more or less affiliated with the Cunningham studio or sympathetic to the company. In general, the students who attended were dissatisfied with composition courses; these, they felt, were too structured for genuine innovative exploration. As Cunningham himself was not inclined to teach composition, Dunn was invited by John Cage, with whom he had studied, to teach his own course. The creative energy unleashed during these classes was to provide the impetus that resulted in the formation of the seminal Judson Dance Theater in 1962.

Judson Memorial Church on Washington Square South did not have a history of involvement with dance before the arrival of the graduates of Robert Dunn's classes, but it did have a sense of community responsibility. The church, designed by Stanford White after Renaissance Italian models, was founded in 1890. During the early part of the century it sponsored nursing care and low-cost pasteurized milk for the immigrant families that lived in the neighborhood. Political causes were commonplace at Judson, and in the 1950's and the 1960's concern for the problem of narcotics addiction developed under Rev. Howard Moody's direction. The church's first excursion into the arts, under the stimulation of Rev. Moody's first assistant, Bernard Scott, was a series of painting exhibitions and "happenings" beginning in 1959. These events were held in a meeting room renamed the Judson Gallery. By 1961, drama and musical productions were being given there. By this time Scott had been replaced by Rev. Alvin Carmines, who is a composer of some skill who was to collaborate on a significant number of productions. It was to Carmines that a delegation composed of Robert and Judith Dunn, and two of the new young choreographers, Yvonne Rainer and Steve Paxton, appealed for space to give a dance concert. Carmines, whose familiarity with dance was limited to his Virginia grandmother's remark, "A praying knee and a dancing foot never grew on the same leg!" decided that he liked what he saw in their audition. In July of 1962, during a sweltering evening, a three-hour concert of dance formally inaugurated the Judson Dance Theater.

Judson rapidly became a focus for experimental work and attracted numbers of choreographers who had not been in Dunn's courses but who were drawn by the open atmosphere of the Dance Theater. The major innovative developments of the newer choreographers are, in the main, traceable to work with Dunn in his course and in the workshop that developed at Judson Church itself. The latter was not a formal course as was Dunn's but operated more as a forum for dancers and choreographers to look at and analyze each other's work.

Dunn did not produce dances and cannot be judged by a personal body of works. He played for and talked to others and encouraged them to find fresh approaches to movement. It seems logical to allow him to speak in his own manner about what he had done so effectively. The following is a conversation with Dunn about his work and that of his students that led to the establishment of the Judson group. Dunn, who was schooled in the procedures of older compositional methods, shows clearly the ways that the new teaching method broke away from the old.

Dunn: I had studied various forms of dance at the Boston Conservatory of Music for about three years and I had taught composition with percussion instruments there. Then I came to New York and I was Martha's [Graham] personal pianist. I worked a great deal with Merce [Cunningham] and the company and studied composition with John [Cage]. I was very unhappy with several things about composition. I had seen both Doris [Humphrey] and Louis [Horst] give recipes for things, which I thought were very stultifying recipes. I enjoyed Martha's much more. *If* there were two lines [of modern dance], Doris was much too didactic for my taste and Martha was far more an intuitive artist. Also there was the whole background of the Orient with Martha and the asymmetry of patterns. I thought that Merce was very definitely in that line, with the asymmetry of pattern having very much to do with Oriental art, rather than Renaissance Western art. John had taught courses previously at Merce's studio and John asked me.

McD.: Composition courses?

Dunn: They were the only classes [at the time] related to anything up to date. Louis was giving a course in modern forms but the most modern piece was something from Schoenberg's six piano pieces. This was called "intellectuality." I thought that this was simply *infra dig.* Those are expressionist pieces. Also, they were written in 1911. However, I discovered while working on Martha's earlier pieces that Martha's mind worked so much on intuition and had so little discipline that while Louis was there he did a lot to form and shape the basic structures of Martha's marvelous dances. But Louis and Doris were presenting forty-year-old students.

McD.: Who were they?

Dunn: Thirty- and forty-year-old students at Connecticut College presenting dances just there.

McD.: Why did you want to teach a composition course?

Dunn: Out of anger. John asked me to and there was no one else to do it and I said, "Yes, I'll do it," and I enjoyed it very much. It was John's idea that we could use Merce's studio and work with some of the people surrounding him. John did not want to do it again and Merce did not like to teach composition at that time. What happened is that I taught four courses and he taught the fifth one. He brought his "Suite by Chance" in and had people toss the coins, you know. He has done that at colleges. They toss the coins to realize the detail of it. In 1964 I did teach one more session at Judy's studio downtown and then that was it. It was something I thought that I could do and it was very nice to think about doing it because I had taught composition before.

McD.: Where?

Dunn: At the Boston Conservatory. It was the old Wigman [Mary Wigman, founder of the German Expressionist School of Dance] percussion composition, teaching students the fundamentals of music, teaching them how to handle percussion instruments and then to compose accompaniments for their own dances. But what I found much more interesting was to compose dances including the students' own percussion accompaniment and having them handle the instruments while performing. I was a student of musical composition and I felt that it was much the same thing. Obviously John's ideas extend very readily to theater and I felt quite secure.

McD.: How was the group assembled?

Dunn: They were mainly people taking class with Merce and interested in his work.

McD.: Your class was very mixed because some of the people were not even dancers.

Dunn: You had people of greater or lesser maturity in the art field. Some of the most delightful ideas came from people who were very naïve. There was room there for everybody. The more sophisticated people fed on the ideas of the less sophisticated. My class was a workshop. It was usually ten or twelve sessions. I gave it four times between 1960 and 1962. It was a class in which two things happened: One was a presentation of a method of analysis from John's book, *Silence:* "Structure in music is its divisibility into successive parts from phrases to long sections. Form is content, the continuity. Method is the means of controlling the continuity from note to note. The material of music is sound and silence. Integrating these is composing."* These four terms are rather neat guideposts in analyzing what you see in any time art—dance being a time art as well as music. Many of the assignments in class were given in these terms; that is, it was a case-study research thing. I had worked with John and John's classes had an incredible effect, which was that everyone was productive at first and then productivity vanished as the classes went along. Partly it was that John would, say, bring in this or that, you know, bring in whatever you had and he would tear it apart thinking that you would do something more far out the next time. I could never quite figure that out, so I said, "I think it needs a little more structure." But each assignment that I gave was only partially defined as to what I wanted and there were many, many choices that were up to the student. And in the discussion, following John's idea of discussing and not evaluating, we concentrated on what we had seen. What was the structure, what were the materials, what were the methods. And it was very interesting to guess how a piece was put together, and to keep throwing people off from evaluating statements to statements of what they had seen. The last person to really confess what he had in mind was the choreographer himself. Often the choreographer's idea was much more narrow than what had come out in the class itself. What was also interesting was that in about the third session of each class there was a great deal of anxiety and some hostility toward me, which I had to get used to, because they had expected an evaluation and I saw how thoroughly people were trying to fill the recipe. And there was simply no recipe to fill for me.

McD.: So you refused to become an evaluator of material. In the sense of judge and jury. That was different from the classes you had seen before.

Dunn: Yes! John didn't evaluate really, but you felt that it wasn't quite right.

McD.: Did the people who came to your class have a lot of bad habits or inhibiting experiences?

*John Cage, *Silence* (Middletown, CT: Wesleyan University Press, 1961).

Dunn: Yes! But that did not come out in what they did, most of which to my mind was very, very fresh. It came out more in the anxiety that they felt and in something that I was very naïve about at first and did not understand: the hostility directed toward me in about the third session.

McD.: You personally as the teacher?

Dunn: Yes, because I simply would not tell them to do this or not to do that. Or even how to structure the class session. The class was always left very loose.

McD.: This was a deliberate thing on your part?

Dunn: Yes! Very deliberate. But I felt very happy about the classes because they were enormously productive. The concert was a very sharp selection out of the material presented in ten classes and, even so, it ran about three hours, which I thought was rather incredible.

McD.: How were your classes shaped?

Dunn: I should say that I brought in nine or ten assignments, and they were all very different. They were brought in to show very different things. We always did three pieces of Satie and that's where Yvonne's [Rainer] dances came from. Everybody in the class took the same Satie "Gymnopédie." I played the piece and gave them a number structure and they composed a dance, separate from the music but structured with the music in a sort of dovetailing way without any mickey-mousing. That's the way Merce did his various Satie pieces.

McD.: What is a number structure?

Dunn: The number of measures of the phrases. You know, this is all John [Cage] lore. The big time structure, leaving out whatever actor material went in the time; eight measures in ¾, two measures in ¾ plus three [measures] plus two [measures]. Then, taking these the dancers regrouped them and did a dance counting this way, without ever worrying about the music until I played it, to give them an idea of the tempo before they came in with their pieces counted out. And then we put it onto the music. I had always felt that that had a very lovely result because it had such freedom. That was one assignment. And then I gave an assignment in games. You know, game time. Always it was a little different. I was always sure to give an assignment so that people were forced to collaborate. They could not control the result because there were two people working the thing out in semi-independence.

McD.: On a piece which they would have to present together?

Dunn: Yes! Rehearse together and present together. The actual assignments were very fluid from time to time. They were structured up to a certain point. I would say, "This is what I would like you to do," and they would say, "Well, how would you like us to do other things about it?" and I would simply say, "You will have to choose." We had a lot of ideas about chance, indeterminacy games.

McD.: Chance is a mathematical concept, but indeterminacy?

Dunn: Chance operations are used to make a piece, and the piece more or less exists as it is; it is performed the same way each time. An indeterminate dance is something which may change each time. It's not necessarily improvisation, but there is a certain amount of improvisatory choice as to how the dancer will perform. The dancer has a choice, in other words. Performing his thing now or performing his thing in relation to someone else, in an unforeseen manner.

McD.: How would you categorize your work?

Dunn: There were two traditions: architecture versus "camp," you might say. I don't know what to call it. It's not quite fair to call it camp. My tradition was much more the architecture Al Carmines spoke about when he said there was a certain classicism about the Judson, and I was very touched because I had no idea that he understood about that. He felt very anxious about the first Judson things when he saw what we were going to do there. When he got used to it, he felt that there was a certain classicism about the way we kept getting down to the very elements of dance expression. I always enjoyed the "camp" element and I never attempted to discourage it but I was interested to get people's minds working on questions of architecture. I was always impressed by John's statement that when you build a structure that strong you can accept all sorts of things into it. It was to the freshness of inspiration, and not to any intellectual thing, that I was trying to open people's minds. To get people's minds working in different areas.

McD.: You really felt that things had closed off?

Dunn: Except for Merce and Judy [Dunn] and Jimmy [Waring].

McD.: What was the relationship between work that was going on in the plastic arts and the work that was going on in dance at the time?

Dunn: [Robert] Rauschenberg and [Robert] Morris did visit my classes. Rauschenberg said that he was not interested in happenings but was interested in dances. What he did were dances. Rauschenberg's things were situations and very striking. They were not so much lyric or dramatic movement things. In terms of John's divisions, I would say that the materials were very interesting. "Pelican" [by Rauschenberg] was one of the most extraordinary things I have ever seen because it was presented as a three-ring circus. The understanding came from the art world and not the entrenched music and dance world. It's really a function of economics. Economics are on the side of the art world. Art is, after all, a form of real estate. One thing about Judson. I always insisted that it was not a stage but that it was an area in which to perform. In class we always said that whatever you do, don't mock up a stage in class. You are in this room, we are sitting on the floor by the wall, here. Do it in those terms. Let's not use the lights or curtains, just let's use the place as it is. The early concerts that we had at Judson had this wonderful feeling of space and of involvement with the audience because the dancers were not trying to mock up a format stage in a church. It was the area it was. That was the start of using various areas and using an area for what it was rather than as a cheap or *faute de mieux* stage.

McD.: There was a tremendous surge of activity at Judson since everyone had so much to show. I was talking to Lucinda Childs about one dance she did which I was not able to see and it was in one of your classes.

Dunn: I remember that we were at Judy's studio and Lucinda went across the street and stood in a doorway. Meanwhile I think that she had left a tape with us, saying various things and when it came to "Everybody go to the window," we looked out the window and there was Lucinda four or five stories down across this crazy, grimy street. Everyone looked out the window because that was the instruction. It was extraordinary, just fantastic.

McD.: It was a time assignment that she had?

Dunn: Yes, I think I got that from Jimmy [Waring] or Merce. You know, people agonize about everything, making a ten minute or five minute or something to bring in next week, so that was a good study. I don't think that it was my original idea.

McD.: I spoke to Lucinda about that dance and she said that she didn't like the deadline but was able to work to deadlines in your class because it wasn't a lifetime commitment. It was just a commitment for the duration of the course.

Dunn: Yes, there were paradoxes involved in that. Which brings me back to the paradoxes that I had so disliked, of seeing dancers presented in a semi-student situation. The last workshop was simply too big to have in Merce's studio, there were too many people in the course, the dances were too big, and too many people were interested to see them performed. I had had workshop performances at the end of previous courses but in Merce's studio there just wasn't room to do the dances, put benches in, and have people sit. So Steve [Paxton] got in touch with Al Carmines. There was that great big space and we started working. Taking the space for what it was. When it came time to do the concert I didn't say anything about this being a workshop for my class. Instead we just gave it as a concert of dance. This whole concert was very classical in approach.

McD.: What did Al say?

Dunn: Steve, Judy, Yvonne, and I went and he said "Yes."

McD.: Did he ask to see any material?

Dunn: I don't remember whether he did or not.* We were coming from Merce's studio, and he was quite sure that we were on the up and up. We gave the concert and it was a very great success. It was a terribly hot night. A lot of people came and a lot of them stayed for the whole concert, for the whole three hours, and it was in the middle of July. We woke up next morning and there was a nice review by Allen Hughes in the [New York] *Times* and the whole thing had been accepted as quite off-off-Broadway. It had been presented and accepted as a professional dance event.

McD.: That was a very important thing to have happen.

Dunn: Yes. I acted as program-maker for the first five Judson concerts. I chose the order of the program, but the actual pieces we chose among ourselves. There was something very special about the shape of the programs. They were not meant to climax. Steve Paxton was marvelous. In ways I think that he was the most anxiety-provoking of all the choreographers in the early Judson programs.

McD.: What did he do?

Dunn: I don't know. His pieces were just so wide open and so slow and they did not take any standard psychological form. I can just feel the effect on my nerves. They were wide open and unencompassable. Dances where Steve

*Yvonne Rainer, Steve Paxton, and Ruth Emerson did in fact show him brief works.

Fifth Judson Dance Theater concert, June 24, 1963: Carolee Schneeman's *Chromelodeon*. Photo by Al Giese

just very solidly and sturdily did a few things just the way they were. And there was a non-psychological or anti-psychological atmosphere surrounding these things, and I don't know whether it was so much their provocation or lack of provocation that made you feel anxious as much as the fact that they couldn't be encompassed by the recipe. You had to look at what was happening, the basic elements of dance, of theater, of light, of space, of sound. There was nothing very much to grasp onto. You just had to undergo them.

McD.: There's an interesting description by John McDowell of the opening of the first concert: "The very first dance that ever happened at Judson was really very extraordinary in a couple of ways. First, the beginning of it, which was Bob Dunn's doing and was beautiful. The dance concert was announced to start at 8:15 and they went upstairs into the sanctuary to find that in order to get to their seats they had to walk across a movie that was going on. This movie consisted of some chance-edited footage by Elaine [Summers] and test footage that I made. . . . And we went on exactly, precisely for fifteen minutes. The first dance which was by Ruth Emerson started on the dot of 8:30. As the movie was just about to go off, the six people or so involved came out, the movie sort of dissolved into the dance, and as the stage lights came up the dancers were already on stage and the dance had already started."*

Dunn: Yes, this was really incredible, the beginning of the first concert. It doesn't sound like so much now but it was extraordinary, my hair stands on end to think how that worked. Nobody ever did anything like that. It was so beautiful and I suppose disorienting. I suppose what I really mean is that it kept the attention alive.

McD.: This would be an attempt to freshen the audience's appreciation, something which had been dulled by the usual concert presentation.

Dunn: Yes.

McD.: Was there any kind of religious feeling in the movement?

Dunn: Well, I don't know because everybody was so different. There were certain Oriental ideas, like Zen, and the people from California probably had some of that. Zen was a big thing to read about then, and John would talk about Zen. Otherwise, nothing that you could put your finger on. Ruth Emerson was a Quaker and she was very marvelous at insisting we do some of these things by consensus. In the choice of pieces, there was a consensus

---

*Conversation with John Herbert McDowell, *Ballet Review*, vol. 1, no. 6.

between the choreographer and the other people as to which were the best dances.

McD.: Did the workshop charge a fee?

Dunn: Yes. It was very small, something like $12 for ten classes. I did give one session of twelve classes for $15.

McD.: Very modest.

Dunn: Well, it was simply a token. Some people didn't pay, and especially to people who came back again I'd simply say, don't worry about it. And of course Merce did not charge me for the studio. Merce actually, during some of the classes, used to sit back in his dressing room and I'm sure he listened; he was concerned about something or other. And I know some of the things we were doing Merce just sniffed at and said they wouldn't work.

McD.: What type of things?

Dunn: Well, things about indeterminacy and letting people decide when to perform certain parts of their movement repertory in relation to somebody else's parts; and Merce said people would knock into each other on the stage. John and other people kept asking Merce why he didn't make an indeterminate dance. Well, Merce didn't think that was practical until he had seen approaches to that through the Judson Dance Theater. And of course he's been doing that very thing for the last few years now. Judson gave him the courage to go quite far.

McD.: His spatial ideas in deploying dancers were quite free within the proscenium stage but he's never moved beyond the proscenium stage really and truly.

Dunn: Well, his spatial ideas are unfocused and asymmetric. "How to Pass, Kick, Fall, and Run" has been done without wings, when I've seen it, which means already that you have a big, open area. He's just had to use the proscenium because he's a touring dancer and that's what he finds. But haven't you seen him perform in non-proscenium situations?

McD.: At the Philip Johnson estate, they built a platform. It was a stage in effect although it didn't have a proscenium.

Dunn: I think Ann Halprin also did non-proscenium things.

McD.: I was always very curious about Halprin. I didn't see her early work and have never felt that I was able to evaluate her clearly.

Dunn: Simone Morris, who was in a workshop or two came from Halprin, and she was extremely important. She did improvisations of a very simple and repetitive nature. She did very simple bodily actions which would only be done extremely slowly or repeated many times, or she would do sheer, outright improvisations with some sort of prop, which were marvelous. And she also brought a dance which was a poem about an onion. And the dance was an instruction, like one of LaMonte Young's instructions—like, draw a line. It was just drawing a line, but a line that lasted all evening, a long line across the floor. It was done with a plumb line and I don't know what-all. I know I did it two nights and for three hours at a time and I'd lean down and draw the plumb line and I was so terribly sore. That was probably 1963–1964, something like that. That was at Yoko [Ono]'s loft. Look how far Yoko has gone from all this.

McD.: Oh, I remember helping to cut her out of a mail sack one time, in Central Park. It was called "Cut Piece," I think.

Dunn: Whose was it?

McD.: Yoko's.

Dunn: Well, Simone was the first person I'd heard of who would say, I've brought a dance and I will *read* it to you. And it was an action not performed, it was an action that was a natural action outside of the human being, it was a situation and that was her dance.

McD.: I'm interested in the important part that your composition course played as the focal point from which people developed.

Dunn: Well, it somehow was an opener when there was nothing else open.

McD.: Nothing?

Dunn: Yes, because Jimmy [Waring] wasn't teaching. Now Jimmy would have been open, but I somehow think the fact that I was a clearing house—that I was not a choreographer—made it just a little more open.

McD.: It's interesting that in modern dance musicians have had such an impact on actual form and structure. You think of Louis' work with Martha, and John, and yourself as a musician.

Dunn: And John Herbert McDowell, who's always been so active, and is always active, when he's involved with something, in a very overall way. He's really a collaborator, to some extent, with everyone he works with.

McD.: The musical aspect seems so much more important than the plastic, the decorative aspect. The dance exists in space and time but somehow the time aspect seems so much more important.

Dunn: Yes, I don't think these things could have happened without the developments in music that John brought and the avant-garde in Europe.

McD.: People like Stockhausen?

Dunn: Yes, but it's a little hard for people like me to say. I do think that art was the most advanced, music the next, and dance the least advanced of these.

McD.: It's my impression that Louis Horst performed a very real function at one time and then became a gigantic roadblock.

Dunn: Once Martha said, Louis knew I really wanted to go to the movies. I think Louis' being around, and Louis' mind, somehow served as container to give Martha's inspiration a structure. And the same thing happened with John and Merce for a number of years. I think Merce probably accepted less of that from John and needed much less, but Merce would not be what he is without John Cage.

McD.: One difference between Louis and the people who came after was the critical hostility of *Dance Observer* to ballet. I don't get that feeling from the later generation.

Dunn: Well, you don't get it from Merce and Jimmy. Both studied ballet. That attitude of Louis' was a holding action when modern dance was fighting for its life.

McD.: That really was an attitude of historic modern dance.

Dunn: It really is true. From Merce and Jimmy on, it's not even "modern dance." Jimmy's idea is that it's ballet, it's theatrical dance. But that's very confusing because ballet people simply won't accept that. Who was it who hit on the word "cisum" for John Cage's stuff?

McD.: Yvonne's phrase [Yvonne Rainer] is "post-modern dance." It's descriptive in terms of time but not otherwise.

Dunn: Well, Jimmy Waring will not bear, or he would not bear a few years ago, the term "modern dance." He uses the term "ballet" in the sense of a theatrical dance, or dance as a theatrical presentation, so it really seems to me that that should be . . . well, I don't know. I don't have strong feelings about a central ballet tradition.

McD.: Do you see any change in, say, the ballet world, as a result of what happened at Judson?

Dunn: Well, I haven't seen that much. But I'm certain from what I hear that there has been, yes, because there's a very different theatrical treatment in the use of space, and use of mixed media, in looser, more improvisatory structures, in lack of story or genre line. And when I say genre I mean you don't have to have the same type of forms that you used to have. Balanchine must have picked up something, as he picks up something from everywhere.

McD.: When did you give your last composition course?

Dunn: One in 1964, a ten- or twelve-session course at Judy's studio.

McD.: Who was at that?

Dunn: Many of the original people and a few extras. Bob Morris came around. Meredith [Monk] was there. Elizabeth Keen. Sally Gross. . . . Yvonne and Steve might have been in for part of the time. . . . Lucinda [Childs]. . . . That's where Lucinda did her wonderful piece on East Broadway.

McD.: Now that is a piece that couldn't be repeated anywhere else.

Dunn: The idea could be adapted so that the audience could discover the dancer in some sort of surprising relationship to her surroundings. But I don't know. That was a time when there was a tremendous interest in the basic elements of dance along the idea of Bauhaus philosophy. I'm not sure there's so much interest in that right at the moment; there are so many more political and social concerns that seem to have taken over. You see, the Judson was partly the work of the semi-silent generation. And also, the money for these concerts was given by contributions, and it covered only the putting out of publicity. They were really free concerts. This was simply a public service on everybody's part. Jimmy [Waring] asked me to teach composition after I had stopped. He asked me, "Why did you stop it?" I said I did my thing and that it was really a sort of utopian thing that had to fall apart. Although it would fall apart, a utopian thing should certainly happen.

A Note on the Judson Dance Theater

After the initial success of the first Judson concert in July of 1962 and a summer filled with activity by those who participated in it, the Judson Workshop was established in the fall and met on Monday evenings. The structure of the workshop was deliberately pitched at an informal level, people just showed up to work and to look at each other's material. In many ways the assemblage of talent that comprised the workshop was similar to an artist's "atelier" in which aspiring artists would apprentice to learn their craft.

At Judson, an important element of the workshop, consensus decision making, was established largely through the influence of Ruth Emerson. Drawing on her Quaker background, she infused the group with the idea that decisions be arrived at by common assent rather than vote. Thus it was that programs were created by general agreement and not (potentially acrimonious) vote tallying. Throughout the first years of the workshop, nothing was ever put to a vote. It was an unusual way to make a revolution but most everything else about Judson and the work that went on there was unusual.

Costuming for its pieces ran from nearly nothing to workman's overalls. Designers like Remy Charlip, James Waring, and Charles Stanley created for themselves and for others costumes full of innovative excitement. The designers and choreographers also worked with other components of Judson's performing mix, like the theater section. They choreographed movement passages for productions and designed costumes and decor. Sometimes they appeared in the productions as well. Lighting designs were created by many of the choreographers themselves or by dancers who had taken a special interest in the technical side of presentations.

At first the church did not have any special theatrical equipment to speak of. The space was ill-equipped to handle any elaborate lighting or sound requirements. The interior had the gloomy charm of an old movie set. It obviously had been elaborately designed, but it had been allowed to run down. But all the space was available to the dancers. The performing area

Third Judson Dance Theater concert, January 29, 1963: Carolee Schneeman's *Newspaper Event*. Photo by Al Giese

was anywhere that the choreographer wanted it to be. There was the church proper. The benches were movable so the performers could arrange an audience at one or another side of the area, split it into segments, place the audience around the periphery of the room, or cluster it in the center. At times performances, or parts of them, took place in the choir loft above the main area. Below the church was a gymnasium which was used for many concerts. The Judson Gallery, in existence prior to the dance theater, was a meeting room around the side of the church which could be entered only through a door leading down off the street. At one time or another all of these spaces were used for dances. Light designs of strikingly imaginative quality were created in these performing areas by Jennifer Tipton, Beverly Emmons, and John Dodd, among others. (In recent years, more modern equipment has been added and the interior of the church renovated.)

With the flurry of experimentation there was at times a certain untidiness about productions, but subsequent viewing of the pieces in more technically polished presentations revealed that their inspiration was sound. Judson conveyed the feeling of amateur genius, of brilliant helter-skelter. There was much naïveté associated with Judson since many people did things that they would not have done if they had "known better." It was part of the special charm of Judson not to be encumbered by the usual rules of approval and disapproval, and it expressed its freedom in its total receptivity to the bizarre. There were, unquestionably, excesses. Many of the dances that were created had a charming air of desecration about them, but all had to be allowed to grow and flourish in order that any might survive.

Judson was run on a shoestring. Every one knew it and no one was able or inclined to do anything about it. Often costumes were physically put together—the materials bought and sewn—by the designer himself. Technical equipment was on loan, permanent or otherwise, and the church was only able to allot a small sum for each production. As a tax-exempt entity, the church was not empowered to charge admission fees but relied on audience contribution to cover the costs. The donations covered the free coffee that was served during intermissions but hardly made a dent in the costs of the productions. From time to time, patrons like Walter Gutman, Jerome Robbins, or Paul LePercq would assist an individual artist in preparing a production. Other sums were generated from friends of the performers. But by and large, a system of cooperation and friendly barter provided the technical and financial assistance needed.

The audience for the Judson dance concerts was unusual in that it basically was not a dance-oriented audience. It was not the audience that would traditionally and loyally attend modern dance concerts at any of the familiar locations in which recitals were given (the Kaufmann Concert Hall or Hunter College). It was a community audience that was interested in all of the activities that took place in the church. The same audience that would attend a dance concert would return to see a play. It was not an audience that was devoted to technique, although it could be charmed by and appreciative of ballet in sensitive pieces like "April" and "December" (choreographed by Remy Charlip). It was an audience that was primarily interested in seeing theater made over and freshened. It was an audience that could not become excited by Broadway's empty facility or its dance that had the tired stress lines of bygone conventions. It was an audience that wanted to see movement and presentation in vital and electrifying terms. It was passionate, prejudiced, and proud of the artists who presented their works at Judson. It was also friendly.

There was the sense of participation among the members of the Judson audience. They identified with the performers. A light, easy banter was the normal conversational tone of Judson intermissions—or during the some-times interminable delays in waiting on the stairwell for a production to open its doors. Difficulties of seating were usually passed off with a shrug and room could always be found for another. Unlike most audiences, the Judson audience was trustworthy about personal possessions. There never was a guarded coat room, just a pipe rack, and one didn't fear that books, papers, cases, and the like would disappear, which is more than can be said for other, more glittering theaters in New York.

The audience was heavily seeded with members of the art world. Many of the dancers were friends of the artists, and a number of the artists participated either as choreographers or as performers. Some galleries in midtown New York, like Cordier and Ekstrom, even went so far as to invite Judson dancers to perform in their spaces. Dress was casual and parents of performers were usually more formally dressed than their friends. On certain evenings a "camp" outlandish garb, such as a fur-coated man with a stuffed parrot mounted on a leather glove, would be seen amidst the working clothes of the rest of the audience. It was a style assimilated as calmly as were the others. A tolerance for individual expression was as prevalent in the audience as it was among the choreographers.

Part Two

The Matter of Movement

Until the development of modern dance in the late nineteenth and early twentieth century, the serious theatrical dancer was the ballet dancer. To be a ballet dancer meant one had been trained in the vocabulary of steps that started and finished in one of the five basic positions of the feet. The positions had been developed out of about three centuries of experimentation with the form. The classical dancer moved through space by seeking to approximate with photographic accuracy various established conformations of the body. This system of dance was soundly conceived, consistently modified, and lent itself to subtle changes that could make it more congenial to various national temperaments. But it was basically a single language with regional accents.

The earliest modern dancers were not trained ballet dancers and had to devise a system of movement that was suitable for their individual expressive needs. Thus it was that at the outset of modern dance an exploration of form became a necessary adjunct to the expression of an artistic sensibility. The exploration started with Loie Fuller, Isadora Duncan, and Ruth St. Denis and accelerated in the 1930's with the specialized technical contributions of Martha Graham and Doris Humphrey and the historic generation of modern dance. Although the schools of modern dance often had vastly differing starting points, they all basically tended to be less concerned with the flight movements that characterized ballet and more interested than was ballet in using the floor. Also, modern dancers tended to have greater flexibility of the torso than the ballet dancer, who generally kept the upper body fairly rigid. What was not questioned by the historic generation was the necessity of technique as a prerequisite of dancing.

This "necessity" was one of the first questions posed by the generation that began to emerge in the 1960's. To be contemporary, a classically established form such as ballet makes relatively minor physical adjustments to its time, while changing its thematic emphasis quite drastically. Evolving modern dance, on the other hand, effects sweeping changes in both its expressive form and thematic content. As a movement approach, yet one without a standard set of school-ordered steps, it has in each of its genera-

65

tions created a radical movement vocabulary as well as an altered thematic structure with which to represent its period. The choreographers who followed the historic generation were strongly concerned with form and asked themselves whether they could logically appear in the highly stressed technical garb of accomplished performers to display their own reality or whether they did not need to revert to a more intimate approximation of shared common movement with their audiences. Just as poetry is the most refined form of speech, a technically trained dancer possesses a physical skill that is a dramatic intensification of ordinary movement. The highly trained dancer takes the commonplace and elevates it for presentational purposes. However, between the day-to-day movement of anyone and the technical skill of the most accomplished technician there lies a range of dance skills of greater or lesser refinement. It was to the more everyday—the more fundamental in the sense of being there first—that the newer choreographers turned in order to express their creative intentions.

The question posed by those who chose to analyze movement was the basic one: What is the nature of dancing? Is it unchanging in its forms from one decade to the next or are differing forms appropriate to different times? The pioneer generation of modern dance sought out lyrical expressionist shapes and the dancers of the 1930's wanted percussive, forceful accents in their works. Each wanted to develop a method of moving that would speak directly to the concerns of the time in which it was living. The generation of the 1960's found that theatrically generated emotionalism was fogging the clarity of movement and some found that technique was interposing its own requirements over those of the choreography. For many it became necessary to find more suitable forms.

This was done in a variety of ways—from total abnegation of standard dance training to major modifications in the trained dancer's body. The choreographic outlines formed by trained dancers were "softened" so as to include those more related to everyday movement. An element of the casual or the related entered into dancing. Choreographers tended not to draw a rigid line between dancers of varying performing skills and often mixed those of widely diverse accomplishment in a single piece. Forms of new movement burst with a volley of differing emphases.

Among those who have produced and sustained a unique conception of movement in a series of works are Twyla Tharp, Steve Paxton, Deborah Hay, Yvonne Rainer, Gus Solomons, Jr., and Meredith Monk. Each in an individual way has a special approach and has continued to explore its implications. A number of other dancer/choreographers have made important though more fragmentary contributions to the exploration of movement and these are discussed in a "round-up" chapter.

Twyla Tharp

Controlled Living Space

Twyla Tharp's main concern in choreography is to throw lines of move-ment across and through space and thereby establish a zone of human mastery over the real estate that is our environment. If space is the enemy, then time is her weapon, although these two related parameters of dance can never be so artificially separated. What Tharp does is to approach a given space and through choreographically inventive motion cross and recross it with differently paced passages, weaving a skein of activity over it. Starting with the proscenium stage as liberated by Merce Cunningham, she moved out to occupy the entire performing space in which she found herself. These spaces have been as different in scale as the "Great Lawn" of Central Park in New York and the main staircase of the Metropolitan Museum of Art. She has progressed in her own performing style to a point in which the upper body has been drastically freed from conventional restraint while the body from the waist down has retained the foundations of strong dance training. Tharp does not display technique for itself but rather assumes it in order to progress to something else.

Tharp was born in Indiana, where she had her first dance lessons. Her family moved to California when she was a child. She had dance training at the rudimentary level, but a long time elapsed between her period of active involvement with dancing as a child and the highly directed performing interest she showed during her college years. Prior to selecting a college, she had decided that she wanted to be near good dance teachers. She chose to attend Barnard College in New York. While pursuing a degree in fine arts, she worked toward an active career in dance. She was attracted to the Paul Taylor company and when she graduated in 1963 was invited to join. She had to get special permission to miss her own graduation in order to appear with the company, which was starting a tour. She remained with Taylor until 1965, when she left to begin her independent choreographic career.

The first year she completed five dances, which ranged in length from a brief five-minute collage of movements with non-dancers, to a twenty-minute stage show for trained dancers which she called "Stage Show." The latter was performed in the Alaska Pavilion at the New York World's Fair and was closed after one performance because of lack of funds. However, Tharp found the experience valuable, since it was her first chance to hire and work with trained professionals.

In the first part of her choreographic career, Tharp interested herself in handling space with linear patterns. "Tank Dive" (1965), her first work, was also the first of her linear structures. Choreographed especially for a small theater at Hunter College, it was done in three sections. Tharp was the only dancer; she entered a half-cleared auditorium and worked around to a previously positioned oversized pair of flat wooden shoes in the middle of the floor. She stepped into these and leaned forward as one might do in a ski-jumping contest. She then slipped out of the prop shoes and went to the small stage where she held a relevé for the duration of a "pop" tune, after which there was a blackout. The second section consisted of two men advancing into the space and accepting two flags which were handed to them by two girls, followed by another blackout. In the third and last part, Tharp started in a relevé position on the stage, ran across the floor to the back of the theater, swung violently around a pole, and reversed direction so that she slid out toward the center of the floor on her side; then she arose to assume the position she had on stage. Blackout and end of piece.

For a first piece, it was interesting as an integration of various types of physical activity, combining in the slide a gesture from baseball with a strictly dance step, the relevé onto the toes. More significantly, the piece indicated that a technical approach was being made that took off from the point to which Cunningham had brought dance. While Tharp did not entirely dispense with the use of a stage, she did bring part of the work into the area traditionally thought of as being the zone of the audience. The work also concentrated quite deliberately and dramatically on the weight of various movements in and of themselves, even emphasizing them by such devices as the oversized shoes which enabled her to extend her range of forward latitude far beyond that which would have been normal.

During the remainder of 1965, Tharp continued to work on a variety of pieces. It was a time of exploring the basics of craft methodically. She made a 30-minute film-dance, "Stride," which afforded her the opportunity to try out a dance of extended length for four people. In "Cede Blue Lake," she created, in the form of a canon, a work for three dancers. The second and third of the identical sections started at some length after the first and second, respectively, and overlapped until, at the end of the work, the three dancers were in unison. Tharp was much concerned with the use of stage properties, from the outsized shoes of "Tank Dive" to the use of a piece of burlap that the four dancers pulled apart into equal sections in "Stride." The dances of this period also used spaces; after the first work in the small theater at Hunter College, she used the non-proscenium space of

Twyla Tharp and Graciela Figueroa in *After Suite*, 1969. Photo by Jack Mitchell
(Courtesy Twyla Tharp Dance Foundation)

the Judson Church for other dances and did her film dance on the roof of a school in Brooklyn.

The following year she produced the first of the works that indicated a maturing sensibility—"Re-Moves." In this work, she further showed her special sensitivity to the problem of segmenting and thereby controlling space by means of efficient dance timings. The dance was designed for a small group, three dancers, and was divided into four sections. The first section was formal, and the three performers were costumed in black with small white triangles of cloth for headpieces, like nurses' caps or modified nuns' habits. Each dancer wore a glove on one hand, leaving the other bare, and a sneaker on one foot, leaving the other foot bare. To emphasize the rigor of the dance, each girl carried a stop watch and moved between points in a carefully calculated set of straight lines. The introduction of a diagonal direction appeared almost like a romantic luxury. The second section was warmer and consisted of a deadpan tap dance which also developed in right angle directional changes. In the third section, a large box was moved into the performing area so that there was some portion of the audience seated on each of three sides. The fourth side faced toward the entrance, where no one was sitting. The size of the box was such that it was impossible for the audience to see activity on more than one side of the box, unless seated right at the corner. Even here, only half of the dance could be seen as the other two sides were blind. The dancers traveled around the periphery of the box with deliberate slowness. In the fourth movement, the box was removed and a dance of a more flowing and warmer nature concluded the work. The piece had a great deal of movement invention and further showed Tharp's willingness to include in a single piece various types of dance movement, including a section of mime flower-plucking at the end of the hard-surfaced and businesslike first movement. (This part of the dance changed on a European tour the company undertook later that year. Instead of doing an illusionistic act of flower plucking, eggs were allowed to roll out of the palm and to shatter on the floor. In each case, something organic had been stopped in its development.)

The spirited concluding movement of the dance was designed in such a fashion that it could utilize some aspects of the space in which it was performed. While touring this piece, various areas presented their own problems, but one of the most interesting was a large iron door encountered in Holland which could be cranked out on the stage. Like other varying things, it was included. In six out of her first seven pieces, Tharp had used music of some description in conjunction with the dance. The music tended to be pop group songs, and in one case a short phrase of a hymn as interpreted by Thelonius Monk. After her European tour, Tharp stopped using music altogether, with the one exception of a curious piece called "Three Page Sonata for Four" (1967) done to Charles Ives' "Three Page Sonata" for piano, the only instance in which she used concert-level music—and in the Ives piece, it appeared that her reaction to this type of musical structure was not particularly inventive. Tharp has avoided music because she feels that it competes for attention with the dance and does not allow one to judge the effects created by movement alone. She has instead used sounds of a rhythmic nature, such as the ticking of an electric metronome and the snapping of fingers and direct voice-call signals between dancers. These calls can be as enigmatic as asking for a section count, such as was done in the incredibly complex "Group Activities" (1968) or as simple as shouting out the name of a person at the end of a line of dancers, which indicated that it was time for the file to reverse direction.

An important characteristic of Tharp's modified-proscenium approach to choreography is her willingness to consider almost any space as suitable for a dance. She has at varying times appeared on a regular proscenium stage with frontally oriented dance works such as "One Two Three" (1966), and in an open field with "Medley" (1969) which, although meant to be seen from the front and looked through, is not suitable for a small stage. She premiered "Generation" (1967) in a gymnasium, and her most recent work, "Dancing in the Streets of London, and Paris, Continued in Stockholm and Sometimes Madrid" (1969) was first seen on two levels of the Wadsworth Atheneum in Hartford and was later presented in a modified version in two different locations in New York, the Metropolitan Museum and the Performing Arts Library of Lincoln Center. Recently she created a proscenium dance for a concert in Virginia. Tharp does not have a specific spatial requirement for her work but will handle the space that is offered to her. It is a freedom of choice which was made possible when the proscenium arch was seen as only one possible way of organizing space and not always the best one.

Tharp has worked in a variety of choreographic lengths from very short to very long, although her present work tends to run closer to the hour-long than to shorter pieces. Since she has not interested herself in concert touring, which would entail using works from repertory, many of the shorter dances have not been seen for a few years. One of the finest was "Forevermore" (1967), which was designed for a soloist in an area visible but physically removed from the main performing area in which a trio of girls in black-spangled costumes perform a flashy and show-stopping highly energetic tapdance variation. The soloist is not only physically separated but also psychically separated from this activity, and passes from side to side, alternately pinning up and unraveling her long hair while sinking to the ground and rising again. In the background is the sound of two snare drums—unseen and of varying intensity. The contrast of the soft, dreamy narcissistic solo with the hard, forceful movement of the trio offers a dual view of reality and one is allowed to wonder about who is marching to the different drummer.

"One Way" (1967), another short work, was a display piece created for a long gymnasium space in which five girls moved from one end of the area to the other. Each did individual variations which together had the precision and flowing charm of a geometric figure tracing itself out on an electronic screen. When they reached the other side of the gymnasium, the piece was concluded.

Among the notable features of this dance were the costumes designed by Robert Huot. (He is Tharp's husband and has designed all of the Tharp repertory.) They consisted of blue velvet pullovers with sleeves that just cleared the ground, so that the dancers' hands were not visible and the sleeves exercised a slight floppy life of their own, following limply the direction of the dancers' arms. As with "One Way," Huot's costumes and properties have demonstrated a great understanding and sympathy for the thrust of Tharp's work. In "After 'Suite' " (1968), a homage to Merce Cunningham, Huot contributed a proper sense of flow to the choreography by designing beige jump suits which extended the dancers' outlines in the arm and the bell-bottom pants' legs. For "Generation," he prepared a series of identically cut costumes and had them made out of five different textures and finishes of silver cloth (from a soft matte surface to a bright metallic brilliance), the variations of which mirrored the growth and decline curve in the choreography.

Recently, however, Tharp has begun to enlarge the numbers of dancers she includes in any piece and has abandoned special costuming in favor of street clothes. Of the larger works she has created to date, "Medley," a dance for over 40 dancers, represents the crowning piece of the first part of her choreographic career. It was the last piece created whose form was unchangeably set. Subsequent works have tended to be more fluid in their ordering.

"Medley" was the warm culminating statement about the members of her company (Sara Rudner, Theresa Dickinson, Margery Tuppling, Graciela Figueroa, Rose Marie Wright, Sheila Raj) that Tharp made in the summer of 1969. She worked on the piece from the outside—as a choreographer only and not a choreographer/dancer—and created it with a great deal of emotional overtones, an element that she had suppressed more or less vigorously in her previous work. "Medley" was given its first performance at the American Dance Festival at Connecticut College and included forty summer dance students as well as Tharp's basic company of six girls. It was the first time that a man had ever appeared in one of her dances—as a matter of fact two men (who were students)—though because they were included in the corps and were not given any distinctive male variation to perform, they could have easily escaped notice.

The dance began with a girl doing a solo that started before the audience arrived and ended with the same girl doing the last slow adagio after it had left. As the viewers sat down to watch, from the sloping lawn above the performance area, various members of the six-person company picked up movements from individuals in the audience and reproduced them. Later, student dancers, who were seated among the regular audience, burst out of the crowd and ran down into the performing area to line up in files behind the six basic members of the company to perform a series of lyrical drill exercises. During another portion of the dance, two groups mirrored the actions of two soloists, one of whom was engaged in a very quick succession of actions and the other of whom had many sustained and slow-moving movements. Toward the end of the dance, all of the performers poured from a cluster and took up individual positions all over the performing area like jewels spreading across green velvet. Each took as long as possible to do a slow identical adagio movement and left the field as soon as it was finished. The idea was to remain as long as possible. The tempo of the dance steadily slowed until the last dancer left the area, and the flood tide of dance energy was stilled.

Tharp now works and presents rehearsal material in terms of a continual and on-going work-in-progress called "Dancing in the Streets of London and Paris, Continued in Stockholm and Sometimes Madrid." The piece in its first form was premiered in Hartford and sections of it, somewhat altered, were presented in New York, first at a benefit at the Performing Arts Library at Lincoln Center and later at the Metropolitan Museum of Art. On both occasions in New York, a serious miscalculation was made regarding the performing conditions and the dance was not seen to best advantage. At the library, the benefit audience was unsympathetic and found it annoying to have dancers rushing around in their midst; at the Metropolitan, there were far too many people present in the performing area for anyone to be able to see anything. At Hartford, the piece received sympathetic viewing from an interested audience and was not crowded out of existence by the numbers attending. Choreographed as it is in portable individual phrases, the piece has a flexibility that lends itself to presentation in a variety of locales, drawing on each for special effects but being incorporated into the basic amorphous structure of the work. It is a logical extension of the variable fourth section Tharp had included in the earlier "Re-Moves," although it does not share the tight, angry tonality of that work.

In Hartford, "Dancing . . ." was performed on two floors and the connecting stairwell of the Wadsworth Atheneum. The audience flowed in and around the performers at all levels and at times trailed them from one floor to the other. There was no set position from which to view the dance, for it took place out of sight and at the viewer's elbow at the same time. The audience was told at the beginning that the piece would be done in its entirety twice, thus removing a great deal of the anxiety from the viewers who would be able to see what had been missed the first time. The nine dancers (all girls) kept in touch with one another by means of verbal time checks called up the stairwell and by the use of video monitors connected to a closed-circuit television hookup between the various galleries. The formation of the dance was one of flow and follow-the-leader cue-taking. At times the follow-the-leader element was directly expressed when a formation of girls would perform in one of the open areas and then follow the leader down the stairs, assemble, and perform movements in unison. At other times, the leader would be located on a different floor and the dancers would pick up the movement from the monitor in their gallery.

At the beginning of the dance, all of the performers were seated on the floor of the first ground-level gallery doing warm-up exercises, and then slowly, as the dance picked up momentum, they spread out over the entire performing area. The audience was drawn into the performance in various ways. Dancers were allowed to incorporate certain gestures which they observed from the audience at certain times during the dance, and the audience was invited to ask the dancers questions. In one gallery, a dancer would attempt to do any solo movement that was requested. At another time, the audience found itself in a gallery where steps had been painted on the floor, much like the footwork patterns one would find in a school diagram for a social dance. The phrase was built on a four count, with the first part being a simple set of "1," "2," "3," "4," and the second a sidewards "1 and," "2 and," "3 and," "4 and" series, accelerating the motion into the third set of crossover steps. This set was to be done in a large circle with a center of two footprints where the performer finally plants feet slightly apart and makes some motion from the waist down. One of the most successful of the set pieces was done for five girls who switched articles of clothing—for example, passing along a sweater and acquiring an outsized shirt or sweat pants. While clothes-switching continued, one of the girls read from a book, but all had to perform the variation.

Toward the end of the entire dance, the performers trickled back from the entire space of the building and began to concentrate in the room where it had begun. In the final section the dancers split into two groups, and one did rote movements in formation while a smaller group did challenge sets for one another. The dancers in this group would try to best one another by attempting to meet the increasingly difficult demands that the others made upon them. They became like human clay which the others would attempt to mold into impossible positions, and it became a test of concentration and skill to maintain balance and to incorporate the requested adjustments. After a while both the formation dancing and the individual contests finished and the dance was over. The dancers simply sat down for a rest before repeating the dance and the audience asked them questions about it.

Like most of Tharp's work, "Dancing . . ." was physically demanding and had a stylish belligerence. No attempt was made to hide the fact that it was hard work and that for the most part it required special training to be able to do it, and yet the movement was not ornate with the performing inflections that have come to be associated with professional dancing. It was aristocratic movement with a vernacular phrasing. It represented a giant step that Tharp has taken in her drive to get closer to the flow of quotidian movement that is the common experience that the audience faces regularly without being aware of it. It was an attempt to set into an artistic frame that which might ordinarily pass unnoticed to the pedestrian ambling down the street or squeezing into some public-transportation vehicle. The dancers often looked as if they were trying to work their way through a dense crowd with a skewed upper-torso twisting motion.

The style of the Tharp dancer is quick, twisting, and strong. The choreography calls for sustained poses, trigger-quick shifts of weight from toe-to-heel, rapid changes of direction, and a general alertness to others with a sensitivity in reacting to them. Tharp's choreography consists of innumerable slivers of movement "compacted" almost in the way that ordinary gesturing would appear in rapid-sequence photography. There is a strong structuring which underlies all of her work, with little or no use made of chance elements, although performers have some choice as to when they will perform certain variations. She is perennially intrigued with dancers as individuals and their special individual qualities which she works into her choreography. "Medley" excepted, her work generally has a cool and finished surface, thus focusing attention on the movement itself rather than on any emotional overlay which might be imparted to it by performer "interpretation."

Tharp is devoted to the possibilities and properties of physical movement. Simultaneously, she is less and less interested in the formal separation of audience and performer and has begun to create her works more and more in such a manner that an audience, which may not see all of a work, will pay more attention to what it can see. It is an element of observing and emphasizing which has been present since the obstructing box in "Re-Moves." It undoubtedly will lead her into more and more public places.

Steve Paxton

People

Serious creative activity and enlightened sponsorship are inextricably linked in the opinion of choreographer Steve Paxton. He has produced a number of dance programs, written and lectured about program sponsorship, and currently finds himself not so much a creator of movement in his dances as a sponsor of choreography. The equation behind the dual facets of his career is that intelligent sponsors enable choreographers to work, and responsible choreographers then make good dances.

Paxton likes to involve himself as closely as possible with the people who are going to perform in his dances, and then give a few simple instructions to allow them to create the dance from their own moment-by-moment experience as performers in front of an audience. What Paxton does is to create the ambiance in which choreography arises. His approach is probably one of the more radical contrasts to traditional theatrical practice, in which so much stress is placed on the possession of technique. Paxton maintains that the current generation of dancers is the first one to have the choice about whether they wish to become technical dancers or not.

Growing up in Tucson, Arizona, Paxton habitually found himself concerned with disciplined movement, first as a gymnast and then as a dance student. He decided to take up dance as a means of improving his gymnastic form and ended up abandoning gymnastics for dance. His two teachers in Tucson, one an Episcopal nun and the other the director of a Jewish Community Center, were both former Graham students and were dedicated to that system of teaching. Both shared many of the same dancers and were involved in putting together dance performances, and Paxton found himself making tours of Texas and the West Coast with a heavy performing schedule. In 1957, the year before he left Tucson, he did more performing than he was to do for the next three years as a student in New York. When he arrived in New York, he began to take class with José Limón and Merce Cunningham. Soon after, he was part of Robert Dunn's choreography composition course when it was first organized. In 1961 he was invited by Cunningham to become a member of the company. He was an outstanding performer with Cunningham, possessing as he does a sensitively attuned weightiness of gesture and a strong, alert bearing. He was to tour with the company until 1965, when he left and pursued his own full-time career as a choreographer and teacher.

When Paxton first began studying choreographic composition, one of the problems with which he concerned himself was the sources of movement. Traditionally, movement is determined by the choreographer and expressed through the body of another dancer. It is a system that works well for many, but Paxton found it limiting both in terms of his own imagination and in terms of movement itself. One of his first attempts to find a new source for movement was to create a small "chance" machine. This consisted of a rubber ball, marked with movement directions, and a piece of glass. He would roll the ball on the floor of a studio and stop it by pressing down on it with a piece of glass. The spot at which he touched the ball with the glass indicated a type of movement, and the amount that Paxton depressed the ball indicated time duration. It was simple and analogous to other methods of developing chance dances, such as the movement charts that Cunningham developed for "Suite by Chance" and from which sequences were developed by tossing coins. Another method that Paxton used at this time was the picture score. For this, he would take photographs of people and in a random fashion arrange them in some sequence. The choreographic problem then became to develop the movement that would allow one to reach or, if one wanted, pass through these pictures as part of a continuous dance development. With his athletic background, it was logical that Paxton find a source for dance movement in sports. On tour in Sweden during 1964, he created a picture score from photographs of soccer players which he clipped from magazines. (He included the score in a piece that was performed only once, "Jag Ville Gorna Telefonera.")

Paxton has not concerned himself with the traditional ideas of climax and denouement, theme and variation, conception and development, but rather with a smooth, even flow of choreographic material. He has deliberately sought to create a dry and almost arid presentational plane in which his performers were thrown in upon themselves in a special way. Paxton has focused his attention on performers as people and not as technicians projecting an image—that is, expressing a conception molded by a choreographer—but has attempted to create a choreographic field which would throw the behavior of the performers into relief. Accepting the untidiness of ordinary life, he has incorporated everyday gesture and action into his pieces with a lavish hand and even finds himself including animals, such as dogs and chickens. He once commented on a chicken with whom he did a duet, "The performance was bad but we had a good rehearsal."

Paxton is one of the most radical of the newer choreographers in his attempt to wrench audiences loose from their habitual ways of looking at dance. In the course of his career, he has found himself verbally assaulted

Steve Paxton in *Backwater: Twosome*, 1977. Photo by Johan Elbers

during a performance, and recently he has been censored and not allowed to present a large dance with all performers in the nude. As one who is calmly rational, he finds it difficult to understand why his studied revolution arouses such passions.

In "Proxy," his first work (1962), he created a sixteen-minute piece in three movements for three dancers. It began with a long walking section, in which the first performer circles whatever forms the backdrop of the stage seven times in the same direction carrying a white basin. He places the basin down at a designated spot on the stage and stands in it, while the other two performers enter. One drinks a glass of liquid and the other eats a piece of fruit. The second section is a "picture score" solo which is done first by one performer and then the second. The third part is a "picture score" for all three performers. Desiring a place to perform the work, he auditioned it at the "Y" to the consternation and hostility of the panel, which refused to allow the piece to appear. It was the last time that Paxton was to attempt to work within the frame of the established modern dance world. He began to seek other outlets for his work and found that the art audience was more receptive to his experimental choreography than was the existing dance audience, and he began to work with artists and patrons of the plastic arts.

Out of his failed audition at the "Y" came a work that created an early scandal at Judson Church, where it was first performed. One of the judges at the "Y" had remarked that "All of the Judson people looked alike." Paxton then conceived a duet for himself and Yvonne Rainer that would present them in an identical fashion. They first attempted to arrange their facial expressions so that they would achieve a somewhat zombie-like identity but found that it was not possible. He then thought of doing the dance in gorilla suits but was unable to afford the rental fees; then he hit on the idea of an almost nude dance, which is the manner in which the piece was presented. Both performers wore only the briefest of costumes, which served to meet the legal requirements but little more. The piece, "Word Words" (1962), was presented on one evening, and the following night he presented "Music for 'Word Words,' " which was the sound made by a vacuum cleaner exhausting an inflatable costume on stage.

This was the first time he had used an inflatable object in any of his dances. Later he was to create several pieces using such inflatable props. These pieces, which he created over a period of several years, culminated in "Physical Things," a giant extravaganza in the shape of the human alimentary canal which was the opening piece in the series of "Nine Evenings: Theater and Engineering" that was presented at the 25th Street Armory in 1966. The piece was basically a set—an inflatable—through which the audience had to pass in order to reach its seats in the Armory. Paxton designed it with a series of narrow and wide spaces and wanted the audience members to look at one another as they passed through it. At the exit funnel, there were a number of performers in black crouched in a long stool-shaped inflatable, the performers to be peered at by the audience. Paxton had designed their postures so that unusual configurations of the body would be apparent, such as the shape of the leg from mid-thigh to mid-calf, independent of the full extension of the body that would make up the normal length. The viewers—that is, the individuals who had walked through the set—were also exposed to a cacophony of music and words broadcast over individual transistors which they were handed on exiting from the inflatable. The piece was marginally successful and the last of the inflatable line for Paxton, who lost interest in such elaborate stagecraft shortly afterward. He did, however, sharpen his focus on individuals and their performance behavior.

Despite his considerable abilities as a technical dancer, Paxton has been reticent about creating display solos for himself. During his career, he has prepared for himself only one dance involving technical display, "Transit" (1962), and has performed it only once. In it he juxtaposed long periods of walking with balletic movements in a smooth continuum of energy expenditure. The work explored the transitions of movement from fast to slow and back again. At times he would perform a movement and then take it down to the sketchiest presentation of itself while retaining the essentials of its direction and timing (in the manner that dancers refer to as "marking"). The bulk of his pieces are for many performers, sometimes including himself and at other times deliberately excluding himself.

One of the things that struck him as a dance student was the abstracted inward look that dancers have in class when they are concentrating on doing a dance movement. It was a chance observation which he developed into an outdoor piece called "Afternoon" in 1964. It was a dance that was conceived on and for trained professional performers, except that the setting for the piece was in an area of alternately wooded and clear terrain. The dancers were placed in the various performing areas and the audience strolled through the piece on a roughly circular course. They might come upon dancers doing a sequence of movements or might find that a dancer would come to them when they entered an area and begin to dance in their midst. It was a constant alteration of focus which variously brought the viewers into immediate proximity with the dancers and then set them at a distance. It was a technique that Paxton was to use again in a later series of performances of "Deposits" (1966), an anthology of small pieces that he presented in various locales in cities and in the countryside. In another work, "Rialto" (1964), he went so far as to take a photograph of the audience from the performing area to indicate to the patrons that he wanted to see them as well as have them look at him.

Unlike many of the newer choreographers, Paxton retains an interest in the concept of repertory dances. He likes to become so familiar with his pieces that he transcends the immediacy of having to worry about remembering things and has perfect security about the choreography. Combining this comfortableness with repeated performances of his works, along with his passionate interest in individuals, he began to develop his series of short dances designed for lots of laymen. In these structurally simple pieces, he does not have to concern himself with teaching and remembering complicated sequences of movement, but can pass beyond mechanical display to stimulate people's performing styles.

In the summer of 1967, he, along with Robert Rauschenberg, Deborah Hay, and Alex Hay, was invited to a three-week workshop in Seattle. Paxton had assumed that the sponsor of the event wanted him simply to perform a piece, but discovered that the intent was for a choreographer to work with other theater people and with a group of students to create a small piece. Up until this time, Paxton had worked for the most part with a small group with whom he was comfortable and whose performing habits and skills he knew reasonably well. The experience of working with strangers significantly changed his viewpoint about the thrust of his work. To create movement, he devised a dressing and undressing competition for the performers which was done by teams against the clock. He included a series of story recitals from each of the individuals, who were instructed to relate their tale in a smooth, uninflected manner. During the three weeks, he found several new ways of dealing choreographically with individuals. Most significantly, he could tell the dance to people and then the choreography would emerge. It was the first time that he had worked in this fashion. Soon afterward he used the story-telling device in "The Atlantic" (1968), in which he instructed one dancer to relate an event in terms of its colors and two others to talk about something professional and a fourth just to talk—because he liked the sound of the performer's voice. He didn't dictate the material but simply elicited it with simple instructions and also cued movements and the light design. From the piece he did in Seattle, "The Sizes," he developed both larger- and smaller-scaled pieces built on the instructional method.

Possibly the best known work from this series is "Satisfyin Lover" (1967), which is a seven-minute piece designed for forty-two performers working within a narrow range of instructions. The structure of the piece is made up of the walking, standing, and sitting styles of the performers. Everyone is asked to cross the performing area once in the same direction. The mode of crossing is the natural walking gait in as relaxed and natural a manner as the performer is able to manage. There are three chairs halfway between the audience and those walking. Some performers are directed to sit in the chairs for varying periods of time or stand for a while at points in the space that they are crossing. When the last person has crossed and disappeared on the opposite side of the space from the one at which he entered, the piece is over. While the time is not rigidly controlled, it usually takes seven minutes for the forty-two performers to make their crossings.

Paxton has performed the piece in a variety of places with varying ease, since some groups are able to enter into the spirit of it better than are others. When it is performed well, the variety of movement produced by individual reactions to the walking situation is beautifully varied. Since those who participate in the piece are not accustomed to stage performance, the theatrical situation produces different body tensions in each. On one occasion, Paxton decided that he wanted to do a performance of the piece in the nude but the sponsor of the concert series in which the dance was to appear, New York University, did not allow him to have nude performers. Annoyed at the authoritarian attitude of the university, Paxton cancelled his appearances and gave a performance in a borrowed loft. For it, he created another seven-minute piece—untitled—designed again for forty-two people. It was performed in three movements and involved minute weight shifts and arm movements. The first instruction to the performers was to imagine that they were going to step forward on one leg and then to imagine that they were going to step forward on the other leg. The second movement was to perform the smallest jump that they could do and the third was to move the arms straight up from their normal relaxed length to the waist and then lower them again slowly. It was a dance that at first was full of small tilts and body adjustments and then eventually found more overt expression in the gentle raising of the arms.

A third large-scale piece that he made for forty-two performers was "State" (1968), created shortly after "Satisfyin Lover." Performers are asked to stand quietly during four three-minute sections, each separated by a fifteen-second blackout. While the lights are on, movement is only barely perceptible. During the blackouts, performers were allowed to make more radical movements, such as altering their position in the space or the direction in which they were facing.

In all of these laymen pieces, Paxton tries to relax the persons who are going to perform and to get them to acknowledge their own movement patterns and habits. Depending on the success he had in such pre-performance sessions, the pieces are more or less well performed. They represent, in any case, an attempt to bring the dance experience closer to the individual and to remove the highly dynamic level of performance created by trained dancers.

All through the course of his work, Paxton has experimented with the psychic and physical distance between audience and performer and has attempted to break it down or recast it in a new and evocative manner. He is especially interested in the drama inherent in any individual's manner of organizing movement. Just as the recital of personal stories is accomplished by different people in different ways, so is the everyday action of, say, taking clothes off and putting them on. Dressing and undressing is a device that he has used in a number of dances and one which he employs in teaching choreographic composition. He has moved steadily closer to the non-professionally trained performer in order to create what he regards as a more and more realistic performance situation. He scrutinizes ordinary movement with a discerning eye and attempts to produce a similar analytic attitude in those who participate in his pieces either as performer or as audience. For him, one of the most interesting parts of his laymen dances is the effect they produce in all participants after the performance. It is an effect that is almost impossible to gauge, although it would be difficult not to have a heightened sensitivity to the performance possibilities of the everyday after concentrated exposure to a choreographic presentation of such material.

Paxton has combined words and movement in a variety of interesting ways and one of the most interesting forms has been the performance lecture, which he gives either alone or with another performer. The most successful of these demonstrations to date has been "Lecture on Performance" (1968), which is a trio for himself, his dog, and a stool. Each establishes its own dynamic level, from frisky to frozen, upon which Paxton comments as he moves around. Other talks of varying success have been "Beautiful Lecture" (1969), during which a pornographic film and a dance film were shown simultaneously, and "Intravenous Lecture," during which he spoke of sponsors and their functions and walked around holding a nutritive feeding bottle connected to a vein in his arm. As in other lectures, he offered here a striking visual image along with trenchant observations on the subject of dancing. These appearances represent an imaginative development of a traditional modern dance specialty, the lecture demonstration. As with most of his work, Paxton has taken a new and somewhat startling approach to traditional materials.

During his career, Paxton has managed to question nearly all of the cherished ways of presenting disciplined movement which have been tried and found satisfactory by previous generations of dancers. Production values such as costuming, decor, and music have all been subjected to his imaginative scrutiny. At times he has used elaborate costuming and at other times none. He has carefully chosen the locations in which he wanted to present dances and at other times he has hardly bothered. At times the lighting of his pieces has been haphazard and conversely at other times highly imaginative. He has presented trained dancers in a casual manner and the untrained in careful settings. Music has virtually been eliminated from his pieces and technique has been seriously questioned as a prerequisite to dancing. His body of work has a savage innocence, asking, as it does, pointedly searching questions about basics in mild-mannered ways. He combines forthright seriousness with a diversity of means that incessantly reiterates his own musing search for the root of theater dance. It is a search carried out almost diffidently but with enormous imaginative persistence.

Deborah Hay

Structures

No one among the newer choreographers has created dance structures of such rigorous order and spontaneous performance style as Deborah Hay. She is exceptionally accomplished in handling the non-trained performer, combining efficiency with soft-spoken directions to achieve her effects. As a trained dancer, she has found herself in effect pushed out of her dances, since the performance qualities of non-specialists are what she is interested in. Her most recent and finest works have an almost mathematical order that achieves expression through the casually clothed and mixed performing skills of the people appearing in them. It is a form of dance that everyone can do, although it takes a choreographer to tell them what to do.

Hay was born and grew up in Brooklyn. She started dance training at the age of three with her mother, who ran a neighborhood dancing school and who had appeared in Broadway shows. She was exposed to ballet and tap training and later was to dedicate a dance with a tap sequence to her mother. She moved on to study at the Henry Street Playhouse at the age of fourteen and was particularly impressed with the dancing skill and teaching abilities of Bill Frank. During the time she was at Henry Street, she did a variety of commercial shows and found herself totally immersed in the world of dance to the exclusion of nearly everything else. Even after a day of rehearsal, she would go out social dancing in the evening. After a full year of almost luxuriant enjoyment of dancing, she decided that she should return to the study of ballet with its particular rigors, and soon after that she began taking class at the Merce Cunningham studio. She passed from an emotional involvement with dancing into a cooler, more structured ordering of her dance life. She became interested in the mechanics of dance and not in simply doing it. Years later she realized that she had ceased to enjoy "dancing" after she had stopped studying at Henry Street. Study at the Cunningham studio eventually led her to join the company for a six-month world tour in 1964, after which she left it and also the performing world of established companies.

Prior to joining Cunningham's company, she had performed at Henry

Street and during one summer in José Limón's company at Connecticut College. She had also appeared in the first concert given at Judson Church, the last workshop of Robert Dunn's dance composition course. After leaving Cunningham in 1964, she devoted all of her time and energy to developing her own choreographic voice. As with many other of the younger choreographers, she found that the established world of dance was not sympathetic to those concerns which were most important to her. She found that she received much more consistent support and understanding from painters and sculptors and those associated with the plastic arts as critics or patrons.

Her reaction to the world of established dance was strong and decisive. She abandoned dance training, traditional choreographic methods, and other affiliations with the dance world. She decided that designing movement to reflect something other than itself was uncommunicative. To her, it became something unreal, being removed from the thing itself. Standard technique, she began to feel, was an arbitrary exercise and really had little meaning. The ballet turnout she found "abnormal" and the traditional style of performance she felt was like a circus where the dancers performed feats for the excitation of the crowd. The training required to develop the conditioning necessary for these feats she condemned as being masochistic, and she decided that ballet class had really done some damage to her body. She found that the ritual Chinese exercises of T'ai Chi taught her more about the flow of the body and its parts than any dance training that she had taken. Having shaken herself loose from the world of which she had been a part for most of her life, she began to do her most serious creative explorations. She had done several pieces in the two years prior to 1964 in connection with the Judson Dance Theater. Strongly colored by dance technique and many of the conventions of the dance world which she had come to repudiate, they carried radical elements which were to flower more fully in her later work.

Hay was and is interested in communication between people and in individuals with their own special capabilities. She has included elements involving personal choice for the performer as well as systems of sight and sound signals—to trigger certain movements—almost from the start of her work. In these pieces, she combined aspects of choice for the performer with emotionally charged situations in a variety of ways that were challenging to the performer both as physical endurance tests and in terms of his own performing "voice"—his presentational stance. In "All Day Dance" (1963), she employed six trained dancers, each of whom was listening to separate sounds in the sound score that formed the "music" for the piece. Each sound represented a certain type of movement and also its duration. After these individual variations, all performers had to do a section of compulsory phrases which each had to repeat until he became tired. One finds the same mix of elements—individual choice, emotionally charged

Deborah Hay's *All Day Dance*. Judson Memorial Church, 1963. Photo by Al Giese

situation, tests of physical endurance—in "Would They or Wouldn't They" (1963), a dance for two couples. In the first section, the men (not trained dancers) suspended themselves from a pipe for as long as they were able while the girls (trained dancers) danced around them. In the second section of the piece, clear signals were sent out by the two girls as they called each of the men by name. As a man was called, he walked to wherever the girl was seated and lifted her in a seated position to another spot in the performing area. At no time did the men evince any interest in the girls as people. The final section of the work had the two frustrated couples hanging and swaying gently side by side from the overhead pipe.

While Hay has retained her interest in signals, in her most recent dances she has given up working with small groups of performers in favor of masses of people. She would rather draw a small motive charge from each of a large number of performers cumulatively than create a high emotional weight from one or two performers, since the latter, as she sees it, is accomplished ordinarily by means of technical artificiality. Instead of arising from the collective interior changes in a mass of people, the performing voltage is fabricated from dramatic confrontations or encounters. One of her first explorations of signals with larger groups was "Victory 14" (1965). It was a dance designed for twenty-four performers, divided into three equal groups, each of which was assigned a different task. One group of three girls and five boys in white costumes stood, each with a rope tied around one leg, and moved directly toward the audience in parallel lines. From time to time, one or another of the performers might turn to do a short duet with a neighbor in the progression downstage. Directly behind each of these eight was a "puller" who grasped the rope attached to the performer's leg and played it out slowly. A short distance behind the eight "pullers" were seated eight "musicians," each of whom had a portable radio turned on. They twirled across the radio band and whenever they found something that particularly interested them they would turn up the volume of the radio so that it could be heard above the din of the other radios. This was a signal for the "puller" to give a warning tug on the rope. The performer would then lie down and the "puller" would draw him or her slowly back toward the starting point until the "musician" turned the radio down. The impression of the piece was that of a rigid and somewhat arbitrary control of life coming from the chatter of the radio spectrum as it became localized in one particular spot. The signal began as sound and was transmitted through a tug on the rope. As a system of control it was efficient enough in its way, but for Hay the desire has been to have a communications network that would be quicker and more readily understood by a large group of people.

Hay has not interested herself much in solo performance or in duets, although from time to time she has created a few such pieces, among them "Elephant Footprints in the Cheesecake-Walk" and "Flyer." The first, a relatively early work (1963), was a collaborative event performed with Fred Herko at Judson Church. Each of them put various dances into their collective effort and presented the whole thing together under its somewhat bizarre title. It was an example of the "camp" extravagance which was so much a part of the Judson scene in the formative years. The occasion provided Hay with the opportunity to do the tap dance she dedicated to her mother. In addition, Herko was an exceptionally gifted dancer, balletically trained with great stage presence and élan, and he afforded her the opportunity to "dance" in a way that she had done at Henry Street. "Flyer," four years later, was a shadowy piece performed in an artist's loft, and represented a less flamboyant Hay, who performed in the piece with the non-technically trained John Giorno, a poet. It was a "peril" piece, though one did not realize it until the end, for it was more easily heard than seen as the dancers brushed back and forth against a wall in the gloom. Until the lights went up and it could be seen that each was standing on a platform and holding on to a stretch elastic band, it had not been clear that their little communicative tugs on the band could have caused one or the other to fall.

Another duet was an outdoor piece called "Hill" (1965)—Hay has rarely concerned herself with the organization of proscenium space—performed at a country club golf course in the Catskills. In it, she came over a hill running toward a man with outstretched arms and rebounded off him. She was to repeat the piece several times, once on the center mall of Wiltshire Boulevard in Los Angeles. She also worked with some solos around the same time that she did "Hill." In the solos, typically, she was not so much interested in technical display as in providing a major visual focus for the pieces. Her performing strength was held carefully in check and an entire presentation was performed at a middle range of energy discharge. In "No. 3," for example, her own dancing had the same "attentional weight" as the amplified sound and sight of bricks being dragged along the floor and formed into little structures.

Hay assembled a number of her concerns in a largescale work with the at first glance paradoxical title "Solo," created in 1966 for the series "Nine Evenings: Theater and Engineering." The engineering part of Hay's contribution was the inclusion of little mechanical carts, which unintentionally broke down occasionally. The dancers deployed themselves in a smooth multi-directional way around the large armory floor where the performances were held. It was a serene work with a sense of controlled flow, and everyone in it was the same, so that it was in effect a solo for sixteen separate people inhabiting the same general field. It started with a few persons and accumulated the full number in a calm and undramatic manner, swelling out to fill the performing area like a pool being fed from an unseen source. There were no climactic motions and the men and women were all given the same movements or non-movements to do. A series of blackouts occurred during which performers would change their stance. The little carts were directed by a group of eight persons seated on chairs in the performing area. Because of certain technical difficulties (with the carts), the piece was not fully realized but it did indicate strongly the direction in which Hay was traveling. She was subsequently to use spaces with a controlled, even level of performing exertion on the part of her dancers more successfully.

The first work to do this—and the first work in her most recent style— was "Group I" (1967). Here Hay showed a given space shaping dancers into formation. On black and white film, she displayed her performers entering a room and going to one corner in a series of five assembling exercises. The performers did not wear any special costumes but dressed as they would in ordinary circumstances. At times they entered in a straggling fashion and at other times in a more organized way. What was consistent in each of the five sequences was that when the performers had been compacted into a wedge by the shape of the room, they then behaved as a unit—moving off in that shape with short, shuffling steps the first four times and remaining still the last time.

After this short film, in which each of the five movements took approximately one minute, the lights in the auditorium were turned up full and a tape recording of soft human voices and assorted cooing sounds began to play. Eight musicians with white wooden poles stood above the performing area and clashed the poles from time to time, directed by an unseen conductor who cued them. Five dancers entered the performing area from two doors and began to do a rote of simple movement. From time to time, one or another would leave the performing area and return. Like the musicians who were directed by an unseen conductor and the people in the film acting under the instructions of an unseen director, the performers made their entrances and exits according to a covert time schedule, one previously agreed on.

The dance was a case of simple elements being timed in a complex way and showed Hay exercising her choreography through the media of untrained dancers, unschooled musicians, and unprofessional film performers. The various units, however, had a beautiful conceptual precision, although only the rote movements of the film performers had any special distinction in the sense of movement invention.

Hay later developed a more robust color version of this dance, called "Group II" (1968), in which the films were shot outdoors in color, the musicians and performers were in variously colored clothes, and the poles that the musicians clashed together were made of enameled metal. The whole thing had a more vigorous air to it than did "Group I," and the film sequences, in terms of movement, were again the most inventive part of the production. In them the people formed themselves into two lines and traversed an open, paved space in a series of straight-line formations, then in circles, and finally in arcs cutting across segments of the space. The film was taken from above the heads of the performers, giving a "mapping-angle" view of terrain to their sequences of movement.

In contrast to the use of chance or randomness, Hay's dominant interest has been the rigorous ordering of a dance substructure which would be fleshed out by the actual performers. However, during a series of performances at the Anderson Theater (New York) in 1968, she created a proscenium-oriented concert piece that contained many elements of spontaneous behavior, and also a traditional musical score played by a rock and roll group. It was a structured piece performed in randomly determined order, and was called "Ten" after the number of performers in it. The stage was traversed by a horizontal metal pole four feet above the floor, dividing the back quarter of the stage from the front three-quarters where the dancers performed. The musicians remained behind the pole. A vertical pole went from the center of the stage upward and disappeared into the "flies." There were three groups of performers: a couple, a trio of girls, and five men. The dancers were all dressed in white and clashed innocently with the garish and casual clothes of the musicians. Each group of dancers had to stay together but could perform any series of exercises that it wished to do at the signal of any one of the group. If the horizontal pole were used by the person who wished to become leader of his group, then all of the others in the group had to replicate his stance further down along the pole. If the vertical pole were chosen as the starting point, then all of the others in the group had to attach themselves to the person in front of them in a chain of links as identical as possible.

The piece was a "natural"—and had an appealing openness of game structure. The performers were like charming bits of sentient cork bobbing around in a din-filled sea of sound. The dance tested their ability to signal to and communicate with one another to the utmost. It was easy enough to see what one had to do when the signal was visual as on the horizontal pole, and one could take a cue from looking to the left or right at the last person in the formation. What became difficult was the dissolving of a chain after it had been completed at the vertical pole. In this case, the signal was to be a shout from the last person in line, whom no one could see, since they were facing away. The dance had a rowdy charm of tracking, stalking, and playfulness, and Hay repeated it elsewhere with success, including a gallery performance in Rome.

In 1969, Hay began a series of rigidly formularized and structured pieces that represent a breakthrough for her in the use of the non-specialized dancer and that fulfilled the promise of works like "Solo" and other of her white-costumed pieces ("Victory 14," "Group I," and "Ten"). In the new pieces, she has concerned herself with a performing order that allows the development and display of a form of proto-narcissism whereby individuals, though performing in a mass, are able to inflect and present the movements in a personal way. To emphasize their differences, she has done away with the standardizing white costumes. At first these pieces, such as "20 Permutations of 2 Sets of 3 Equal Parts in a Linear Order," required much rehearsal and developmental time to drill non-dancers in the patterns and formations that they were to follow. It was much like the work that a precision military team does in preparing a silent drill. The signals for the movements have to be generated from within the group in such a manner as to be unobtrusive and yet be effectively transmitted to all other members of the group so that they can act in concert. For Hay it was tedious work, but out of it she produced a substantial body of pieces that have a restrained purity of tone and performing texture. Rather than present the pseudo-excitement aroused during the usual performing situation, the pieces call upon the small emotional adjustments made by the non-professional performers who are not technically trained and find a genuine and valid emotional response generated by the very act of performance. Thus the movement in these pieces is about itself and not anything else.

Hay has presented these works in a variety of situations, including Damrosch Park at Lincoln Center, in an area in front of a band shell. In such a situation, the structured actions of the performer are seen to special advantage as they are a contrast to the casual movements of the crowd forming and flowing past the performance area. The performers and spectators are dressed in exactly the same manner, that is, in accordance with the situation. For this performance, Hay asked everyone to dress as they would for a mild Sunday afternoon in the fall. For a performance of other pieces at the Whitney Museum, she asked performers to dress as they would for an art opening or a theater show. In each case, the effort was to keep a resemblance between performer and spectator. (Among the pieces performed at the Whitney was "Half Time," a work for twenty-five girls that was a sensuous and joyous celebration of female charm.)

Hay has continued her work with the non-technically trained dancer but has moved away from long rehearsal periods. She now ideally would like to be able to have only a single rehearsal before a performance. In the early part of 1970, she presented in a gymnasium (of the Emanu-El Midtown YM & YWHA in New York) the first of the pieces produced under these conditions, "20 Minute Dance." In it, half the performers were hidden behind the other half and were instructed to make themselves visible at any time up to twenty minutes after the start of the dance. They were then to walk to any part of the gymnasium to stand, except that they could not block the visibility of any of the other performers. When the last person emerged, all formed two clusters and mirrored the actions of the other group for forty-five seconds, then assumed their original positions and the piece was over. It combined precision, spontaneity, and instant communication between performers, fulfilling Hay's desires. As a little girl performer in one of her pieces remarked, "It's like modern dance except that we are standing straight."

Yvonne Rainer

Why Does It Have To Be That Way?

In the early part of 1970 Yvonne Rainer realized with some surprise that she had been choreographing for a decade. She was filling out an application for a foundation grant and found she had qualified for the higher amounts allotted to those who had a span of ten years serious work behind them. It was a bittersweet discovery, since in the public mind her generation of choreographers as well as others considerably younger were still being lumped together in an undifferentiated mass labeled the avant–garde. Indeed, this classification, with sublime indifference to time, reaches back even further, including Merce Cunningham along with choreographers who were born the year he made his first dance. Little critical effort has been made to distinguish between the varying approaches that the individual choreographers of the post–historic modern dance period take to their work, and to the casual outsider it might appear as if they were all doing the same thing. The failure of critical acumen particularly irritates Rainer, who has published a number of articles outlining what she does in her work.

As with many of the post–historic modern dance generation, Rainer has been deeply involved in the world of painting and sculpture—in her case, not only through interest but also by marriage. When she came to New York, she was married to hard-edge abstractionist Al Held, who introduced her into the New York art world. Since their divorce she has maintained friendships with artists (and sometime choreographers) Robert Morris, Robert Rauschenberg, and Alex Hay, among others, although she has never asked any of them to design either costumes or decors for her works. She has, rather, shared with them their interest in exploring formal problems of their respective crafts, included some of them in pieces she has choreographed, and appeared in works that they have devised. One of her few appearances that achieved notice in large circulation, national publications resulted from a nude duet, "Waterman Switch," choreographed by Robert Morris, which she performed with him at the Albright-Knox Gallery in Buffalo and later repeated at Judson Church in New York.

Rainer, despite the sometimes wearisome length of her pieces, is vitally interested in presenting the human body and the human psyche in their raw, "fresh" state. She is not interested in feigned emotion or characterization, nor, if it interferes with the body's natural bearing, is she interested in the technique of dancing as such. At times, as in "Trio A"(1966), she is interested in displaying a smooth, even flow of natural motion, but consistently she is interested in the sheer act of moving. She regards the body as a system of gears and levers with an infinity of motor options, and attempts to create a performing situation in which various of these possibilities are explored at length. She finds that emotional concerns, and particularly those that are connected with sexual feelings, often clutter the viewers' eyes as to what the actual physicality of the action is. In an attempt to demythologize the body sexually she has, from time to time, introduced nudity into her work with precisely the same detached sense that she would produce any unexpected prop. At times she has appeared nude, as in "Waterman Switch," or nearly nude, as in the earlier performance of a duet which she did with Steve Paxton, "Word Words" (1962). As a part of her own "Rose Fractions," a piece she did for a concert at the Billy Rose Theater in 1969, she included an anonymous couple in a pornographic film, and had a nude Steve Paxton and dancer Becky Arnold filmed in a sequence of movements involving the tossing of a balloon along with simple tumbling movements over a sofa. In each case, the bodies in motion were supposed to provide the primary focus for viewer attention, without any emotive overtones. (These overtones, however, are never entirely banished from the works presented.) However, the effort to return to unspoiled appreciation of the body has logically led Rainer into a systematic exploration of sexual effect. Just as logically, it has led her to discard various theatrical devices which she feels have outlived their usefulness. Included among the things jettisoned were "spectacle, virtuosity, the star image, and any type of theatrical 'magic,' " as she herself noted when making "Parts of Some Sextets" (1965).

After the elimination of so much, one might wonder exactly what was left. What was left was the human body clothed or unclothed, in motion or at rest, reacting to the situation in which it found itself. For Rainer the theatrical setting has been the proper place for this exploration of human motion. She has found herself attracted to "neutral space" and not to environments. She has compared her placing of somewhat organized physical activity in rigorously emptied-out gymnasiums, factories, and ballrooms to the action taken by the painter Marcel Duchamp, who exhibited a urinal in an art show. The setting revealed the art. Neither the object nor the movement would be noticed in an ordinary space. In regarding her own work, Rainer has observed, "I do not wish the audience to participate in my thing; neither do I wish them to focus on themselves, but rather on arbitrary and carefully focused situations external to themselves within clearly delineated spatial areas. If I make them mobile, it is only to avoid their being 'captive,' not to narrow the separation—either physical or psychic—between audience and performer." Placing herself thus in the theatrical tradition, not as an assassin bent on its destruction but rather as an analyst bent on its reformation, Rainer has created a body of twenty-nine pieces (some of them reworkings of previously used materials) dedicated to test whether dance theater as presently constituted can long endure.

Rainer was born and raised in San Francisco and began her performing career there as an aspiring actress. She joined a little theater group and did crowd scenes but enjoyed being "up there." She did not have any dance training and had seen very little dancing at this time. As a child, her mother had taken her to some opera and ballet performances, but the one that made an enduring impression on her was one in which the spectacular Jean Babilée appeared with the Ballets de Paris de Roland Petit.

She came to New York in 1956 and began acting classes, which she did not like. Her particular dislike was the theater's confusion between what was "real" and what wasn't "real." The following year she was introduced to the work and theories of John Cage through a friend who was studying with Cage at The New School for Social Research. In the same year, she went to her first dance class with Edith Stephen. She found Stephen's classes were just right for her, since they contained a little bit of everything in movement, including, very importantly, the opportunity to improvise.

Her first experience with improvisation was extremely pleasureful. She simply dove into a box of props at the Stephen studio and reacted in a very uninhibited manner. After this first kinesthetic epiphany, she went to a variety of ballet and modern dance teachers, reaching a peak of three classes a day during 1959 to 1960. That summer she returned to San Francisco to take Ann Halprin's summer course at the Dancer's Workshop Company, and in the fall, having returned to New York, prepared her own first work, not shown until the next year, 1961.

In 1960, she enrolled in the Dunn composition course; the next year she danced first in her own work and then with James Waring's company. Later, during a program organized by Waring at the Living Theater, she was given the opportunity to show her first work, a solo, "Three Satie Spoons."

As in many of her early pieces, she used music in this work in an ironic manner—as something to be worked against rather than collaborated with. In "Satie for Two" (1961), a duet with costumes by Waring, there was a similar usage of music. The punnish titling of these first pieces contrasts strongly with the determinedly descriptive appellations of later works, such as "Ordinary Dance" (1962) and "We Shall Run" (1963), and no doubt reflects the influence of Waring, who is a master of incongruous, florid, and comically imaginative titling. After her early pieces, the only subsequent dance that has any evocative associations in its name is the large-scale "The

Yvonne Rainer in *Three Seascapes*, Judson Memorial Church, January 29, 1963. Photo by Al Giese

Mind Is a Muscle" (1966–68); a phrase that occurred to her while riding on a bus.

The Judson Workshop, established in the fall of 1962 and meeting every Monday, was an extremely creative period in Rainer's life. She produced nearly half of her total output of twenty-nine dances in the three years of the Workshop.

From the beginning of her work, Rainer has used the human voice in dances. Her own first solo ("Three Satie Spoons") began in silence; Rainer then began to emit beeping sounds and then words and phrases of no particular consequence. It was her first experiment with having two types of action—audible sound and visual motion—arise from a single source. Somewhat later, in "At My Body's House" (1964), in which she had contact microphones taped to her body, she accompanied herself with the sounds of her own muscles, bones, and breathing. In another early work, "Three Seascapes" (1962), she used several kinds of sound, including some she made while dancing. "Three Seascapes" was a solo in three parts, the first of which employed a Rachmaninoff score, the second, the scraping of chairs on a wooden floor, and the third, screaming from the performer herself. In terms of its movement, the work went from romantic swaying to frantic thrashing amidst a pile of bridal-weight material. "Three Seascapes" also exemplified the understated but real developmental thrust present in Rainer's work before she returned to dances for groups and to a structure of non-climactic field activity.

Some of the dynamic concerns that had been latent in her work became active in "Parts of Some Sextets," first seen in New York at Judson Church during 1965. The previous year she had worked on portions of the dance in Philadelphia. "Parts of Some Sextets" started as a duet, was reworked further as a duet, and finally emerged as a dance for six people. Rainer had begun to evolve a working methodology in which dances sprang from one another with considerable areas of overlapping material. It was dance creation not in the sense of preparing individual pieces dealing with the same problem in movement but showing sections of one work, almost as if they were stations along the path to a solution. In a manner similar to the enlargement of "Parts of Some Sextets," "The Mind Is a Muscle," which started out as a trio, was enlarged to include six performers and reached an apparently definitive stage with eight performers. Since 1968, Rainer has shown no interest in reworking "Mind," so one can assume that that work has reached its final statement.

With the creation of "Parts of Some Sextets," Rainer also began the systematic exploration of movement that concentrated on the weight and operational workings of the body, paying little mind to theatrical considerations that would in any way alleviate viewers' difficulties in concentrating on sheer physical activity. It is an uncompromising road to which she subsequently has adhered. Rainer's basic assumption in her work since

1965 is that activity exists and has a value in and of itself, and she declines to falsify it with what she considers extraneous trappings. Her refusal to use such trappings is so strong that, at this time in her career, she refuses to perform again in Judson Church, where so much of her work was first seen, because of its associational echoes. The space, she feels, is no longer an empty vessel into which she can place her theatrical concerns, but brings with it an unwanted atmosphere of dance and theatrical history.

It is this Puritan rigor that in part has commanded the loyalty of those dancers who have been associated with her for a number of years. These generally tend to be "dropouts" from regular concert touring who have spun off from their original affiliations with other performing companies, notably Merce Cunningham's, to work on their own and perform with Rainer when asked to do so.

Rainer quite freely acknowledges the debt that she owes to Cunningham's work. From him, she recognized that there was a different manner in which to organize space than the one of central focus, which had prevailed throughout the development of modern dance. A second debt, perhaps more clearly pertinent to her own concerns, was the possibilities that Cunningham's work demonstrated for breaking up the movements of the human body. It was not necessary for, say, one limb to do something to counteract the stylized motion of the other; there were numerous options open and she saw that many had not been thoroughly examined.

Another dancer/choreographer who had a strong impact on her was Erick Hawkins. During a performance of Hawkins's "Here and Now with Watchers," in 1958, she was struck with the theatrical force that very simple movements could produce, and she wanted to be able to achieve a similar effect as economically. She was also impressed with the work of Aileen Passloff (with whom she had worked for a while when she first began to dance) and in particular with a solo by Passloff (1961) that involved little movement but had an extremely strong impact on the audience. In the dance, Passloff was seated with aristocratic self-assurance in a floor-length red dress. She slowly took a pencil and placed it in her teeth and grimaced at the audience and then outlined the configuration of her body with the pencil in the air. The sheer power of a simple action again affected Rainer's theatrical sense. The contrariness of the piece also appealed to certain mischievous impulses which she drew on in the early part of her career, such as deliberately going against the mood of a musical accompaniment or making sounds instead of remaining docilely silent.

Rainer is fond of the spontaneous, unrehearsed response and in much of her work has prepared elaborate schemes in which to bring it about. Although she had prepared dances using chance methodology such as John Cage had employed in composition—for example, overlays of paper on which the imperfections of the sheets were marked to indicate placement for the movement of performers—the device of sophisticated game-playing has proved more appealing to her. By means of signals which she gives to her dancers, she is able to have them alter the sequence and shape of a dance. In some dances, the movement is agreed upon beforehand and its performance is then put under the control of the performers, who by word or movement signals can cause the other dancers directly or indirectly to react to what they are doing. Some of these signals are quite complex and others are as simple as a cry for "Help!" In an early work, "Room Service" (1963), done with Charles Ross, Rainer used another device to create opportunities for the spontaneous. She established three teams of performers and Ross's group was assigned the task of enlivening the dance by placing obstacles of their own choosing in the path of the other two teams. The obstacles included tables, bedsprings, and other such litter and became a junk landscape across which the performers had to maneuver. Yet another device that she has used is the secret instruction. One of her group, secretly instructed beforehand, is allowed to insert a piece of movement into a dance at any point and the others have to cope with it. Another element of secrecy that she has used is the unexpected stage property which she will produce at a particular point in a dance. The unplanned reactions of the other dancers then become part of the performance.

Rainer likes to work with an intimate group of about five people, which is the size of her current group, because it presents conditions in which it is relatively easy to create. She can leave a great deal up to the performers and feel confident that they will handle the responsibility in an intelligent manner. At times she herself is surprised and somewhat taken aback at the results of this delegation of responsibility, such as the time when "Trio A" (1966), one of her best-known sequences of movement, appeared in a dance and she did not want it to.

Basically, Rainer does not differentiate between the type of movement she makes for men and the movement she creates for women. It is by and large the same, with the only difference a consequence of the fact that men are obviously able to sustain certain strength moves more easily than women. Rainer was active athletically before taking dance training and a wholesome rough-housing element is clearly visible in her work. For both men and women, the choreography is physically demanding and in fact involves some hardship for the smallest members of the company. But Rainer sees no satisfactory escape from this dilemma. She is endlessly interested in seeing the human body and its configurations engaged in game or task activities. In her work "Carriage Discreteness" (1966), she laid out a large number and variety of materials across a grid-marked floor and then from a balcony with a small radio transmitter directed her performers to move them. For her the interest in the work lay in the amount and type of effort needed to raise and carry objects of different weight.

Her current interest has extended to the actual working conditions of her and her performers, and it is these raw rehearsal movements along with more polished dance movements that comprise her newest piece, "Continuous Project—Altered Daily" (1970). During a rehearsal, the dance material is worked upon, then repeated and in the process added to or just incorporated into the performance in its entirety. The original material then becomes like a script which is worked on repeatedly in the course of actual performance. She feels that there is an enormous amount of audience interest in what goes on in rehearsal, which accounts for this current extension of her previously developed work-in-progress methodology to include the raw material of dance. In order to preserve the naturalness of the rehearsal situation, she and her other performers deliberately refrain from learning some movement sequences in the studio and acquire them during the performance. In addition, a series of microphones are placed in the performing area so that the audience can hear the discussions that are the normal part of a dancer's rehearsal.

"Continuous Project—Altered Daily" is a further step in tearing away the facade of artificiality, the dissolution of which Rainer has dedicated herself to. Thus far she has demonstrated that she is an effective demolition expert, for no one who has ever been exposed to her work can again succumb to theatrical illusion with quite the same innocence. She is post-modern dance's most dedicated iconoclast.

Gus Solomons, Jr.

Logic

Nothing distinguishes the career of Gus Solomons, Jr., more than its rigorous adherence to the rules of logic in the pursuit of choreographic expressions. Solomons has been persistently devoted to the analysis and systematic isolation of the elements that go into making a dance. The uninhibited examination has inevitably brought him into conflict with audiences' conceptions about the nature of dance.

To Solomons the logic of the situation is clear: audiences have become the unwitting prisoners of previous ages' definitions of dance. To him, such definitions have become the enemy. He feels that the word "dance" imprisons an audience behind a forest of preconceptions through which it is difficult to perceive what is actually being shown to them. He would like to present his own work free from any associative titles and allow it to have its own existence. People would then be free to categorize it as they wished.

The catalytic transformation in his own creative trajectory was his performing experience with the Merce Cunningham company. He joined it after it had completed a long world tour in 1965 and remained until a painful back injury in 1968 forced him to give up the arduous grind of concert touring. Since then, despite injury, he has chosen to pursue his own choreographic career. As he observed, "After Merce it's either yourself or nothing. He demands that you are yourself as a human being and then from that a dancer, and he goes on from there. Everybody else's work seems to be about something instead of being something."

Solomons is originally from Boston, where he had jazz and tap experience as a child, but he did not begin to study dance seriously until he was a sophomore in college. He attended the Massachusetts Institute of Technology and while completing the requirements for a degree in architecture, he actively pursued an extra-curricular dance career. While in Boston he attended classes at the Boston Conservatory of Music, which had Jan Veen as the director of its dance program. Veen, a student of pioneer German expressionist dancer Mary Wigman, gave his students a large amount of expressionist dance training. Solomons also took ballet class with E.

Virginia Williams, the founder of the Boston Ballet Company. At one point in his student years he was rehearsing for nine separate productions of dances or plays while attending classes at M.I.T. His energy is exceptional (although he has had to ration his time more carefully since sustaining his injury).

In 1960, Solomons joined Dance Makers, a modern dance company in Boston, both to dance and to make dances of his own. Solomons' first dance was "Etching of a Man," a three-minute solo which covered man's life from birth to death with all of the crises in between. Murray Louis, who was an adviser to the Dance Makers (and also taught a course at the Dance Circle in Boston), was perceptively critical about it. As Solomons tells the story, Louis asked simply, "Gus, what do you know about suffering?" Solomons has not done a specifically dramatic—that is, with a narrative theme—piece since. His very next work, "Construction II," which used white elastic and stretch jersey, Solomon humorously refers to as his "Nikolais piece," alluding to Alwin Nikolais, who has made such imaginative use of these materials.

Solomons moved to New York in 1962, found a studio to share with eight other dancers, most of whom were dissatisfied with their work at the Tamiris-Nagrin modern dance company and were looking for something else. Among the others were the sympathetic and aspiring choreographers Elizabeth Keen, Cliff Keuter, and, later, Phoebe Neville, Kenneth King, and Meredith Monk. They called their studio "Studio 9" and began to work, sometimes collaborating with one another, at other times appearing independently.

In his early pieces, Solomons worked easily with conventional music and showed a skilled grasp of the mechanics of assembling dances. His first New York piece, shown at Clark Center of the 50th Street YWCA (at that time a haven for younger choreographers), was a duet for himself and Abigail Ewert called "Rag Caprices," done to the music of Stravinsky. Later that year he prepared a formal quartet, "Fogrum," to baroque music. "Fogrum" was a formal, courtly dance of an abstract nature in which two couples kept greeting each other with elaborate gestures, until the greetings developed into a slightly absurd game. The most elaborate of the situations was performed with the two girls perched on the men's shoulders as the bearers bowed to each other.

With "The Ground Is Warm and Cool" (1963), a solo he designed for himself, his work showed a change in choreographic attack, developing in bursts of movement separated by periods of calm. It depended on more intimately shaped phrasing than he had used previously.

Later in 1964 he collaborated with Elizabeth Keen on a duet called "Match." The stage properties were three wooden boxes which Solomons and Keen manipulated and moved into and out of. Unlike Solomons' previous work, it was not done to a specific score and the interest of the dance was based on the complex movements of the boxes, which were of varying sizes and weights. "Match" combined obvious physical difficulties, as the performers worked with their feet to manipulate the props, and a high level of inventiveness.

During the time that he was preparing these pieces, Solomons danced with several companies, among them those of Martha Graham, Pearl Lang, Donald MacKayle, and Joyce Trisler. He also performed on a television series directed at younger audiences (NBC's "Exploring"). When he joined Merce Cunningham in 1965, he had satisfied himself as to his own dancing skills—which are considerable and indeed unique in his generation of dancer—and he was ready for the creative stimulation that is the special aura of the Cunningham company.

With Cunningham, Solomons had the opportunity to observe the close harmony of the dancers and the special rapport that they had for one another in performance. He could watch the creation of the company's new works rather than come upon them as finished products, and he thought about what he was seeing. For someone of a reflective nature such as Solomons, the stay with the Cunningham company provided an extended period of observation and analytical reassessing as well as a great deal of performing. It was, he reports, one of the most enjoyable periods of his life—cut short because of the degenerating spinal disc which had once troubled him early in his career.

Solomons now had three options: the first was to continue working with the Cunningham company, which meant that he could continue dancing for two more years at the most; the second was to take up an independent but modified dance career, which meant that he could count on ten years of more or less intense dancing; and the third was to give up dancing entirely. He chose the second.

After leaving the company, he began to sharpen his choreographic focus on the issue of the border between dancing and something else; this has meant involvement with everyday gestures and, in terms of performance, involvement with audience. Solomons, typically, set about his work in a systematic manner. He had, during his years with Cunningham, decided that one motion was equal in value to any other motion for making dances, and he began assembling combinations of simple movements which he arranged and combined in a variety of ways. For the most part, his works have tended to be solos (although he has also worked with group dances).

Solomons, unlike many who demand audience participation in their work, invites rather than commands the audience. A series called "Kinesia" demonstrates a variety of his ideas for performer alone and performer with audience involvement. In "Kinesia #5" (1968), a solo, he first address-es a few remarks to the audience and asks whether it would use some of the normal crowd noises in a slightly more organized manner than usual to make them form an accompaniment to his dance. The members of the audience were requested to shuffle their feet or clear their throats at certain points in the work rather than distributing them randomly and unselfconsciously throughout the dance—as these sounds would have been.

While it takes a certain type of fortitude to join a performer on stage, it requires very little to remain seated and participate, and the noises that Solomons asks his audience to provide serve the function of making the audience more alert to the movement pattern of the dancer. Pushing the idea one step further in "Two Reeler" (1968), Solomons did not even appear on stage but had two tape recordings played in his stead. In fact it was given for the first time without Solomons' presence. (He had prepared it while teaching one summer at U.C.L.A.; the dance was given in New York, at The New School for Social Research.) He had devised a simple set of motions that could be accomplished by anyone, and as these were suggested in sequence on one machine, the other tape, coordinated with the first, rattled off a series of action words. For example, the soft-spoken statement, "If you move your left foot along the floor you can feel it in your spine," would be accompanied by words like "easily," "softly," that indicated the motive force of the movement. "Two Reeler" was one of Solomons' most direct attempts to involve audiences without in any way determining precisely what they had to do. They were free to try any or none of the movements, depending on their own curiosity, and they were not given visual cues by a performer moving through space.

At other times, he has attempted to loosen up audiences' viewing habits by having the elements of his dances operate in an autonomous fashion. In "we don't know, only how much time we have . . ." (1969), he tossed three white wooden shapes on the stage periodically during the course of his solo. The position of the three shapes—a circle, a square, and a triangle—in respect to each other indicated to the person in charge of the sound which portion of the piece's tape accompaniment he should play, and to the light designer whether he should dim, flash, or bring the lights up full. To Solomons, the point of the triangle indicated the direction his next sequence of movements would take. In each case, the three elements—sound, sight, and movement—were combined in accordance with a chance procedure. In a variation of this technique, Solomons later formed three shapes with tape on the stage itself, and he would trigger off some sound or light process by his movements when they crossed or impinged on a shape. Either way, spontaneity during the actual performance was achieved.

The game concept is one that interests Solomons a great deal, and with it he can prepare a dance that will look different in its shape from moment to moment, depending on the operative variables, but which will retain its integrity because of its structure. This technique is a way of creating dances that allows for wide variability within a chosen area of concern. Even when he is performing such dances himself as solos, the parts of the dance change

Gus Solomons, Jr., c. 1968. Photo by Guy Cross (Courtesy Dance Theater Workshop)

when one of the instructions directed toward himself is, "Never do the same movement more than once."

In working with a television station in Boston (WGBH), he prepared a multi-channel dance which partook of both a game element and the chance elements of "we don't know, only how much time we have . . ." The title of the piece was "City Motion Space Game" (1968), with the words of the title appearing in alternating sequence on two channels. Two separate sets were required for the viewer to appreciate properly the piece, which was made possible through WGBH's multi-channel capability. Light, sound, and picture processes were prepared, and different locales in Boston were selected for filming. Solomons did dance sequences in the varying locales and gave independent and individual programs of action to the lighting, sound, and camera technicians. Not only were the technicians not coordinated with one another, they could not take their cues from the action of the dancer. The cameraman might feel that a certain series of movements required a close up but was bound instead to follow the timed sequence of camera positions with which he had been supplied. These sequences were randomly developed beforehand for all of the technical aspects of the program. The end result was a combination of randomness and preplanned game structure.

Despite the fact that Solomons would prefer to present his work without an identifying tag word such as dance attached to it, as a performer with an extremely high level of technical dance skill, it is difficult to imagine Solomons as belonging anywhere but in the category of dancer. His height and bearing attract instant attention. He cuts through space with a blade-like efficiency and changes direction effortlessly. The pauses in his work emphasize the alertness and grace of his habitual quickness. He has a way of skimming lightly over the performing area, like a dragonfly darting rapidly over the surface of the water.

Concerned though he is with the mental logistics of current dance expression, he nonetheless choreographs highly dramatic dances from time to time. In "Neon" (1967), a solo, he prepared a piece that was a commentary on the restless energy that is symbolized by rock music. Designed to preserve a distance between the performer and the pulse of the music on which it comments, it at times slips out of its detachment in some performances and becomes simply a rock dance. In the most successful performance of the piece, Solomons danced in black leotards and tights and hung the bright-colored costume in which he usually performed the piece over the back of a chair in plain sight. It helped to keep the distance.

In his most recent theater work, "Obbligato" (1969), he prepared an "old-fashioned" dance in a highly imaginative manner. In creating the piece, he joined two seemingly unrelated impulses. First, he felt like doing a tap dance, which he had not done for a number of years, and second, he wanted to employ the static picture of unmotivated nudity. He appeared on stage fully clothed, and for the first half of the dance moved unconcernedly around the stage area doing a tap routine to the accompaniment of crisis- and emotion-laden voices culled from radio broadcasts of the 1930's and 1940's. He moved independently of and unconcerned with these voices until a dull and commercialized jazz sound of no inspiration and much borrowing from original black sources began to play. He stopped, his attention caught for the first time, and then in silence began to remove his clothing until he had worked down to his dance belt, the undressing coinciding with a decreasing light level on stage. The contrast of the deliberateness of the second part heightened the nonchalance of the first and formed a strong dance image.

His latest work is a choreographed arrangement of original prose com- missioned by his college, The Massachusetts Institute of Technology, "A Dance in Report Form/A Report in Dance Form" (1970). In it he proposes his own view for the inclusion of "the creative art experience into the education of an M.I.T. student." His comments are witty and laid out on individual sheets of paper that do not have a sequential relationship. Except for the cover sheet—the title of the piece—the parts are meant to be read in any order of the reader's choosing. Under Solomons' hand, even the act of reading has been enlivened, since the words run at different angles and motion is required to cant and tilt the pages into a readable plane. After finishing, the reader is encouraged to shuffle the pages and read them again.

Solomons calls the work a word-and-motion piece and suggests that its tempo and texture should be leisurely, allowing for indulgence in the activity. That same indulgence in sheer activity for its own sake and pleasure is what he offers to all his audiences.

Meredith Monk

Mixed-Media Kid

When Meredith Monk decided to go on Broadway—in 1969 during a week of performances at the Billy Rose Theater, sponsored by the Ford Foundation to acquaint a wider audience with the work of new choreographers—she opened her concert with a recording of brassy-voiced Ethel Merman singing "There's No Business Like Show Business!" but there was no one on stage. There were, however, people crouched in cardboard containers in the lobby and in the balcony, where performers are not usually found. And, during the intermission, there were movies of Monk in various poses, which the audience could look at or not, as it chose. The option was pure Monk, operating as she does in the spaces between the accepted categories of dance and dramatic and musical theater. For many in the audience, the ambiance of the choice offered by Monk was unsettling: to stay in the theater and look at repetitious movies or to go to the lobby there to peer through little holes in cardboard containers and to see people sitting inside. For others, the situation was an opportunity for conversation and for the development of a light-hearted camaraderie produced either by a common confusion over or a common comprehension of such a mixed environmental presentation.

Monk, representative of the second avant-garde generation that followed closely upon the heels of the formation of the original Judson Dance Theater, was one of four choreographers invited to show their work in the Ford-sponsored week of dance. Though the theater had the standard Broadway proscenium stage, precisely the sort of stage she had spent much of her career avoiding, she decided to try to fit her non-proscenium concerns to its structure. The attempt was not entirely successful. Of the two concerts she gave, her first had more organic internal relationships than the second. Press reaction to the entire week was lukewarm at best and straightforwardly hostile at worst. For Monk, the experience of being pushed again behind a proscenium was as frustrating as an earlier experience in her career when she was trying to dissociate herself from what she considers the narrow category of "dancer" and then found herself cast as a "dancer" in a theater work by Roberts Blossom.

Meredith Monk studied dance as part of a performing arts major at Sarah Lawrence, where she received a strong background in movement of the Merce Cunningham technique from Judith Dunn and from Beverly Schmidt, who taught there. At the time, she was undecided as to whether she wanted to pursue writing or dancing as a career. During a composition class, she once created a dance using a chance methodology employed by Cunningham, but she did not feel at all attracted to this method of choreography. She was attracted, however, to the Cunningham technique, particularly its use of the back, and she still retains elements of the training for her own personal barre each day. Some of her early dances, such as "Timestop" (1963), show traces of Cunningham physicality, but Monk's interests are not exclusively confined to the physical activity of movement. She has pursued Cunningham's ideas about the development and use of space more than she has interested herself in his style of dancing.

Her first important solo, "Break" (1964), indicated some of her spatial concerns and showed the vitality of her talent. She used a series of automobile noises as a sound accompaniment, and as she worked around the stage area she would utter a non-emotional "Oh!" whenever she encountered the limits of the proscenium arch. She wore a transparent plastic raincoat over black leotards. The sound accompaniment was programmatic in the sense that it matched automobile noises with appropriate points in her dance—a starter turning over at the beginning of a dance or crashing noises when she would encounter an obstacle—but basically the sound was not rhythmically used. The piece was strongly autobiographical in motivation as were several other early works such as "Me" (1963), "Cartoon" (1965), and "Beach" (1965). In these works, Monk unhesitatingly appropriated her own experiences while growing up as subject matter for her dances. While this highly personal approach has continued to play a strong part in ordering her later works, the subject matter has not been so tightly concentrated on her own history.

"Break" was selected for inclusion on the educational television program "New Voices in the Arts" (prepared by WNDT-TV), but was not photographed to best advantage in the television studio. The dance was designed as a frontal proscenium piece, and the television cameras swooped around it, ignoring its intended flat presentational plane.

Monk insists that she is not exclusively a dancer but rather that she does a type of composite theater work that could only have been arrived at by a dancer. She is interested in combining various theatrical elements, and in her pieces has paid special attention to the music, much of which she composes and performs herself. She has involved herself with music to such an extent that she subtitled her most elaborate work, "Juice" (1969), a theater cantata. Monk has a great deal of difficulty in identifying her own multi-media concerns with the concerns of the "dance" world as she sees it. Further, it has been her experience that far more serious and sensitive appreciation of her work has come from persons outside of the regular dance world than inside it, and it is her intention to cultivate an audience that represents all of the theater-going public. She is strongly concerned with the communicative aspect of her theater work and has little patience for those choreographers whom she considers to be working with modes of alienation. She wishes to make her work accessible to a wide audience, although she refrains from making the work simplistic in the attempt to do so.

As with many of the younger choreographers, she sees the problem she faces in the dance/non-dance dichotomy as a matter of definitions, and so is loathe to relegate herself into any one category, any one of which she regards as a trap. She feels that the public should just come to attend an "event" and not to place it into one category until after having had a chance to feel it and participate in it.

Monk's first few years of performing and choreographing (1963-1966) indicated that she was not averse to using any movement device in exploring her concerns. In a work from this period, "Blackboard" (1965), she simply wrote words and pushed a large portable school blackboard around the performing area. In "Portable" (1966), she created a small house-like enclosure on stage into which her performers were free to move and which was portable. In "Beach" (1965), she had platforms and boxes, and at one point wore tap shoes. In "Cartoon" (1965), one of the performers wore sloppy bedroom slippers.

In this early work, Monk's conglomerate approach to choreographic concerns placed her precisely between a variety of different media approaches rather than within a single one. It was a position that would naturally alienate her from traditionalist expectations. She exercised her freedom in the choice of means with considerable skill and in the relatively short space of two years produced a half-dozen works that displayed an exceptional multi-media approach to theater.

After she left college in 1964 to become a full-time choreographer, she was one of the first beneficiaries of the initial wave of avant-garde activity that was drawing to a close at Judson Church. Without any difficulty she was able to find performance space at Judson and at a variety of other locales in New York which had become available for so-called avant-garde dance. She moved into an ambiance of experimentation as easily as a dancer from a graduation class might have moved into one of the established companies. For her, the avant-garde was a fact of performing life. She didn't have to create it, she simply had to join it, which she did with alacrity. She worked at "Studio Nine,"along with Gus Solomons and the young choreographers Pheobe Neville and Kenneth King, and she showed some of her work at the Clark Center for the Performing Arts. She also made a summer trip to California, where she became involved with the work of Ann Halprin, with whose approach to theater she felt an immediate kinship. Halprin insisted that the place where one performed should have an effect on the work produced. She herself had worked in open fields, in nets slung from trees, as well as in the conventional theater, to try different choreographic formulations.

Monk's concerns with her surroundings are strong, and her feel for architectural structure is vitally important to her choreography, which draws from and expands to the amplitude of the space available for it. Many of Monk's early pieces had to occupy proscenium or semi-proscenium areas, and in all of these she always tried to create her own organization of the space by using an elaborate number of stage properties. The use of these properties was not a matter of clothing or objects for the dancers to manipulate but one of sculptural constructions. It is interesting to note parallels in her work to the type of spatial organization that Martha Graham has so frequently employed during her career. Monk, however, employs stage properties with a respect for their thingness and does not attempt to use them in an illusional way. She does not attempt to transform a screen into the simulacrum of a city wall, as Graham might, but simply allows the screen to perform its function of visually blocking off a certain area. Similarly, when she wanted something to enable her to indicate mountain climbing to accompany a part of "Beach," she placed an inclined platform on top of a box, climbed it, and jumped off.

"16 Millimeter Earrings" (1966), a work from this period, shows an interesting combination of such spatial organization. The piece alternated between the actual and a recording of the actual. Monk created a physical ambiance on stage with a large white box from which red streamers fluttered in long flowing patterns during part of the dance. Later a film showed a small nude doll being consumed by fire. At one point, a steamer trunk was presented, just as it was, as a real object from which things could be taken out or put in. Monk climbed inside of it toward the end of the dance to remove her clothes for the final tableau, which was a reenactment of the nude doll crumpling into the flames. At another point, she placed a large globular screen over her head and had a film projected on it which detailed some of the actions which she had performed earlier. Her head, which had spawned the movement, thus became the place of its reshowing. After the film was over, she removed the screen, the streamers collapsed as their fan was shut off, and Monk moved into the steamer-trunk conflagration.

One of the last works in which she specifically organized space with the use of architectural properties was a duet she prepared for herself and Kenneth King called "Duet with Cat's Scream and Locomotive" (1966). In this work, by the use of fluorescent body striping, stilts, clogs, and blow-up

Meredith Monk in *16 Millimeter Earrings*, 1966. Photo by Charlotte Victoria
(Courtesy Meredith Monk—The House)

photographs of facial expressions registering various emotional states, she expanded parts of the human body out of normal scale and projected the duet into a mechanized and futuristic locale. The entire piece was an enlargement of a simple pas de deux in which everything had a specialized mechanical and dehumanized functionality. There was both a masculine thematic sound—the monotonous chugging of a locomotive—and a feminine leitmotiv—the yowling of a cat. Whenever the man fell to the ground, the girl would indicate distress by holding up a large wooden block with a photograph of her mouth calling out. Alternatively, she would show happiness by the photograph of a smiling mouth rocking from side to side. "Duet with Cat's Scream and Locomotive" was one of the finest pieces Monk created during the earlier part of her career. However, like many others of the newer choreographers who have turned to choreographing in environmental space—that is, doing a specific new piece for one place at one point in time—she is not interested in the concept of repertory performance, so that it is unlikely that this basically repertory piece will ever be seen again.

The following year, in 1967, her work took a new direction and began to develop strongly and directly out of the physical surroundings in which she found herself.

Monk had been invited to perform at the Youth Pavilion of "Expo 67" in Montreal and was a resident in Woodstock, New York, during the rest of the summer. Woodstock, which traditionally had a flourishing artist's summer colony since the earlier part of this century, saw the formation of Group 212 that summer. Founded by a painter, it included representatives from the world of music and dance as well. The group drew its name from State Highway 212, on which its living quarters were located. It was with this group that Monk did the first of her new works. She created two works; one was shown at the Pavilion and the other in Woodstock, and though the titles—the Woodstock Piece was called "Blueprint" and the Expo 67 piece "Overload"—have been used again for works done in different places, the material and organization of each piece has been quite different wherever it was performed. Thus, neither the piece shown at the Pavilion nor the one shown at Woodstock has been repeated elsewhere. For the next two years Monk created five works in the "Blueprint" and "Overload" series, in addition to the ones created for Woodstock and Expo 67.

Parallel with her work on this series, Monk began to issue to her audiences programs that were in the nature of theatrical maps, indicating both where the audience was to be seated during a performance and the various parts of the buildings it had access to. The approximate duration of each section of a piece was also included. Many have found these maps to be of use, but many others have not. Monk feels quite strongly that the audience needs them, particularly if a piece involves simultaneous events. The maps, in any case, are an example of the importance that Monk places on communicating with her audience. During one of her pieces, done in the Smithsonian, she had members of the dance company directing the audience to the concluding section, when the dancers had finished performing the material that they were directly involved in.

The situation at Woodstock was relatively simple and did not require such elaborate aids. Two three-story brick buildings faced each other. The audience sat on the ground floor of one and watched some of the dance there. Viewers then moved outside to the space between the buildings and sat on benches to watch the rest of the performance, which consisted of various tableaux in the windows of the facing three-story house and, finally, after a blackout inside that building, of the sight of a man standing on the roof and pouring out a bag of flour onto the ground. When the bag was empty, the piece was over.

When she did her first "Blueprint" and "Overload" pieces in New York, she chose Judson Church as she had done when she began her career. The work was divided into two parts taking place about a month apart. It had a rhythmic flow and some lovely music composed by Monk and Don Preston. The first part, "Blueprint," took place in the Judson Gallery, a small basement room ordinarily used for art shows. For these performances, the audience entered through a curtain on which was being projected films of a girl standing in an Isadora Duncan drapery-like costume in the woods. A man and a woman (Alfred North and Monk) sat in two chairs facing the audience. The couple moved very little and very slowly, and their eyes were later masked. They hefted small objects—North had stones dumped at his feet by a woman attendant in white—and then got up and walked out of the room and into the courtyard, which could be seen through windows in the room's far wall. Each carried a small satchel. They moved out of sight. In the courtyard, effigy figures of the two were to be seen seated in chairs with backs to the room that had just been vacated.

Several weeks later, North and Monk were joined by five other girls and another man for the second part of the work, which took place in the sanctuary and loft of Judson Church and in the gymnasium directly below the sanctuary. Viewers entered through a doorway, again carrying a projected film of a girl doing Duncanesque movement in the woods, and proceeded to their seats at the far end of the sanctuary. A girl in a white dress and red wig walked down the stairs from the choir loft to the sanctuary and the sound of bells was heard. Monk then did a point solo that closely resembled Fokine's "The Dying Swan" and howled into a microphone. The sound was recorded and played back. She played a few chords on the church organ. Films of children riding up and down escalators were shown. A man in the loft—reminiscent of the rooftop figure pouring flour at Woodstock—emptied a box of slinky springs on the floor and a girl shone a light on him; the section ended with Monk leaving the sanctuary with a naked baby in her arms.

After a short intermission, the piece resumed in the gymnasium. There, Monk was in a rocking chair in a niche above the floor level, and the man in the loft who had tossed down the springs was sitting down at floor level. Monk opened a mesh window from her niche and a film sequence of a mesh window being opened was shown. A group of performers crossed the gymnasium on a diagonal and knocked at and entered a door leading to the niche. Various films were shown, including one of "Part I" of the piece, the duet of North and Monk in the gallery. North then tipped a pitcher and poured out stones that he carried out of the gallery part of the work. Film sequences of feet moving slightly as well as a film of microscopic pulsing cell life were projected above the audience's head. Finally all the performers rushed out of the gymnasium and the piece was over. Altogether, the work contrasted the escape of objects and people from constraints of one sort or another at alternating accelerated and retarded rates.

Shortly after this, Monk injured her knee and had to curtail her activities considerably; other workings of "Blueprint" and "Overload"were presented in an intimate series of performances at her loft. Her next larger-scaled piece was also scaled to fit its performance area,"Co-op" (1968), and was presented at the Loeb Student Center of New York University. The next works were the two evenings presented as part of the Billy Rose season, and as far as she was concerned, represented a serious compromise, since she repeated much of her earlier work and had to be behind a proscenium; she managed to organize only one of her two evenings. The direction of her work was carrying her away from the format of the familiar theater and yet the opportunity to be seen by a Broadway audience was only possible within this format. Nonetheless, she did create much of the ambiance of her theatrical approach involving the juxtaposition of varied media such as film, sound, and lighting along with both stylized gesture and more traditional dance movement. Even so, the evenings produced in her the frustration of having taken a step backward.

When the opportunity arose in early 1969 to give a concert at the Natural History Museum of the Smithsonian Institution in Washington, she prepared the first of her latest series, "Tour: Dedicated to Dinosaurs." The second in the series, "Tour 2: Barbershop," was given in a Chicago Museum, and the most ambitious, "Juice," was performed in several locations in New York. All share an imaginative use of space, considerable use of local community members, and an audience-freedom generally unknown in the regular theater.

"Juice" was the largest-scaled of the three museum pieces, involving as it did seventy-five performers and three separate parts, each of decreasing size. The first took place in the Solomon R. Guggenheim Museum, the second, three weeks later, on a regular proscenium stage at Barnard College's Minor Latham Playhouse, and the third, a week later, at a loft on lower Broadway. The most theatrically effective part of the work was the one that took place in the Guggenheim Museum, with its six-story spiral ramp and resonant acoustics. At the beginning of the dance, the audience was seated in the center of the main floor, the ramp spiraling up and around them, and banks of performers in white appeared and retired from portions of the spiral, humming. Four performers in red costume and red body makeup entered the main floor and began a deliberate clomping walk to the top of the spiral. They paused at each level to do a climbing or crawling exercise. Their ascent was interspersed with vocal music from individuals or groups both seen and unseen. At various levels, three girls in period costumes simply stood or turned slowly in place like mannequins in a window display, the first in formal court dress and white wig, the second in 1890's musical costume, and the third in somewhat Biblical dress. After the four red performers had ascended, Monk sang a song that resembled a muezzin's call. All of the performers in white who had retired out of sight reappeared and rushed down in a stream of running bodies to spread themselves around the first level railing. All performers froze as a man cut some wood with an electric saw. A girl in black with a life mask of herself affixed to her stomach was carried to the second level, after which there was a blackout and the first section was over.

In the second part, all of the performers formed living exhibits in various niches and stairwells scattered throughout the museum. The audience wandered among them, pausing or going on. At a signal, all the performers descended the spiral in a beautiful run, clustered in the space the audience occupied at the beginning, and then exited. It was the end of the first installment.

The second part of the work consisted of the four performers in red, along with a few property men and musician Don Preston. This portion showed the themes contracting in size from the large theatrical presentation at the Guggenheim and becoming more intimate as the performers revealed themselves in personal recitatives like the "sprechstimme" of contemporary opera. What had been a stylized hike up the ramp was broken down into the component pilgrimages of four individuals. Small improvisational games were played by the group, the members feeding off their knowledge of one another's characteristic gestures.

The final section of the work (presented in a loft) did not have any performers. It was a display of the costumes and stage properties used in the other sections, along with a videotape monologue and performance by each of the principals (Monk and the performers in red). It represented the complete compression of the performing material into the natural and untheatrical personalities of the performers from which the piece had developed. Monk had presented the full, somewhat allegorical and religious expansion of the group mystique in the Guggenheim portion, the transitional, partially staged and partially improvised performance at Minor Latham, and the raw materials at the loft. The entire piece was the most impressive work that she had created to date, presenting as it did a specialized life cycle of great subtlety and variety.

The theater of Meredith Monk is centered strongly on locale and personality. While on tour, she requires at least three days in any place in order to work, and prefers to have a week or more. Since she does not like to do a piece that she has prepared elsewhere, feeling that each piece should grow partially out of the site in which it is performed, she spends some time familiarizing herself with a given locale. She gives students classes and answers their questions. A further creative interpolation is to include students and audience members in the realization of a work so that it will have some personal meaning for them. She is currently interested in doing a new piece in every place that she visits and is not at all interested in repeating past work. Her past and future combine in the work of the immediate present. She believes in theatrical magic and is enthralled with the idea of stars, in the film sense of spectacle personalities. She even uses film techniques such as the close-up as she brings her audience into close proximity with her performers. But Monk's notion of a personality is not quite Hollywood's. Like a "pop" portrait artist, she dotes on the "star" potential of the ordinarily unexceptional.

Some Others

A Round-Up

One of the first of the newer choreographers who pondered the question of technique was Simone Forti, later and most widely known as Simone Whitman, who had studied with Ann Halprin in San Francisco. In 1961 she moved to New York and in that year offered one of the most influential single concerts ever given by a dancer.

Whitman herself is not a particularly strong performer, nor has she shown any great desire to appear frequently on stage. In the course of a decade and a half, she has organized but three concerts of her work. What has interested her is the discharge of energy in simple game or task-oriented situations. Movement, any movement, could have a beautiful quality if done with purpose. She has sent people clambering up an inclined plane, or spinning in slow circles after being wound up inside a rope hoop suspended from the ceiling, or sent them jumping off one rooftop onto another. It was motion and its qualities which one directed attention to—to, say, the man who was wound up slowly and jerkily by a girl assistant to then spin smoothly down to a state of rest accompanied by a grating electronic score. In other pieces she has sat in a wheeled cart which was pulled in one direction or another by long ropes, or she has assigned teams of performers the task of forming a football huddle over which each clambered one at a time.

Another element of theater that interests her greatly has been the combination of sound and motion. In one dance, seated on a stool, she played a penny whistle which was attached to a recording device that traced the lines of the slide's movement. It was notation that had more in common with an oscilloscope pattern than conventional note indications, but it did show sound in an unusual fashion. Whitman has worked with other sound experiments, such as singing a short song against the powerful Beatles rendition of "Fool on the Hill" or preparing a "ghost" opera called "Steam." In the latter, she secreted herself and another performer in long boxes from which whistling sounds emerged. After a time they stopped, and she was helped out by her partner. End of piece. Whether fully realized or not, her work had an against-the-grain charm that provoked thought as much after as during a concert

All her pieces have been presented with a disarming simplicity and have been of varying but definitely nontraditional theatrical length. They have tended to be short and smooth in dynamic presentation. At times, the performer would address herself to the audience and make a comment about the task she was engaged in. The remarks were usually made in a conversational tone and underscored the use of everyday material that was only once removed from the ordinary. There was no attempt made to theatricalize movement. It existed and was to be considered for what it was. It was presented in non-theatrical time. It took exactly as long to "perform" the motions of a Whitman piece as it would have taken to do the same motions in actual non-theatrical time. The difference that existed between them was similar to the difference between spoken words and sung words. The latter become elastic and lend themselves to endless repetitions which would be totally out of place in normal conversation. So with Whitman's movements, but otherwise she has worked on the basis that there would be only one time in the theater and it would be common to both audience and performer. It was an idea that many of the choreographers interested in developing new ways to move would adapt to their own purposes.

Another response to the problem of creating clear, unambiguous move- ment was the treatment of Tony Holder and Ruth Emerson, who both were members of the original Judson Dance Theater. Each of them brought the technique of athletic gesture to dances that they choreographed. Holder, in a piece called "Plus" (1964), performed a sequence of movements with considerable physical exertion in a white, weighted vest. At the end of the sequence, he stripped off the vest and allowed it to fall to the floor with a solid thump and then repeated the same sequence. This time unhampered by the constricting weight, he soared through the movements, strikingly contrasting the thrust of gestures pushed down by weight and the same movements in liberated conditions. In another dance, "Lightweight" (1965), Holder again showed his concern for the visual weight of gesture. The piece was a solo for himself in which he appeared in the flicker of a stroboscopic light which froze the dance into a series of still photographic images. The movements were presented almost as one would show a slide sequence, with the resultant jerkiness. During an early Judson concert that was a collaborative event between various dancers and sculptor Charles Ross, Ruth Emerson presented "Sense." The basic situation for the dance was created by Ross, who designed a series of pipe constructions and placed them in the performance area. The dancers were free to do whatever they wished to with them. Emerson approached a trapezoidal figure and began a series of gymnastic explorations of the form. Possessed of a beautifully supple and strong body, she created a tracery of movement around the piece in which she became the questing ornamentation of this obdurate and unyielding shape.

Two more dancers who concerned themselves with the architecture of movement were Lucinda Childs and Kenneth King. Both tended to use stillness in a variety of interesting ways. Possibly Childs' most successful piece was one that incorporated the street movements of people and vehicles. Childs stood as the focal point of the activity and the audience tended to judge and relate everything to her quiet organizing presence. After five minutes, she left her position and the dance was over. The activity continued but was now chaotic, without the central focus which brought one's attention to it. Childs has tended to work privately and quietly at her own deliberate pace. She moves to the beat of her own drummer and has in recent years reduced her active performing to a minimum.

King has similarly diminished his own performing rate but retains an active interest in the problems of dance movement. He was a philosophy major in college and his approach to motion is compulsively logical. In his first dance (1965), he attempted to handle two live performers, a transistor radio, a cup, and a saucer as equally interesting dance elements. Later he created two works, "Camouflage" and "Blowout," which further examined the problem of movement for the contemporary dancer. In "Camouflage," he appeared in a green skin-tight costume with a military helmet and female toe shoes. The sound accompaniment to the dance was a reading from Robbe-Grillet's "Labyrinth," and a light dusting of artificial snow fell throughout the dance, which was performed on a grass-green mat. It was eerie and strangely fitting to see this odd dance in a tightly constricted area from which the man sporadically attempted to escape. In "Blowout," he was tethered to the room he was in by means of long elastic strings extending from the fingers of the gauntlets he wore. King's movement was even more restricted this time, since he was confined to a chair from which he rose and from which he later toppled. Both pieces had great theatrical impact and intensity. Most recently King has eliminated such theatrical intensity from his work and is concentrating on the question of flowing movement in repetitious waves. His costuming, often a white laboratory coat, is designed to hide the body so that only the motion of the feet is seen. He is also interested in the combination of words and movement, often accompanying his dances with slides of a continuous and amorphous essay or declaiming it on a tape recording. Like Childs, he goes his own way at his own pace.

Judith Dunn, who assisted in her husband's composition courses, and from time to time continued in her role of assistant in staging the Judson programs, was a graduate of the Merce Cunningham company and had had considerable theatrical experience. It was almost inevitable that she would

Lucinda Childs in *Carnation*, Judson Memorial Church, April 29, 1964. Photo by Al Giese

work in her dances with audience anticipations and expectations. Dunn is a dancer of great physical control and can enter into a movement that should logically develop in one direction and can smoothly change it in mid-flight to another direction, thereby putting the first movement in an entirely new perspective. Dunn constantly changed the presentational context of movement by decelerating it or taking the force out of it entirely so that it collapsed before having reached its logical conclusion. One of her most effective uses of altered gesture came in a duet called "Speedlimit" (1963), which was performed in white coveralls. Most of the action of the piece takes place on a mat and initially consists of balances and supporting gestures by the couple. These strong, simple gestures slump into a series of flowing moves that bring the two into falls and rolls which then are tautened into a series of bumping, rebounding, and grappling motions.

Dunn has often included much naturalistic detail in her work. In "Acapulco" (1963), she playfully developed a string of incidents alternately teasing and rewarding audience expectation. She placed one girl on a chair and choreographed a slow rising, sinking, and twisting phrase for her. A man walks over to stand by the chair in anticipation of a fall. A little later, she topples off the chair into his arms. In another section, a girl is seated in a chair, quietly waiting. Another girl begins a minute-stepped, slow approach to her, like an assassin stealthily approaching a victim. She finally reaches the seated girl, after suitable tension has been built up, only to innocently comb her hair. The audience, expecting the worst, is at least rewarded with the girl's drawnout cry of "Ouch!" Another girl performs the ordinary task of ironing a dress, except that she is still wearing it. A girl arrives to play a game of cards, but rather than walk she is wheeled on in a cart. Instead of wondering why she was wheeled on in a cart, her partner begins to deal out cards.

There is an element of dadaist play in Dunn's work which erupts in dislocations of timing, gesture, and incident. Dunn is a teacher of dance, and when she first started (switching from a program in anthropology to dance) , she had few preconceptions about the dos and don'ts of dance practice. She has retained an equally open attitude after years of professional performance and training. Technique for her is a term that covers all of the physical activity needed to achieve a choreographic end, whether it be of a high order of physical training or of a common garden variety that is within the capabilities of anyone.

Dunn likes to let viewers savor movement, and the pacing of her dances tends to be adagio. When she includes a rapid sequence of movement, she will often just stop short to allow an audience time to recollect and ponder her next directional change or gesture development. One of her most elaborate dances was "Last Point" (1964), which had a series of right-angle screens arranged in triangular fashion in the performing area. Films were projected during the dance and both dancers and screens caught bits of the images as they poured indifferently through the forest of bodies and objects. A sound score made up of inconsequential chitchat was read and Dunn did a long, sensitive solo in the center of the work that was like a resumé of growth and maturation. At one point she squatted, tapping a stone on the floor, and then looked up at the audience. The final section, like the first, was choreographed for the group. For her, life is the pleasure of movement which she attempts to share in carefully measured-out phrases.

Another choreographer concerned with exploring movement, who sees it as a form of sensuous play, is Trisha Brown. Like many of the original Judson group, Brown does not concern herself overly with the niceties of technique if they get in the way of choreographic realization. There is a rough, direct attack about her work which was demonstrated early in her career. Prior to her own choreographic development, she worked with Yvonne Rainer, and in one particular dance the two performers tumbled and rolled about the stage area with yowling abandon.

She is as likely to perform in hip waders as in bare feet. A member of the original Judson Dance Theater, she has in recent years been less active than she was in the early 1960's, although she has retained her interest in teaching. Brown as a performer has suggestions of untidy athleticism. There is a direction and physical drive to her work that is earthy and concrete. For Brown, the energy is paramount whether she is throwing herself into a tub of cold water or sending five non-technical "dancers" out to play "Rulegame 5." The latter is a dance constructed in the form of a game. Five parallel lines are drawn across the performance area and the dancers start to follow one of the lines and then the other. The trailing dancer or dancers are allowed to pass the person in the lead, who in turn is allowed to try to prevent such passing. The rules are simple but their working out is the dance. Any group of persons can participate whether they are trained performers or not.

Most of Brown's dances develop from a simple and demonstrable physical idea that is relentlessly pursued. The posture of the dancers in any of Brown's pieces is that of the physical combatant ready to go. She is fond of the athletic stance, and in a duet, "Lightfall" (1963), threw her dancers into a football arms-on-thighs attitude in a variety of sequences. She is to a great extent oblivious of the finer points of production. The technical values of lighting, decor, and costuming take a decidedly second place to the brute reality of movement. She is not oriented in any special manner to the priorities of the standard, theatrically arranged stage, where things are positioned from back of the stage to the front in increasing order of importance. To her, vigor rather than vicinity is the criterion of value.

As with many of the choreographically playful dancers, she does not differentiate between the man and the woman on an artistic level. The rules of the game are set down and all who wish to play are welcome; they must only abide by the common book of standards. For Brown and for many of the newer choreographers, sexual differences inhibited choreography. If the male dancer had a special vocabulary of movement and the female had her own vocabulary of movement, the problem of bringing them together became more and more difficult. One of the solutions was to handle men and women as if they were the same physical machine and to emphasize the similarities rather than the differences. There was the common ground that each had two legs and two arms and one thinking head, so that if dances were made for arms and legs and not female arms and male legs, then certain natural similarities would have a chance to make themselves felt. For many this uni-sexual view of performance is disturbing.

It is argued that to ignore obvious sexual differences is to create an unnatural performing situation. While this to a certain extent is true, modern dance prior to the most recent period had become overly dependent on boy meets girl stories that were becoming more and more constricted. The suspension of sexual differences choreographically followed from the rejection of such stories and allowed greater freedom in the deployment of dancers.

Another choreographer who has made herself choreograph in the non-sexually differentiated manner is Batya Zamir. Having spent her formative years dancing in the Alwin Nikolais company, she was thoroughly familiar with the idea of human movement in and of itself without any sexual differentiation. When she decided to leave the company and work on her own, she resolved to have a group of sympathetic people who would not question the single-sex approach, as well as the other elements of what she was trying to do. Zamir had decided that movement resulting from game situations was the most interesting and spontaneous way of creating a contemporary dance theater. Accordingly, she sought a group outside of the dance world, as so many of the newer choreographers have done, and found a series of interested persons who were connected with the world of the plastic arts. She met regularly with them and conducted weekly classes in the basics of movement.

For the pieces that she choreographed for them, she did not draw on the technical resources that she was able to command. Instead she decided that the form of the dance should be set down in verbal terms and the execution of it should be handled on a purely physical basis during the actual performance. It was a combination of the rigorous rule and spontaneous reaction that was to interest many choreographers attempting to break free of the stranglehold of technique. Choreographers like Zamir attempted to point out that dance structure is what makes modern dance interesting and not any physical feats, pre-established or otherwise.

Zamir selected or rather let a group of people select themselves to appear in her work. The only requirement was a certain dogged persistence on the part of the student in showing up for exercise class. Zamir first presented her people in a loft, a space that was totally unsuitable for the type of movement that she was attempting to present. Later she was to secure a gymnasium in which to perform. She set her performers a series of tasks which included sequences in which they followed the lead of the person in front of them and other passages in which they attempted to thwart the will of the person in front of them, similar to Trisha Brown's "Rulegame 5." At other points in the dance, it was decided that everyone in the piece would carry every other person in the piece for at least a few moments. This brought about the logical absurdity of a tiny girl having to support the weight of a massive man.

After pieces such as these dances without trained dancers, it may have been only logical for someone to conceive of a dance without performers of any sort. Joel Mason, in early 1970, decided that the idea of performance was one which was saturated with the concept of the performer. The only way to properly present a "performance-cleansed" dance to the viewer was to allow him to create it in his own mind without the interpreter. The "dance" Mason offered was composed of two sheets of paper. The first was a listing of various parts of the body with dictionary definitions and the second sheet was an article from a computer programmer's book which indicated various ways of putting parts of things together into meaningful wholes. The combination of the two was designed to produce a dance in the mind of the reader. It was the logical extension of the Judson revolution, and it had the virtue of throwing into relief some basic features of dance.

As an idea, Mason's piece was fascinating, but as a dance performance it was disappointing. It lacked that measure of audience response which is one of the irreducible elements of any theatrical presentation, whether within or outside of a proscenium. One of the most important facets of any dance is the type of audience resonance which is received. The dance as idea was ultimately illogical. Dancing is a physical discipline and one which relies upon the alternation of movement and stillness in order to achieve its effects at a particular time. The dance as idea was not controllable. It was too dependent on the experience of the individual who might or might not have been exposed to any form of serious theatrical dancing. The person who had never had the vocabulary of dance presented to him would not have been able to construct interesting choreographic patterns. The dance as idea was too much like the projective psychological test in which an ambiguous shape or drawing is presented to the subject who can make of it that which he will. Dance to a great extent is performance; it does not have a life outside of its realization. Music has a score but dance has a tradition of presentational continuity. Dance is a time art and not an art concerned with producing objects from its activity. It is an art of being and not of product.

Out of the performing turmoil that surrounded the Judson Dance Theater emerged a significantly different attitude toward the dancer than had existed in the minds of historic modern dance choreographers. The dancer at Judson was an individual possessed of his individual worth and not of "impersonal" values of a society. The Judson dancer did not have to conform to the heroic mold of another age. Instead he tried to integrate the actualities of his daily existence with those of a performance situation. He tried to close the gap between performance and life by altering his performing scale to one that was more closely related to the scale of the other facets of his life. Elements of play, random activity, and non-stressed movement appeared alongside or even in place of conventionally conceived dance. Technique had become personalized.

Part Three

The Matter of Presentation

Modern dance, like most serious theatrical dance, was shaped by the conventions of the proscenium stage. There were always occasional presentations in other spatial areas, in connection with benefit or festival performances, but basically modern dance was designed for the nonthrust stage; that spatial area is fundamentally a black box into which can be poured light and motion. It is a frame and provides innumerable possibilities for surprise. People leaving one side of the stage can appear a moment later from the other side. Dancers, properties, and whole sets can be "flown" out of sight or dropped through the floor. The system invites "magic," but the demands of the literary have exercised an inhibiting effect on the use of such magic.

When the more recent choreographers freed themselves of stories and began to work with dances from moment to moment without literary strictures, the first thing that happened is that many found that they could use the proscenium stage more imaginatively. There also arose a new familiarity with the use of modern technology in the forms of the tape recorder (with its possibilities for unusual editing), the videotape machine, and varieties of film and slide presentations. The technological turn, together with the fact that the rejection of stories freed dancers to present isolated bits of movement in varying sequences, resulted in the appearance of a certain extravagance that had been rigorously purged from traditional dances full of social content or concerned with psychological studies.

Newer choreographers who concerned themselves with novel production values and forms included both those who had been trained in the skills of dance techniques and those who did not have this special technical ability. At Judson, both were accepted in the group. The concern of these choreographers centered on creating an effect through imaginative costuming, decor, and other such theatrical elements. This group of choreographers, whose pieces necessarily were more romantically skewed than were the classically rigorous dances of the other major group of younger choreographers, who were interested primarily in ways of movement, brought back to modern dance an interest in the "illusionism" that had been eliminated in the 1930's.

Few of the choreographers who work with production and presentational methods use chance in their dances. The new presentations have been a mixture of the novel and the naïve. They offered possibilities for performance to trained dancers and also to those who were not primarily dancers, among them, musicians, artists, and, at times, the imaginative amateur.

Without the need for characterization, costuming was liberated to produce any effects the choreographer wanted. He could conceive of his dancers in terms of color harmonies alone or he could break up the body lines by appending lumps and bulges in bizarre anatomical places to convey a sense of the grotesque. The setting of a dance could be as neutral as a bare stage with all the lights turned up full or as defined as a microscopic world created through projections of colored slides. The determining factor for all of the new possibilities was their suitability to enhance the mood of the dance. It was not a question of thinking through the demands of the situation in terms of conventional logic but of selecting those elements that would combine to produce the proper emotional tone.

Many of the newer choreographers became interested in the technical possibilities of industrial materials and methods. For example, infrared sensitive television cameras were used to film activity in a darkened area in which objects were made electronically alive so that a dancer breaking their energy field would trigger off film or sounds. Some performers used dime-store instruments in place of conventional instruments to create their own music. Everything was considered suitable for a choreographer— nothing was out-of-bounds if it contributed meaningfully to the final result.

Alwin Nikolais

Wizard of Oz

Alwin Nikolais is a theatrical magician, a magus of movement conceived of in a pictorial fashion. He has effected a style of dance that draws on the technical resources of the medium of the theater in the most imaginative manner of any contemporary choreographer. When he found many of his contemporaries disturbed by the fact that he called his pieces dances, he began to call them theater works or presentations. He refuses to be bound by the concerns of the dance audience that demands emotionally charged and linearly developed stories. He creates his pieces as if they were Byzantine mosaics, assembling distinct units, each of which will cumulatively take its well-ordered place in the overall panorama. The kinetic impulse of dance is subsumed in his work into the ordering requirements of visual design.

Nikolais was born in Southington, Connecticut, in 1912, and was first exposed to theater at the age of nine. During his mother's weekly shopping trips to nearby New Haven, he and his brother were left at a matinée at the Hyperion Theater. It was the era of vaudeville, and Nikolais saw a variety of performing styles, including burlesque—until his mother discovered that the theater had changed its family entertainment policy.

Nikolais expresses his interest in theater in a variety of ways. He was a piano accompanist to a ballet and drama school, played piano accompaniment for silent movies, and once ran a marionette theater. In each job, he became interested in the technical aspects of what was going on. For a yearly recital of the ballet group, he devised a lighting design, the first of his career, and for the marionettes he designed decor and costumes as well as the lights. He began work in the theater at a time when the "roll-up" (rather than "draw" or "flown") curtain was still in use, and once devised a light dimmer by raising and lowering a carbon rod in a brine solution. He was technically interested in all of the aspects of production and the way in which each element contributed to the final presentation. At the age of twenty-three, he began to study dance.

During all of the time that Nikolais had been going to the theater, he had not had the opportunity to see serious theatrical dancing. Modern dance came as a revelation to him, and his mature decision to become a dancer plunged him into the idealistic vortex that was historic modern dance in the 1930's. He went to Bennington in the summers and immersed himself in the currents of the dance world. He admired Martha Graham's technical dancing skill, Louis Horst's composition course, and John Martin's critical-writing course and his general good sense. He was dedicated to dancing with the devotion of a crusader.

He choreographed his first pieces as part of a Federal Theater Project drama series in Hartford. In one of these pieces, "Sabine Women" (1936), he worked with an all-black cast whose members were not trained dancers. He devised group movements for them and also drew on some tap dancing which he found in an instruction book. For "World We Live In" (1936), an "insect" comedy, he staged movements appropriate for ants and beetles. The first pure dance piece that he choreographed was in the Hartford series. "Eight Column Line" (1939), done for soloist and group, made his reputation in Hartford.

The man who designed the sets and costumes for the piece was Chick Austin, a local arts patron who had also commissioned Gertrude Stein and Virgil Thomson to do "Four Saints in Three Acts," had commissioned the music for the Lew Christensen ballet "Filling Station," and had staged the first big Picasso show in the United States. Austin was typical of the multi-directed esthetician who did not specialize but was active in a variety of artistic fields. He was like H. T. Parker, the critic of the *Hartford Courant,* who had received Nikolais' work favorably and who reviewed all of the theater, concert, and plastic arts for the paper. These men represented for Nikolais a type of broadness of interest which he developed in himself and which he was to find lacking in a later generation of critics. As his own interests spread beyond the narrow confines of just one aspect of theater to include all the means of dance presentation, he found that he was told that what he was doing was not dancing.

But before he emerged from the story-telling and Freudian-saturated psychodramatic dances that comprised much of historic modern dance, he participated in them and the accepted manners of their approach to the fullest. During this period, in the late thirties, he selected the music of composers like Riegger, Honegger, Prokofiev, and Horst for accompaniment to his works. In addition, he choreographed socially minded pieces, like "War Themes," and, as was the custom, opened his programs with a curtain raiser. All of his creative activity at this time took place in Hartford, and to all intents and purposes he closed the first part of his career when he entered the Army during World War Two. He did little dance work in the Army, although he did develop a notation system in his spare time. After release from the service, he returned to Hartford to stage a number of opera productions that included dance works which he had created in a summer at Colorado College, where Hanya Holm ran a summer course. Nikolais had studied with her earlier and was an admirer of her work.

Then in 1948 he was invited to become the director of the Henry Street Playhouse in New York. Henry Street had had a substantial theatrical history, having seen Bernhardt and Duse as well as Graham, but it had fallen into a somnolent state during the war years. When Nikolais inherited it, it was not only disorganized administratively but also needed considerable work on the physical plant to make it useful as a dance theater. For the next five years, as he physically rehabilitated the theater which he had inherited, Nikolais also developed a children's performing group, for which he choreographed many pieces, including "Lobster Quadrille" (1949) and "Sokar and the Crocodile" (1951). Most of the restoration work was carried out by members of the performing companies. Meanwhile, dancers like Murray Louis, Phyllis Lamhut, Beverly Schmidt and Gladys Bailin received a considerable amount of their early dance training through the performing activities of the children's troupe. At one time the troupe was giving over a hundred and fifty performances a year. The dancers matured as, in effect, did the theater in which they were to perform those works, starting in the early 1950's, that represent Nikolais' mature achievement.

From the very start of his career, with the movement designs he developed for plays, Nikolais had worked with large groups and had interested himself in mass movements. He was never a particularly outstanding solo dancer and concentrated more on the design of dance configurations than on their kinetic flow. When he arrived at Henry Street, he inherited a hulking and almost immobile set of "The Dybbuk," an evil lurking spirit of the past. He had to get rid of it as well as of the spiritual dead wood of the 1930's before he could achieve his mature body of work. In a joking aside to Louis Horst in 1948, during the intermission of a concert of someone else's work, he remarked, "We've already had four!" meaning the number of simulated fornications. At Henry Street, he did away with Freudian symbols and began to concentrate on movement, as a mime representation of characterization or universal archetype, but for its own sake. He worked on improvisation classes with his students and began to strip away the layers of training that he himself had received in the search for bodies that were "clean" and not stressed with the emotional tensions of traditional modern dance. He gave up active performing in 1953, the year that he presented "Masks, Props and Mobiles," the first of his new dance explorations.

The critical reaction to the piece was a shock to Nikolais. The most common difficulty was that critics could not accept it as dance. The consensus was that the work was interesting, but was it dance? Since Nikolais had never wanted to tie his productions rigidly to one category, he conceived of other ways of referring to his pieces so that the mere categorizing of them would not produce a restrictive set in the minds of viewers.

"Masks, Props and Mobiles" had a musical and percussion accompaniment that was in a recognized tradition. However, Nikolais had been working privately with sound-recording equipment, and the advent of the tape recorder came as a godsend to him. Previous work with wax recording discs proved unsatisfactory for a number of reasons, including the infuriating likelihood that the needle would jump grooves when jarred by the dancers' motions. With the tape recorder, editing became a possibility and Nikolais recognized this potential almost from the time of the device's appearance. He prepared his first sound accompaniments in 1953 for two dances, "Forest of Three" and "Kaleidoscope." The latter was a short work and Nikolais was later to expand the title and elements of it for a full-evening piece. Still, he considered the first version a significant work in that it was to open the way for him to begin what was characterized by a hostile press as the "dehumanization" of the dancer.

This "dehumanization" consisted basically of regarding the human body less as the center of significant emotional turbulence and more as an articulated form with a variety of energy potentials and possibilities. Thus it was that, freed from stories and accompanied by sound freed from linear development, Nikolais' dancers were free to participate in movement incidents, in short bursts or pulses of activity that did not have a connective thread running through them. Events did not follow one another in a strictly logical form in Nikolais' works but clustered in related bunches. To emphasize the shape and plastic possibilities of the dancer moving in space, costuming was designed that broke up the outlines of the human body in the way that a prism might separate the component colors of white light. A performing style was developed that emphasized a cool, "exterior" presentation of movement. Movement was not generated from an emotional flow; it spurted out, flickered briefly, and disappeared, only to turn up again in an unexpected but pleasing manner. It was dancing that demanded exceptional physical control, the ability to abort a gesture cleanly but without any suggestion of a jerky spasm. It was dancing with a strongly physical import.

The bearing of the Nikolais dancer is one of alert reserve. He is ready to go but is liable to get there in an unexpected manner. He does not offer clues as to what is to follow in any sequence of movements. A movement phrase may be given a humorous or terrifying coloration by appending a slight gesture to the end of it. He does not prepare you for what is to come next in the dance; he merely presents himself on a moment-to-moment basis and asks that he be regarded in the same way.

In the short space of about seven years, from 1953 to 1959, Nikolais produced a substantial body of work, including the expanded version of "Kaleidoscope," "Prism" (1956), "Cantos" (1957), and "Allegory" (1959), each of which occupied an entire evening, a most unusual arrangement for modern dance. He presented a new, increasingly accepted style of dance theatricality in which lights, costuming, tailor-made electronic sound, and choreography shared the audience's attention. In each succeeding piece, Nikolais showed himself capable of producing theatrical astonishment.

It was inevitable that he would catch the eyes of theatrical producers outside of the dance world. Nikolais' company made its first appearance on television in March 1959. One of the directors of the Steve Allen Variety Show had seen his work at Henry Street and asked him to prepare for an appearance on the Allen show. Without a moment's hesitation, Nikolais agreed. He confessed later, "If I had waited, I would have said no!" During the next year, be presented a series of seven pieces, some of which were choreographed for television. When he started to work in the new medium, he merely had selected elements from dances that had been created previously. But he found the limitations and possibilities of television interesting in themselves. He began to experiment with the medium and to discover those things that could be done with it but were impossible in the live theater.

His most ambitious television project, "Limbo," was created nearly a decade after the first Steve Allen show. Nikolais presented his project to the Columbia Broadcasting System and was told that it could not be done. To prove that it was possible he had to make a demonstration test show before they would allow him to proceed. His own feeling was that he did not invent any new techniques but just saw the use of the medium from a slightly different angle than did television people. He won his argument with the producers of commercial television, just as earlier he had convinced his detractors within the dance audience.

"Limbo" (1968) was an imaginative display of dancers collectively and individually inhabiting a surrealistic plain that contained no recognizable geographical signposts. The choreography was relatively simple and kept carefully within the confines of the small scanning area of the television camera. The technological work, however, was of a high and imaginative order. Nikolais had prepared everything with meticulous care, and he spoke to the engineers using their own vocabulary to establish a rapport with them. Through the techniques of the medium, he created an invisible hole in the center of the screen into which dancers could disappear, or preserved the outline of a dancer while supplying another camera shot of bubbles or swimming fish to fill the shape of the dancer's body, and used an elaborate series of overlays to achieve other effects. In all, he spent nine-tenths of his time in the control booth away from the dancers. The result was a dance that would only be possible on television, so closely was it wedded to the properties of the medium.

In addition to his work in television during these years, Nikolais continued his vision and motion exploration in the technically well-equipped Henry Street Playhouse. His creation of a school at Henry Street enabled him to keep his company well supplied with dancers, and the availability of the Playhouse allowed him to have regular seasons. It was a great advance for a modern dance company to be able to appear with such a degree of constancy without having continually to tour. His productions could be scheduled to appear for a month or a month and a half, so that they were given adequate exposure to a variety of audiences. Ordinarily modern dance performances were limited to a few appearances on a weekend, and companies were unable to build a broad base from the general theater-going public. His choice of the full-evening work as his habitual form was another departure for modern dance. In an age when the short piece was the norm, he returned to the nineteenth-century conception of dance as an evening-long spectacle.

In the decade of the 1960's, Nikolais' most outstanding creations included "Totem" (1962), "Imago" (1963), "Sanctum"(1964), and "Galaxy (1965), each of which had an amplitude of conception and execution that character-ized his finest work. "Imago" is perhaps his most famous and widely known piece. It was created in 1963 and first seen in Hartford, after which it had a six-week season in New York. It was shown again in a half-dozen performances during 1963 in and out of New York, and parts of it were telecast over the Columbia Broadcasting System in its Repertory Workshop series. Five of its eleven dances were also presented at the Lincoln Center New York State Theater during the American Dance Festival season in 1965, and the entire production was revived for a four-week season during 1967 at the Henry Street Playhouse.

"Imago," subtitled "The City Curious," is a colorful view of a seemingly microscopic world full of electromagnetic energy, light waves, and force fields, through which the inhabitants move in accordance with the pull of various forces. The work is divided into three acts, the first of which has four parts, the second, five, and the last, two. Individual parts have descriptive titles based on the number of dancers who appear in them, such as solo, quintet, trio, and duet. Each of the acts closes with a group dance for the company. In the first act, the group has two dances in which they do tolling movements from side to side and later appear like notes on a musical scale as they move back and forth behind lines of elastic tapes spread across the stage. The men do a dance with long biomorphic extensions of their arms, stamping around in a semi-anthropoid manner, and the girls move flowingly in long overblouses. The contrasts have been made between the male and female of this "city curious" and their common plight of being under the control of a larger force emphasized in the driven look of the dances. One of the most effective movements is the rippling lines of the arm extensions that the men wear as they stand directly in line and move their arms from side to side in sequence.

The second act shows a female and a male solo re-emphasizing the respective differences of movement between the sexes—her sinuous squig-gles match his somewhat mechanical assertiveness. The men perform a dance with pennants which are attached to them by means of invisible cords which cause the pennants to dart at them as they jump from side to side. In the finale, the group appears in enveloping robes in which the arms are confined. The context again invokes a sympathy for their encased situation.

The last act has two movements, a duet in which the man and woman assert themselves individually, neither of them able to accommodate to the other completely. The work ends with the entire company in capes that come to the floor, moving as if on invisible wheels, encountering and recoiling from one another, finally being swept back like reeds in a wind at the explosive sound that concludes the work. Throughout, Nikolais has added bits of choreographic incidents until he has created a miniature world that is frantically and insularly busy in its own somewhat odd manner and at the same time calls up an identifying sympathy from the audience.

Nikolais' view of mankind and the world that it inhabits seems at times the view of a visitor who can take a detached look at the comings and goings that make up daily existence and see them simply as units in a flux of energy change. There is a broad line of pulsating life and melancholy that runs through his work. With wry amusement, he delineates the hurly-burly of activity and asks drily what the sense of it is. The question is posed in such a colorful and imaginative manner that its darker import is hidden at first glance.

In one of his shorter pieces, "Tower" (1965), he provides each of his dancers with a section of aluminum fence. Throughout the course of the dance, the dancers form various structures with the aluminum, including an enclosure that always seems too small to accommodate all of those wishing to get inside. As a result, one or another dancer keeps being popped out by the entrance of another. At the end, all of the sections are fitted together to create a contemporary-looking tower of Babel with pennants hung from it. But once again, as in "Imago," a concluding explosion and flash sends it tottering. In "Tent" (1968), the group enters with a tent folded and then hooks it up with great enjoyment and confidence, but at the end of the piece all are reduced to groveling beneath it. In "Sanctum," which is the epic of an individual, a sadness again develops as the man who first swings idly over the company descends to be with them and then ends hung back limply on the same trapeze.

Nikolais is like a man with a private malaise who wishes to indicate something of the ruthlessness of life in its essential operations. It is axiomatic in biology that nature's solutions to the problems of life are simple, brutal, and direct in their concern for preserving the species at the expense of the individual. Nikolais' choreographic methods are none of these—being complex, graceful, and subtle—but they lead to a similar speculation about man and his world.

Nikolais Dance Theater in Alwin Nikolais' *Tent*, 1968. (Courtesy Nikolais-Louis Dance)

Nikolais has moved far from (in his phrase) the "mad,glad,sad" world of choreography that he grew up in and which was commented on with a critical nomenclature that included such terms as "foetal," "fertile," and "phallic." The development of his choreography has been toward an ever-decreasing emphasis on the individual and toward an ever-growing presentation of an overall pictorial movement structure. Some of his most successful pieces have made his dancers creatures of light, nonexistent outside of its glare but busily operative within it, like motes in a sunbeam. He uses light as a sculptor would use three-dimensional material. One of his most brilliantly achieved light designs was in "Triptych" (1967), whose three sections are "Putti," "Scrolls," and "Idols." In "Putti," he used needlepoints of multi-colored lights sprayed on the slowly twisting bodies of dancers suspended by ropes to create a pointillist outline of them; in "Scrolls," he washed, slashed, and poured lights on three large sheets of paper to give them a bright-hued magnificence; and in "Idols," he created a spinning basket of light with ultraviolet lamps and fluorescent dyes.

When traveling with his company, he carries a compact and complete assortment of technical equipment, consisting of thirty-five spotlights, eighteen dimmers on three boards, twelve projection machines, his sound equipment, and three lengths of cable. With these and his stage properties, he can create his environmental pieces indoors and out. In 1969, in a six-thousand-seat Roman theater, he played his projections on the columns and presented "Tent." He favors large theaters so as to give the maximum scope to his technical means. He is superbly professional and impatient with anything less than his own rigorous high standards of performance. He has not found it easy to work with unskilled collaborators and has become habituated to designing his entire productions by himself. He is the chief choreographer, lighting expert, sound, costume, and decor creator. He has achieved the mature body of his work by being all things to all elements of production.

His interest in many forms of theater has steadily involved him in varieties of projects, including such anticipated spectacular ones as an environmental light-and-motion production for a set of cathedral-like caves in Baalbeck, Lebanon, the movement and technical design of an opera for the Hamburg Opera, a multi-media building environment with Buckminster Fuller, and, finally, a selection of sound scores for a record release. In composition class, he encourages creative exploration of space and tries to get students to concentrate on their craft and not their personal emotional states so as to be as professionally competent as possible in their chosen field. He himself is the thorough professional.

Paul Taylor

Advanced Ideas and Conventional Theater

Paul Taylor is the likable prodigal of modern dance. He began his career in 1953, dancing first in the company of Pearl Lang then briefly with Merce Cunningham; he started to choreograph his own works at this time and then became a leading soloist with the Martha Graham company. Taylor originally was the darling of the avant garde in the middle and late 1950's, when his strikingly unconventional works dispensed with the then prevailing narrative line of dance development. When he turned to explore more traditional theatrical forms in the early 1960's, the vanguard coterie abandoned him, and the traditionalists, who had previously reviled his work, embraced the supposed reform in his choreographic outlook. Neither adequately perceived the path that Taylor had taken for himself. In the space of a decade, he managed to delight and infuriate almost every faction in the modern dance world. What has distinguished his career more than any other thing is the desire to go his own way regardless of the tugs and pulls of factionalism. Taylor does what he wants to do when he wants to do it and significantly in his own way.

His career is finely balanced between the traditional theatrical dance presentation and more contemporary thematic concerns of his own generation, a generation that had to explore the origins of movement before it could begin to synthesize movements and gestures into formal dances again. During the radical experimentalist portion of his career, Taylor isolated human postures in order to examine them out of their conventional context. He used heartbeats, wind rushing, and telephone time signals for sound accompaniment. He introduced a dog onto the stage as a performer; he wore street clothes; he did everything that a well-behaved dancer was not supposed to do. He dispensed with the severe technical stress that had been imposed upon the dancer's body in favor of finding the natural accents of movement. When he had satisfied himself about fragmented movement, he began to work in a style more familiar to audiences that had been exposed to historic modern dance—a style, however, that had been formed out of his own experiments and his performing experiences with Martha Graham and Merce Cunningham. He also added his own special quality of exuberance.

He is an athletically formidable figure and on stage exerts a muscular command over his choreography. It is one of the charms of Taylor's work to see his directness of approach, which combines easily accessible theatrical elements with subtle, non-verbal dance ideas. Taylor's skill at showmanship, in conjunction with his warm, humorous approach, have made his work widely appealing to large audiences that otherwise have not had any patience with modern dancing.

Taylor's basic choreographic sympathies are toward people, in the sense of their being personalities, and not toward the intense investigation of form which has been of special interest to Merce Cunningham. Taylor was the first modern dancer to reflect on a sustained scale an approach to choreography that was attuned to the personalities of his dancers while maintaining many of the formal traditions of historic modern dance. At one and the same time, he is careful not to present his dancers as musical acrobats or as characters in a drama gesturing to one another. To a great extent, it is this approach that has resulted in his periods of extended popular touring both in the United States and abroad.

Like many of the first- and second-generation modern dancers, Taylor had been exposed to the theater at a formative creative age and has remained enchanted with the ambiance of theatricality. For Taylor, even moving props with the Graham company had its own special pleasures. He was and is possessed of a showman's sense of presentation, while also being conscious of the recent formal developments in the craft of dancing. The swooping choreographic course he has taken between the poles of formalism and dance drama adds special interest to his career.

Taylor arrived in New York after leaving the University of Syracuse without having been graduated; he had little more than the desire to become a dancer. Only the rudiments of training were behind him. Moreover, during his career at the university, he had pursued the one sport which almost without fail is harmful to a dancer, swimming. He swam not with the aim of becoming a champion-caliber athlete but to receive an athletic scholarship and so relieve himself of waiting on tables. It was the classic case of the boy working his way through college (in Taylor's case as an art major) who saw that there was an easier way toward his goal.

In his junior year at Syracuse, he observed some dance classes, engaged in some student dance work, and decided that he wanted to become a dancer more than anything else. To do so meant that he had to give up competition swimming, which lengthens the muscles and tends to take the spring out of them, and it also meant that he would lose his scholarship and would have to give up Syracuse. He did both without any serious misgivings and came to New York.

Taylor had so little idea of the direction that he was going to take in the dance world that he showed up for an audition in socks, for he had heard that modern dancers worked barefoot and ballet dancers worked in dance shoes. So he took the middle course. The choice was indicative of his creative approach as it was to develop—an eclectic tendency which also was evident in his career at Syracuse, where he originally went for a degree in painting, swam to support himself, and ended up in the world of dance.

Taylor had no difficulty in securing a series of dance scholarships in New York, from the Juilliard School of Music Dance Department, the Martha Graham School, and the Metropolitan Opera Ballet School. He met two artists, Jasper Johns and Robert Rauschenberg, who were to work with him later and were to have a marked effect on his creative approach during the early part of his career. At the beginning of their association, he simply earned some money working with them doing window displays for Fifth Avenue stores.

Taylor's career began to develop along several routes. He was attending dance class and at the same time was being exposed to the advanced ideas then bursting out of the painting and sculpture world. In 1953 he became a member of Merce Cunningham's company and danced with him at Black Mountain College, where John Cage had produced the first "happening" the year before in collaboration with Cunningham and Rauschenberg, and he continued with Cunningham through Cunningham's critically ignored season at the Theater De Lys. Also in 1953, Taylor prepared his first professional piece, "Jack and the Beanstalk," which was given on a program at the Henry Street Playhouse organized by James Waring two years later in 1955. The decor, designed by Rauschenberg, was a series of helium-filled balloons attached to a string, which Taylor and Rauschenberg released into the air after the performance was over. The dance was not a particularly good one and did not satisfy Taylor, but for him it was the start of his serious choreographic career.

In 1954 he left Cunningham to form his own company. While dancing with Cunningham, Taylor was able to observe and participate in one of the crucial turning points of modern dance choreography, the introduction of chance as a means of composition. While not really sympathetic to such choreographic structuring, Taylor was strongly influenced by his exposure to the idea of chance. When joined with his own innate theatricality, such formal devices however were molded into a form of neo-dada choreography, as in "Public Domain" or "Piece Period" (1962), which persist in Taylor's work alongside more narrative choreography, as in "Agathe's Tale" (1967) and "Big Bertha" (1971).

Another area where Cunningham and Taylor differ is in their use of music. One has only to point to Taylor's "Post Meridian" (1965), a dance that matches an electronic score to a series of movements which had been worked out beforehand, to see his semi-cavalier treatment of music. Taylor does not work with music either the way that Cunningham does, as a parallel artistic act to the dance, nor does he rely on its rhythms in the manner of the previous Graham-dominated generation. Taylor uses music for its suitability to his choreography. He started choreographing one of his pieces, "Scudorama" (1963), to Stravinsky's "Rite of Spring," but then switched to another score for actual performance. It is commonplace for Taylor to change music well along in the creation of one of his dances. The change shows the type of choreographer's independence of an adjunct discipline that is characteristic of the newer modern dancers although each achieves it in his own way. At times Taylor's use of music is reminiscent of a nineteenth-century ballet choreographer who has a libretto firmly in mind and just needs it aurally decorated. This approach was brought to a high degree of perfection in Russia where the post of ballet musician meant, in effect, a skill at writing non-demanding music to precise measure. The practice fell into disrepute shortly before the Russian Revolution and was despised by the naturalistic school of choreographers who followed, the greatest exemplar being Fokine. Taylor has blithely returned to the tradition whenever it suits him, as in "Aureole" (1962) , a modern dance "ballet blanc" performed to selected and unrelated scores by Handel, a work that has proven to be one of the most popular of his repertory among ballet as well as other dance audiences.

Taylor's dance vocabulary tends to be restricted to a small palette of movements which he combines and recombines in a variety of interesting ways. There is no choreographer outside of the ballet tradition who is able to derive so much variety from such a restricted range of movements. Taylor's dance posture is modified balletic with free swinging arms for gestural comment. Taylor will take the classical carriage of the arms extended to the side with palms facing forward and bend it so that the palm faces upward and the elbow tucks slightly in toward the torso to form a shallow "W." Or again he will thrust the torso just slightly too far forward so that the repose of a strictly vertical classical beginning position is disturbed. His work is ordinarily composed toward the front with conventional dance sense, and his distribution of dancers in the performing area is done in terms of a hierarchy of significance, beginning with the center stage as the area of greatest prominence and moving outward in diminishing intensity.

One of Taylor's most successful theater works, "Four Epitaphs" (1956), (altered in 1960 to "Three Epitaphs"), dates from the early years of his independence. The decor and lighting were by Rauschenberg and the music was discovered by James Waring. It is a recording of blues played in a proto-dixieland slow stomp by the Laneville-Johnson Union Brass Band. The dance consists of a man and four women in various combinations.

There is deliberately little virtuosity in the piece, and the performers slump forward and move from a virtual crouch. The impression is of something less than human and more than brute animal. These humanoid figures have a pathetic but friendly bearing. The viewer is alternately depressed and exhilarated by their slouching clumsiness and erratic bursts of energy. At one point, a figure scuttles out to center stage and assumes a preparatory position only to realize that there is nothing to follow and then shambles off in dejection. It is the briefest of the work's "epitaphs."

When the piece was first performed, it was done exactly the same way twice through. The first time the lights were up high, and the second time they were pitched at a very low level. Rauschenberg remarked, "It was either the funniest or the saddest thing you had ever seen." Some time after the first few performances, Taylor decided to simplify the piece into "Three Epitaphs" and the light design was altered to accommodate a single performance of the choreography rather than the original two.

For all that he differs from Cunningham, in developing his own choreographic voice Taylor was strongly influenced by Cunningham's work and also by the experiments that were taking place in the world of painting. The most extreme example of his personal explorations of gesture—an area of Cunningham's concern—occurred in 1957 during a Sunday afternoon concert at the Kaufmann Concert Hall of the Young Men's and Young Women's Hebrew Association, 92nd Street. The program was made up of seven dances, all prepared by Taylor. It was a scantily attended concert and one that was even more scantily reviewed. During the course of one dance, "Epic," Taylor stood in ordinary street clothes and assumed small posture changes as the recorded voice of the telephone company time signal woman recited the ten second interval changes. In another piece, a duet for two girls, "Events 2," the dancers sat, got up, and moved around slightly, and had their dresses blown by the wind. Another solo for himself consisted of a series of unrelated gestures divorced from the context in which they ordinarily would be encountered. By his own admission, it was one of the most difficult dances he has made. It involved counting of a specially complex order, and just in physical terms was exhausting. It was an attempt on Taylor's part to explore the possibilities of natural movement and the theatrical possibilities of stillness. The piece was the culmination of a line of development for Taylor which began with the premier of "Jack and the Beanstalk" at the Henry Street Playhouse and extended through his work over the next four years at the Master Institute with James Waring and Dance Associates, a period concerned primarily with exploring movement possibilities outside of those favored by historic modern dance.

For the next three years he continued working in this exploratory manner but with a diminishing interest in exploring novel forms. His pieces during this period include "Rebus" (1958) and "Tablet" (1960). Then, at the 1961 American Dance Festival at Connecticut College in New London, he produced "Insects and Heroes," a work that opened the second phase of his work.

"Insects and Heroes" was cast in the form of an allegory, as the ambivalent title suggests. It involved the use of a serio-comic monster with a cactus-like exterior and five dancers who occupied telephone booth–sized cubicles on stage with lights which the dancers switched on and off. The dance had the thematic development of a metamorphosis. It was a dance focused on the balance point where the human and the not-quite-human meet. The piece was ambiguous in the comic-tragic way that "Three Epitaphs" was ambiguous.

The previous year, Taylor had appeared at the Festival of Two Worlds in Spoleto and was clearly headed toward a totally independent concert career for himself and his company. In 1961, the year he created "Insects and Heroes," he left the Graham company after having danced some of the most important roles in her repertory, among them Aegisthus in the full evening "Clytemnestra," Tiresias in "Night Journey," and the Stranger in "Embattled Garden." When Graham and George Balanchine collaborated in 1960 on a project to do two different ballets back-to-back, both set to music of Anton Webern, Taylor was chosen by Balanchine to do a solo in Balanchine's portion of the program. The solo was choreographed for Taylor to display his special qualities of muscular control, and it was not performed when Taylor was not available. In recent years, in fact, it has disappeared from the repertory and neither Balanchine nor Taylor can remember it.*

In 1962, Taylor created "Aureole," one of the company's most popular dances. Its combination of a classical poise of the torso with angular accents of the feet provides an unexpected tang to the work. The piece represents Taylor's debt to his modern dance and ballet training in a way that nothing else in his repertory does. In 1969, Taylor even mounted the piece for the Royal Danish Ballet, which accepted the discipline of dancing in bare feet when it took "Aureole" into its repertory.

The line of choreographic development which started with "Insects and Heroes" culminated in Taylor's first hour-long work, "Orbs" (1966). He had become adept at the shorter twenty-minute dance and wanted to develop his ideas further. The work that emerged had a depth and gravity that complemented his venturesome choice of late Beethoven string quartets as an accompaniment. In it he explored the area of changes that are not

---

*It is an interesting sidelight that the two ballet masters of the New York City Ballet, Balanchine and Jerome Robbins, had entirely opposite experiences with Taylor. Some years before the solo for Balanchine, in a production of "Peter Pan" which Robbins choreographed, Robbins fired Taylor after he crashed into the proscenium while doing a back flip off stage. Taylor not only lost a job, he broke his nose. Several years later, at a dinner in London when his fame had been firmly established, Taylor spoke with Robbins about the incident. True to his convictions, Robbins averred that he would still fire him if Taylor didn't do it right.

produced by dramatic choice but, in effect, just happen in a natural—inevitable—developmental way.

He had examined a similar situation in an earlier work, "Scudorama." Here a group of persons recognizably dressed in street clothes strip off their garments in the course of the dance to reveal the dancers' garb that lay beneath. "Scudorama" begins with the entire ensemble prone in a circle on the stage. Slowly one man raises himself from the prostrate group. The effect suggests the aftermath of a party in which all of the guests have passed out and one is finally reviving. The man looks around and others begin to revive as well. He tosses off his checkered coat and begins to move in a more spirited manner. The other dancers now rise and begin to leave the stage hugging the ground. Then one by one they reappear in leotards and tights. Each person has a distinctive color. Various combinations of duets, trios, and solos transpire until at the end the dancers huddle under massively gaudy beach towels, unable to face one another and recoiling at a physical encounter. It is the end of a series of meetings, most of which had the furtiveness of back-alley romances. From time to time, the dancers would reappear with their street costumes, giving them the semblance of being absurdly sane people caught in a maelstrom of uncontrollable behavior—almost like a perfectly intact house being whirled away in a twisting cyclone.

For "Orbs," Taylor chose to have three-quarters of his dance performed in stylized dance costumes and one-quarter danced in ordinary, middle-class clothes. The balance was about the same as in "Scudorama," except that the dance began and ended in the dance costumes, and only in the third section did the dancers wear street clothes.

In both of these works, Alex Katz was the designer. 'Orbs" was the seventh production he designed for Taylor. Katz, a pictorial painter of exceptional color sensitivity, created the dance costumes in a timeless heroic mode that could as easily be conceived of as Persian-Greek or Mexican or Minoan, providing a definite and meaningfull contrast with the supremely "average" appearance of the naturalistic clothes of the third section. But these also were conceived of as timeless in their own way and were designed not to suggest any specific locale or social class but merely the idealized middle ground of conventional dress in the twentieth-century United States.

In his working plan for "Orbs," Taylor had started to develop a detailed outline on which to build his conception. The idea of changes that were outside of human volition—that just happened—at first suggested seasonality to Taylor, which led in turn to the agencies that cause the change of seasons, the motion of the planets in their courses. The work finally resolved itself into a cyclical pattern of six parts, titled with a mixture of straight descriptive titles (Introduction and Conclusion for the beginning and end) and poetically evocative ones (Venusian Spring, Martian Summer,

Paul Taylor (center) and company in *Orbs*, 1966. Photo by Jack Mitchell (Courtesy Paul Taylor)

Terrestrial Autumn, and Plutonian Winter for the middle sections). Despite all of the seemingly cumbersome preliminary theorizing, "Orbs" is a work full of dance ebb and flow and is not visibly encumbered by its schematic framework.

After his sustained work on "Orbs," Taylor returned to shorter dance pieces of an extremely varied nature. He created "Agathe's Tale" (1967) which was a medieval story of a maiden, her protector, and a seducer. "Lento" (1967) was an abstract work that seemed much concerned with the career of dancing and with both the dedication it requires and the pleasures it offers.

Then, separated by a season, he introduced "Public Domain" (1968), a knockabout movement farce that had the weird charm of a dadaist collage, and, in 1969, "Private Domain," a dance of subtly erotic power and one of his densest and most enjoyable pieces to date. Once again Alex Katz designed the decor, large panels that rule off the stage into windows, and costumes that are bathing suits. The panels obscure the dancers' movements from time to time, and one has the feeling of being on the outside of an aquarium looking in at the swimming denizens as they move to the glass and then away again. There are three major openings in the panels through which to observe the action, which prevents any one spot from receiving all of the spectator's attention. Thus, Taylor has opened up the performing area in a way that he had not done in previous works, allowing himself to dispense with the hierarchy of center-stage placing for the most important personage. Dancers seem heedless of whether they are performing upstage or downstage, thus spreading the focus of the dance across the entire depth of the stage with a uniform intensity.

At every stage in the career of this exuberant and talented choreographer, Taylor has proven receptive to technical and formal developments in the utilization of dance space, while always measuring them against his own special sensitivity for the nuances of character and personality. This ability has enabled him to incorporate an extraordinary range of elements in his work and still retain its organic unity. He disavows having any revolutionary theories about dance but has during the course of his career managed to outrage both the most conservative and the most radical members of the dance audience—which indicates an authentic creative voice making its own synthesis out of the current transitional flux of modern dance.

James Waring

Capturing the Past

Choreographer James Waring stands at the crossroads of so many currents in the dance world that it is difficult to think of him in any but paradoxical terms. He is at once very contemporary in his experimentations with dance forms and at the same time exceptionally traditional in his theatricality. He is as likely to do an abstract dance incorporating liberal amounts of balletic movement as he is to do a period recreation of a Victor Herbert operetta. He is a brilliant costume designer (which means that his dancers are always impeccably dressed), a dedicated teacher, and a polemicist of charm and irreverence. He has a form of personal modesty that is rare in the ordinary course of life and almost unheard of in the world of theater. He is selfless in advancing the careers of contemporaries and wittily acidulous in deflating pomposity.

On occasion he has been one of the harshest critics of his own work, judging certain of his dances to be harmless entertainments, and he has never attempted to thrust his own work forward at the expense of others. He is also prolific. He has been an active choreographer since 1946, creating over eighty "choreographies" (to use his own term) for student dancers as well as for such international stars as Toni Lander and Bruce Marks. Perhaps most characteristic of all is the fact that Waring is undoubtedly the master of the new nostalgia—that contemporary malaise which is attracted to the idea of shoring up the fragments of the present with the idealized remains of yesteryear, not through the wisps of memory from younger days but through conscious exploration and deliberate dipping into the past.

Waring was born in California and started his dance training in 1939. During his first years of training, he was exposed to a variety of dance styles, including plastique or interpretive dancing with Raoul Pausé, Graham technique with Gertrude Shurr, as well as classical dance at the San Francisco Ballet School. It was dance schooling of a form that appears to be the direct descendant of the Denishawn method. (Interestingly enough, it was also the method used in another California city, Los Angeles, where the teacher Lester Horton encouraged a variety of pupils, among whom are Alvin Ailey, Carmen de Lavallade, and Joyce Trisler.)

After Army service in World War Two, Waring began his active choreographic career with "Luther Burbank in Santa Rosa" (1946), a dance for five which was performed at the Halprin-Lathrop Studio Theater in San Francisco. It of course had nothing to do with the noted naturalist but displayed Waring's special dadaesque gift for titling. It also included a duet for himself and the then-pregnant Ann Halprin. Another work he did at this time was a suite of dances based on Cocteau's "The Infernal Machine." Shortly afterward he was to choose two more dramatic frameworks for dance treatment, using a Japanese Noh play and Poe's "Fall of the House of Usher." Among the influences on his early work, Waring lists primitive art; Balanchine ballets such as "Apollo," "Le Baiser de La Fée," and "Danses Concertantes"; and the performing of Alexandra Danilova. From each source, Waring chose that which was congenial to his own working methodology. As the possessor of a variety of performing disciplines, Waring felt free to mix balletic movement with modern dance or even to include non-dance gesture in the body of his pieces long before it became the practice with contemporary choreographers.

He possesses a particularly facile turn of mind which can entertain notions of elevated whimsy and of poetic sensitivity at the same time. It combines the refinement of the connoisseur and the leer of the social voyeur and gives a rapidly alternating focus to his work. His own performing style is also an amalgam of highly disparate elements, combining correctness, waywardness, intimacy with and distance from his audience. At times his partnering in a pas de deux is like that of a naughty "danseur noble" who, in movement shorthand, will sketch in what should be danced out in full or will present a relatively minor gesture with elaborate performing élan. He is attracted by formal order almost as much as he is intrigued by the grotesque distortion of such order. He has dedicated his dances to such contradictory personalities as the classical painter Nicholas Poussin and the Austrian decadent Gustav Klimt. In each case, the dedication was used to lend a certain emotional resonance to the piece in question.

His use of music is eclectic, alighting on and juxtaposing the singing of Fanny Brice with a score by John Cage. His phrasing has traditionally shown a musical sense that was somewhat out of the ordinary, appearing almost like embroidery around rather than on the music. Waring at different times has used music as a rhythmic base for a dance, as an aural element simultaneous to a performance, and as an activity performed by the dancers themselves. Recently, while preparing a series of duets and quintets in a strong balletic style, Waring used music by Schubert, Debussy, Liszt, and Chopin. On the other hand, in one of his recent works, "Purple Moment" (1969), he has alternated a Bach orchestral suite with popular songs of the 1920's. Just as he is fond of using collages of dance movement, so too is he intrigued with the possibilities of sound collages. He is also an enthusiastic devotée of electronic tape scores and has frequently used the sound assemblages of Richard Maxfield and John Herbert McDowell for his work.

Waring's choice of music and movement is strictly dependent upon his current interests. He does not take a doctrinaire position to use or not to use one or another type of music. He has taken all music, including music scored for dime-store instruments (as in "Poet's Vaudeville" [1963]), within his purview. Early in his career, he tended to work mainly with scores that had been specially composed for his dances, but he has since shown himself equally adept at selecting existing scores from the standard repertory.

One of the strongest elements in Waring's work is a painterly sensitivity to images. He worked as a collagist before he was a choreographer and tended to structure his early pieces by means of collagelike pictorial conceptions. Currently (1970) he is working on a dance which has several provisional titles but which has yet to be choreographed or finally named. Yet he has most of the dance mentally worked out in painterly terms, even to the coloring of certain sections. One of these he sees in a hot steamy pink, another he sees set in a darkened garden with a white Pierrot-type figure patiently waiting. The middle section has not presented itself in terms of pictures, but choreographer Waring knows that he needs some connective material to unite the other two sections.

At times, one has the feeling that his is a form of designer's choreography, especially in those pieces in which he sets out to create the ambiance of another period, an object of great fascination to Waring. The movement is tailored to fit his conception of what the piece might have looked like if it were to be done at the time in which it is set. The "reconstruction" is not always serious. Sometimes he has consciously set out to create a burlesque version of a performing style and included only enough characteristic movement to stand apart from and poke gentle fun at it. One such piece, "In Old Madrid" (1965), he refers to as his "fake" Spanish dance. (The only other two titles possible for such a work, he maintains with a smile, would be "In Old Barcelona" or "In Old Seville.") The work includes, in a solo for himself entitled "Tambourine Dance," an affectionate jibe at the use of the percussive instrument for ethnic flavor.

Waring is highly conscious of period style. One of the things that he admired about the dancing of Danilova was her ability to capture and vivify so many types of dancing styles. In preparing choreography or costumes for his own "period" works, he goes to extraordinary lengths to make as exact a replica as is possible of the period being represented. If he sets a dance in 1919, he will try to insure that the costume is not 1918 or 1920 but is precisely 1919 in its details. He has a large collection of pictures of clothing styles and spends time researching exact nuances in the costume collection of the Metropolitan Museum of Art or in the print room of the New York Public Library.

Waring has attempted to "revivify" the past in a variety of ways, from the simple creation of a solo such as "Salute" (1967), done to the music of Berlioz in a romantically "plastique" style, to the choreographing of an avant-garde operetta to the music of Victor Herbert in "At the Cafe Fleur-ette" (1968). He attempts with each of these reconstructions to place and define a specialized stylistic rendering of a single-time reality. It is as if one were to turn the pages of a photographic album and have the figures from the past suddenly become animate.

The tonality of these reconstructions has been the subject of some debate as to whether they are a cynical—that is "camp"—celebration of the charm-ingly grotesque, or whether they are, as they represent themselves to be, true homages to times and places of other persuasions. It would seem unlikely that they are anything less than sincere recreations of that which they attempt to portray. In watching these pieces, their picturesqueness at first produces a warmth in the viewer for what is obviously past. Then it becomes progressively obvious that opportunities for callous asides about other mores have been allowed to "slip by" and that the piece is hewing to the high and more difficult road of simulation rather than denigration.

Waring fingers these shards of patina-ed conventions with true affection, much in the manner of the connoisseur examining the household treasures of a vanished civilization. More than any other of the newer choreogra-phers, he has a passion for the past—a passion for order, taste, and delectation.

Despite his concern with precision in the matter of costuming, Waring has never interested himself in lighting design or in decor. The set of "Dances before the Wall" (1957), one of his few dances that had a formal decor and a good example of his collagist's approach, was designed by Julian Beck. It consisted of many wooden liquor boxes piled up on one another to form a wall. The boxes contained objects of various sorts—an old shoe, a mannequin head, a vase of flowers, etc. Some of the boxes had a colored gel covering their fronts and contained lights. The lights were independent of any element in the dance and were controlled from their own board. The wall of boxes also had a door and a window in it. The musical score was a mixture of periods and, in effect, formed a wall of sound all its own.

The dance itself was in twenty-two sections and was created for ten performers. The fact that the various elements of the production were handled in a non-linear way and that the development of the choreography did not proceed in terms of theme and variations made it a difficult work for many to grasp when it was first performed. In it, Waring also indulged in repetitive movement—such as the simple gesture of a man rubbing his hands along his thighs for a long period of time—the monotony of which

James Waring's *At the Cafe Fleurette*, Judson Memorial Church, 1968: Teri Loren and Ann Danoff (dancers), David Vaughan and Nancy Zala (singers), Al Carmines at the piano. Photo by Teresa King (Courtesy of James Waring Dance Foundation)

further distressed viewers. The dance as a whole was a tour de force in which he assembled fragments with a collagist's sensitivity. It was a combination of arid and dramatic fragments, a parade of elements that had only tangential relationships to each other, and were of kaleidoscopic variety. It also was Waring's first evening-long work of importance, and most likely the first evening-long modern dance work done in this country. He was to create other full-length entertainments but none with the special qualities of "Dances before the Wall."

Waring abandoned dramatic and narrative structuring of his works— excepting his reconstructions—in the middle 1950's, and at this point began basing his dance on strictly musical structures and non-logical associative relationships. The better known of the two methodologies, the second, constituted the dance theater of the absurd, created by the free-floating relationships of objects and people. The mode of these dances was the creation of spontaneous inanities through the juxtaposition of the highly serious and the amusingly inappropriate. Movement was regarded almost simultaneously within a dramatic context and outside of it. At times dancers would break out of their roles as "abstract movement machines" to assert themselves as persons. The audience thus in effect was invited behind the scenes to see the performer as well as the performance. This effect has been the most strikingly unusual aspect of Waring's work, since the audience and performer gap had always been regarded as a sacred gulf across which each retained its own hierarchy of separate but equal privileges.*

Concurrent with the examination of the possibilities of the breakdown of such barriers, Waring has created a substantial body of dances of an abstract nature. These works, though part of his regular output, have tended not to have the public appreciation accorded to his other pieces. For the most part, they have been created in a style of choreography which could be termed balletic-modern dance.

Although he created a proto-ballet, "Jeux d'Enfants," in 1955, Waring did not then have the services of skilled ballet dancers for whom he could choreograph—which he obtained with the creation of the Manhattan Festival Ballet in 1966—so he chose to emphasize the less technical side of his abstract works. One of the more unusual of his modern dance works created during his "pre-ballet" period was "Phrases" (1956). It is a piece for which Waring has a special affection, and he has presented it both in a three-duet and a two-duet version and maintained it in his repertory for ten years. It was also included in a special program arranged for Russia's Bolshoi Ballet in 1966 to introduce the members of that company to modern dance when they were touring the United States.

*Waring's handling of this whole techique was a full-blown exploration of lines of creative development that previously had interested two other choreographers, Charles Weidman and Katherine Litz.

"Phrases" begins with a couple crossing and recrossing the stage seven times with seven different patterns of movements. These crossings are done in silence. The "repetitive" stillness is quite different from the second movement, performed by a second couple to the accompaniment of some of Erik Satie's quasi-mystical piano music. The final section begins with the original couple in the center of the stage moving outward from the center while the other couple passes back and forth behind them.

In 1960, Waring created an hour-long dance, "Peripateia," which had a set and "concurrent events" created by George Brecht, the author of scores of "happenings." The dance progressed in front of disjointed activities presented in a series of tableaux seen behind a scrim. For example, a man with flags is seen standing in a snow storm; he then sweeps up the accumulated stage snow and later carries a pole adorned with lights, all while the dance moves heedlessly on.

Collaborative events were new to Waring's work but were obviously congenial to his sublime sense of the ridiculous, and he continued to participate in them. A few years later he collaborated again with Brecht in another concurrent activity-dance called "Double Concerto" (1964). Each of the partners in the proceedings had one-half of the performing area to do whatever he wanted. Waring chose to create an abstract movement for six performers to the music of Bach while Brecht concocted a bizarre domestic situation in which two people end up murdering each other.

The most ambitious of Waring's associative presentations was "At the Hallelujah Gardens" in 1963, choreographed for six dancers and performed in the ambiance of scenery, costumes, objects, and events prepared by Brecht, Red Grooms, Al Hansen, Robert Indiana, Larry Poons, Robert Watts, and Robert Whitman. It was scored with a tape assemblage of music that had an imposing classical sound which was only indifferently and lightly reflected in the movement designed for the piece. The presentation included such elements as a balloon tree, a live goose, performers addressing each other by name, buckets of potatoes, noisemakers, some beautiful solo dances, streamers, and paper hoops. It was the most elaborate of the object-and-movement collages that Waring attempted and represented the climax of a period in his work that was dominated by the seriously absurd.

A later collaboration of shorter length but striking unity was "Poet's Vaudeville" (1963), with a text prepared by Diane DiPrima, music (for soprano, cello, and dime-store percussion instruments) by John Herbert McDowell, and choreography by Waring. The members of the dance's vaudeville troupe begin banging a drum as though they were a traveling company of performers attracting attention in a town square. Two of the dancers display a banner that announces "Poet's Vaudeville." The musicians arrange themselves, as does a singer. The percussion instruments are of the cheap toy variety and are played by the composer sitting on stage. The first part of the work is a series of dances, climaxing in a four-section exploration of "Spring, Summer, Autumn, and Winter," in the final section of which the dancers are momentarily "frozen." The singer renders a repertory favorite in an elaborate aria style after which the dancers now become serious, dance a lovely variation, and then go off. The chords of the ridiculous, serious, and mistily poetic, have been strummed lightly and the performance is over.

Within the past three or four years, Waring has tended more and more to create movement enchainements that have been more balletic than modern. One of the most successful of these is "Amoretti," a pas de deux created in 1969 and premiered at the Jacob's Pillow Dance Festival by Toni Lander and Bruce Marks. The pas combines balletic rigor enlivened by some of the freedom associated with modern dance gesture. The couple meets in a friendly sense of combativeness and the two people evolve their warm relationship in a series of serio-comic encounters. Aside from the quality of the piece, it represents one of the few happy couplings in Waring's abstract dances.

There is a darker side to the usually witty Waring, and it can be seen in such group works as "Dromenon" (1961) and "Three Symphonies" (1965). The latter was dedicated as a memoriam to the dancer Fred Herko; and it developed interestingly from allegro to adagio. The first section was full of hesitations, the second, rapid engagements and turmoil, and the third showed a type of transcendent reflection. "Dromenon," too, was full of turmoil and inconclusive encounters, as was the later "Northern Lights" (1966) created for the Manhattan Festival Ballet. It was with the creation of this company, for which he became a regular guest choreographer, that Waring for the first time had a core of dedicated dancers who also possessed the requisite technique for his balletically inclined dances.

In all, Waring is one of the most versatile figures in the dance world. He has created a solo for modern dancer Paul Taylor (in "Three Pieces for Solo Clarinet," 1954) and also produced a pupil, Richard Colton, who danced in the Bolshoi Ballet production of "Ballet School." In addition to choreographing his own dances, he has contributed dance movement for off-off-Broadway productions and maintained regular dance classes. He has created opportunities for other dancers to perform through the formation of Dance Associates in the 1950's and by maintaining his own company—though he no longer does so. He existed as a focal point for dance experimentation before the existence of the Judson Dance Theater, and thus permitted dancers like Taylor, Yvonne Rainer, Fred Herko, Lucinda Childs, Aileen Passloff, Deborah Hay, and Arlene Rothlein to gain valuable performance experience when few other opportunities were available to them.

The "underground" impresario phase of Waring's career now appears to occupy less and less of his time in favor of his own independent choreographic interests, but it was a valuable contribution to the development of many dancers and choreographers. Waring has always delved deeply into whatever area of dancing interested him and currently is working as a guest choreographer for other companies, further expanding his work in the area where ballet and modern dance touch upon one another and where the past has meaning for the present.

Rudy Perez

Emotion Under Tight Control

A vibrant stillness that is unique in the work of the newer choreographers encloses the work of Rudy Perez. He is the most emotively charged dance maker of his generation, but his emotionalism is strictly controlled and measured out in carefully placed spurts of movement. Surprisingly enough, his passionate involvement with material is not joined by the concomitant desire for center stage that is usually the handmaiden of such theatrical intensity. Almost alone among the younger choreographers, he has distributed his own roles among the members of his small company with a lavishly generous hand. It is not that he is averse to performing, wishing, say, to save his energies for choreography, but rather that he has resolved to see his own work from the outside—the audience perspective— as well as from the inside as a performer.

Perez came to dance relatively late in life, starting at the age of twenty-one to take regular dance classes. Prior to this time, he had interested himself in social dancing and to this day makes a special point of keeping track of current sub-adult dance interests. He can remember dancing at home and in the homes of relatives and being encouraged to do so for their entertainment, but he had not considered dancing as a possible career. It was only a diversion for him, and in school he was more interested in art than he was in dance.

He began formal training at the encouragement of friends and relatives and began taking class at the New Dance Group and then the Martha Graham school. He remembers, with particular pleasure, classes given by Graham herself. She took possession of the room in a way that none of the other teachers did and brought her own special dramatic intensity to the class. He also studied at Merce Cunningham's school. After a time he began to feel that he was becoming a professional student, without any special prospects of becoming a member of any of the established companies.

He had some performing experience with small non-professional companies which prepared entertainments utilizing Spanish or Hebrew thematic material for community center presentations. There was a certain exuberance in such performing which he liked, but it was at the Judson Workshop, with which he became associated in 1962, that he found a dance structure in which he could flourish. Dancers were encouraged to work freely outside of the mainstream of traditional concerns without the stringencies of technical demands if they so chose. He learned at Judson that technique was only one element in a dance presentation and bore only as much importance as the individual wanted to give it. It was a special revelation for Perez.

He clamped a rigid control on his natural buoyancy, and rather than demonstrate his energy through a whirlwind of activity, began to channel the harnessed emotion into creating an intense physical weight or presence in his choreography. It was a question of a naturally warm, intense sensibility coming into contact with the rigorous mental discipline and dedication of the Judson group. In his first piece created there, his first work of choreography, "Take Your Alligator (Coat) with You" (1963) , a duet, he showed that he was not afraid to stand still. The reflex action of most starting choreographers is to create frenzied activity lest audience interest be lost. Perez demonstrated that he could hold an audience without having to raise his choreographic voice by forcing out string after string of movement.

"Take Your Alligator (Coat) with You" was a wry comment on fashion magazine advertisements. It partook of their surface glamour at the same time that it illuminated some of the more ridiculously stylized physical attitudes assumed by male and female clothes models. In the dance, Perez showed an interest in combining street clothes, the spoken word, and carefully selected gestures outside of the traditional dance vocabulary.

Almost all of the elements that are to be found in his current choreography were present in some form or another in this first piece: meticulous workmanship, unusual juxtapositions of visual and aural material, and a weighty intensity. "Take Your Alligator (Coat) with You" does not have a story. It is a series of tableaux strung together almost like photos on a commercial photographer's contact sheet. Movement is succeeded by deliberate pauses that heighten the contour of the picture/tableau it is dealing with.

Perez has maintained the piece in his active repertory and it has a surprisingly finished look for a first work. The dance is created with craftsman's care and has the smooth, precise, and almost machine-tooled look that is characteristic of Perez's work. He does not like to leave his material until he has thoroughly explored its possibilities. He recoils from theatrical excess, is sparing with the use of gesture, and relies on performing presence to give movement its meaning.

Many of Perez's works at Judson were solos, among them "Countdown," "Monkey See, Monkey Wha?" "Bang, Bang," and "Fieldgoal" (all 1966). In addition to his own choreographic work, he also helped as stage manager and lighting designer and as general consultant to others. At each particular job, he observed carefully and selected elements for inclusion in his own performances. He freely acknowledges the influences of his fellow choreographers and speaks with great admiration about their performing and conceptual strengths. For Perez, Judson was an education.

After his initial work at Judson, he was incapacitated for almost two years with hepatitis. Later, in 1966, after intensive study with Mary Anthony, he went on to give studio performances of other new pieces. "Countdown" and "Fieldgoal" were first seen at Mary Anthony's Studio at this time. In "Countdown," Perez stood directly beneath a beam of light dressed in casual clothes. He moved slowly during the entire solo, completely self-absorbed. The music accompaniment was two French folk songs from Auvergne, one sprightly and the other more lyrical in tonality. Perez's movement reflected their tempos in a minimal way. He did not so much work against them as resist the seduction of their pacing in favor of his own more tightly controlled movement. He sat on a stool and puffed a cigarette, stared at and through his audience. He put the cigarette down, stood and blew a kiss to the left side of the space, and gazed in that direction. His fingers brushed his cheek lightly and left streaks of green paint like stylized tears on his face. He picked up his cigarette and puffed on it as the lights dimmed. It was a ritual farewell presented with monumental calm. The piece is a very personal one for Perez, who uses it as a touchstone against which to measure his own choreographic progress. He makes a point of performing it at least once in every season.

"Fieldgoal," also done in 1966, showed him progressing from total non-movement into a rock-and-roll spasm. For this work, he selected two pieces of music at polar extremes of expressiveness. The first was portions of Gounod's "Sanctus" and the second a popular tune by Martha and the Vandellas. Each represented a tidal pull in opposite directions, one to meditative stillness and the other to pounding activity. The dance developed with washes of first one sound and then the other as the performer found himself increasingly caught up in the surge of the popular sound. The costuming reflected the varied nature of the score in that it looked like an old-fashioned patchwork quilt. Both "Countdown" and "Fieldgoal" have been performed by members of Perez's company but achieve their special impact from his own renderings of them.

His use of music, as in these two dances and in later works, is extremely eclectic. Music for Perez is evocative sound. It is not relied upon for its rhythmic ordering of time but as an element of emotional decor. On occasion he has chosen random noises such as a dog barking or the sound that roller skates make on a wooden floor to convey some nuance of feeling that he wishes to include in a dance but does not want to use movement to describe. As in his use of movement, his employment of music is strictly dependent upon the circumstances of the dance on which he is working. He may choose to include music or not. He may use a collage of sounds or

Rudy Perez in *Countdown*, 1966. Photo by Steve Sbarge (Courtesy of Dance Theater Workshop)

he may work in silence. He once selected a description of cooking aspara-
gus by television cook Julia Child to accompany a dance. Its juxtaposition
with the athletic movement was humorous. A dancer once remarked that
she learned how to prepare the vegetable from listening carefully at one
performance.

Perez does not have a musical profile in the sense that other choreographers do. His use of sound is without predictability and he is not committed
to any particular period when he does elect to use music. In a dance, his
sense of time develops out of his own ordering of the parts of the dance
rather than from an element like music. Things take as long to develop as
they need, and no outside organizing agency is required to assist them.

One of the most dramatic elements of Perez's work is his sense of time. It
tends to be far slower than the ordinary. His works have a deliberateness to
them which asserts itself in the quietest manner. Where others would
jump, Perez will walk; where others walk, he will shuffle; and where others
would shuffle, he will stand still. During the course of an experimental
afternoon performance in the Barnard College gymnasium entitled "A
Space Ruckus," this particular quality of Perez's work was strongly framed
by the dances of fellow choreographers.

The event was planned with certain chance elements in it to provide
choreographic freshness. Five teams of dancers were created, each with a
distinguishing color jersey. Five choreographers were then each assigned
to work with one of the groups, and the gymnasium was divided into five
performing areas. At certain intervals a signal was given and the assignment of choreographers to teams and spaces was changed.

While the gymnasium began to fill with noise and motion, Perez created
a zone of stillness. His first act was to lay down on his back with the
instruction to his team members that they should remain as tranquil as
possible while performing some simple motions. As the frenzy grew and
Perez's assignments changed, he progressed up to an upright slow-motion
walk with another team. He included a two-count stride and forward fall for
another group which had to move in a straight line no matter what the
obstacles in front of it were. Perez himself easily handled the volleyballs
littering the area by passing them dreamily off behind him. The strict
control of time and motion that are hallmarks of his work were in clear
evidence in the afternoon presentation.

Perez is not so much a choreographer of motion as he is its disciplined
overseer. Movement is released from his dancers; it is not thrown off or
flung around carelessly. Sometimes it almost looks as if the dancers are
going to snatch it back after letting it go. Perez is ruminative and exhaustive
in his development of thematic material, all of which has to do with the
personalities and performing skills of himself and his dancers.

An example of concern with the particular personalities of the people
with whom he works is the fact that he took an early dance "Monkey See,

Monkey Wha?" (1966) and rechoreographed it entirely for Barbara Roan of his company, renaming it "Re-Run Plus" (1968). The piece originally showed Perez in a moment of uncharacteristic skittering and jumping. He was filmed running and leaping across a beach in trunks and a panama hat, and the film was screened as part of the dance. It was speeded up to make a complete contrast with his own in-person deliberate ritual of simian movement that included the familiar hear-see-and-speak-no-evil gestures. When he reworked the piece for Roan, he eliminated the film and created a dance replete with jumping, running, and swimming gestures vaguely derived from the film. The piece was tried out with a variety of lighting effects to set it more precisely in its new context. The athletic sequence was done twice. The first time with a white spotlight and the second time with a green light. The reworking is also evidence of Perez's interest in using material a number of times and in a variety of ways. He likes to create dances that repeat themselves internally almost in mirror-image fashion, as in "Re-Run Plus" and "Topload–Offprint."

Perez does not develop themes in the sequential way that has beginning, middle, and conclusion. He prefers to choreograph in an associational way, so that repeated images, in effect, swim to the top of the dance at different intervals and at different places in the flow of movement. It is a method of organization that skips much of the connecting material and simply presents the significant parts.

Perez is strongly affected by the space in which he works, and he moves with apparent ease between the proscenium stage and the open spaces of other areas. Perez tends to organize his space with simple diagonals, straight lines, and judiciously inserted circling movements. At times it is almost as if one were watching a traffic interchange where cars on seeming collision courses pass harmlessly on their individual tracks.

During 1969 and 1970, he presented two concerts of his work which were divided into proscenium pieces and open-area pieces. The latter was a collage of work that he had done during the year and was entitled "Annual." It had some striking moments and concluded with a spotlight following a roller skate slowly turning in small circles with all the dancers still.

Perez's use of props is deliberate and enigmatic. Dancers in his works are not called upon to "sell" their movement but merely to present it as carefully and as forcefully as possible. So too with their handling of stage properties: They are presented suddenly and with no preparatory build-up. A man abruptly stops, blows up a balloon, then releases it. Another man stops in a circling movement, produces a pair of plastic disposable gloves, puts them on, and then continues.

Each use of the prop is concentrated at a particular moment. It has the effect of an object in a dream. There is a connection with the underlying themes but the connection is tangential, and the prop yields up its import slowly and, in the dance, undramatically.

Perez's dance creations are a curious hybrid, almost as if they had been achieved by programming passion through a computer. The use of carefully modulated movement with concomitant still periods puts a great deal of performing weight on his dancers in a way that is not common with choreographers who have abandoned the story tradition of modern dance. Perez deals with a type of theater in which the drama of the situation does not arise from outside, as it would in the course of a confrontation between characters, but from an individual interior conflict which is allowed to infuse the performer's actions but not to flow over into "dramatic" situations. It is a pageant of personal symbolism under rigorous control, which projects itself with a minimum of animation. As Perez said pithily in an interview about the lean economy of his work, "Anyone can go around screaming."

Elizabeth Keen

Eclectic

Elizabeth Keen is a fascinatingly expert choreographic dabbler. She is constantly picking up, putting down, and fingering diverse moods and ideas. She once even made a dance about fidgeting. There seems to be no special form of dancing to which she is totally committed. She herself has trained in a variety of disciplines, including mime, and she also throws massive dollops of natural gesture and movement into some of her dances. What unifies the scattered look of her body of work is a passionate emotional intensity and genuine feeling for movement. There is a pulse and choreographic shape to her pieces that conveys a self-aware delight in the act of purposeful motion. Though she has dispensed with technique in some of her pieces, she does not turn her back on it. Technique and its disciplinary requirements infused with emotional fire have been the source of her finest pieces.

Keen was born in Huntington, Long Island, which to non-native New Yorkers may sound like another borough of the city but is in fact more country than town in its atmosphere. At the age of six, Keen received her first exposure to dancing at a summer camp she was attending. It was not a camp that specialized in dance but offered it along with other physical activities. By the time she was eleven, she was taking ballet class at Adelphi College (on Long Island) once a week, though she was not yet committed to dancing as a career. She appears to have inherited some of her enthusiasm for physical movement from her father, who was a passionate social dancer. He himself did not have any career aspirations, or even an inclination to see serious dancing in the theater, but he did draw great satisfaction from just moving rhythmically.

Keen had not determined to have a dance career even by the time she was sent off to Radcliffe. But during her sophomore year there, she decided that she was far more interested in dancing than she had thought, and she transferred to Barnard College in Manhattan so that she could continue serious dance training at one or another of the dancing schools in New York. She took ballet with Karel Shook and modern dance classes at the

Martha Graham school. When she graduated from college, she entered the Tamiris-Nagrin company and toured with them and also with Paul Taylor. Touring was a mixed experience. She disliked the physical grind, which she eventually found tiring, but she did enjoy the theatricality and the special status of the visiting performer. She decided to establish her own choreographic career. She stopped touring, settled herself in New York, and was faced with the problem of supporting herself. This was resolved through a variety of part-time teaching jobs—to her, not very pleasurable ones. Until recently she hated teaching and did it of sheer necessity. Currently she has been able to integrate teaching into her choreographic concerns and enjoys it much more. From time to time, she would appear with other dance companies in New York, but she basically was concerned with presenting her own choreography, on which she began to work seriously in 1962.

Keen's first pieces were all solos and mostly danced to jazz scores. The one exception was "The Perhapsy" (1962), given at the second Judson concert (at Woodstock, New York), which was set to a poem by e. e. cummings. In it, she tried not to use movement just illustratively, and at times allowed dance phrases to go "across" the words. "The Perhapsy" was not a totally successful dance, and Keen does not consider it one, but it has some interest in that it was her first attempt to integrate words with dance movement, a vein of exploration that she was to take up more successfully later. It should be said that many of the dances with which she is currently dissatisfied did have an educative value for her personally.

Like most choreographers who work at their own deliberate speed, Keen favored appearing in group concerts. In this way she could present only the one piece that was ready and did not have to prepare an entire program of dances, some of which she might not have finished to her own satisfaction. The group concert, however, is ordinarily limited to one or two performances, which is not enough for a choreographer to examine his work. One of the better aspects of touring, Keen found, was that it gave a choreographer the chance to find the life of a piece by being able to perform it numbers of times in front of different audiences. Keen, like most of the newer choreographers, was not attracted to presenting her work at the Kaufmann Concert Hall of the "Y." Rental was, in the first place, too expensive, but more importantly, it was not as sympathetic or flexible as were other performing spaces open to her.

After the emergence of the Judson Memorial Church as a receptive hall for dance, many of the difficulties in presenting the work of new, young choreographers disappeared. Keen was not one of the original members of the Dunn workshop that gave the first Judson concert, but she participated in various Judson programs during the two years after the initial concert, offering her own work or appearing in the work of others.

At the second Judson Dance Concert (at Woodstock) , which was organized by Elaine Summers, she offered, in addition to "The Perhapsy," "Dawning" and "Sea Tangle." Both of these latter pieces were danced to jazz scores, the use of which is very important to Keen, and represented a working-out of thematic material that Keen had first developed at the Tamiris-Nagrin studio. These pieces were created under the compositional rules which were favored in that company. Movement was supposed to be dramatically motivated and to be about something. In a superficial way, "Sea Tangle," which at Tamiris-Nagrin originally had the title of "Magnetic X," was about space travel, but Keen's primary interest in the piece was in the idea of being able to move as easily in one direction as in another. The shift from space travel to the "Sea Tangle" of the title came about because, other than space, the only other medium that offered an approximate simulation of weightlessness was water, the ocean. There one could move in any direction as easily as one could while "swimming" in space. Keen initially approached the dance by imagining herself into the part in much the way that an actor might prepare himself for a role, and tried to conceive of her body magnetized and pulled in different directions. As she developed the dance, the sea parallel exerted more influence on her imagination, with its images of strands of seaweed floating and entwining. It was an interpretive rendering of reality and at the same time offered the abstract-movement interest of parts of the body working independently of one another. "Dawning" took its name from the jazz score by Don Friedman and portrayed an agitated restlessness. Though as dances neither of the pieces now exerts so strong an attraction for Keen as to make her wish to maintain them in her present repertory, the use of jazz continues to interest her.

In her first pieces, she used jazz by working directly with the music and choreographing on it in much the way that generations of choreographers have worked with other kinds of music. After she had been exposed to different compositional techniques, however, she tended to use jazz privately in the studio as a pump primer for movement. She came in contact with other compositional techniques during 1964, when she enrolled in the last of the composition courses that Robert Dunn was to conduct. This was two years after the original series of courses had been completed, and there was a feeling that something was needed to get things moving again at Judson after its first flush of choreographic experimentation. Keen was given sustained exposure to the ideas of chance and indeterminacy through Dunn's various assignments, but did not find the same creative nourishment in random work as she had received from jazz. A year later at a course at Sarah Lawrence College, where she took some post-graduate credits, she again worked with chance. This time she selected the movements from charts and threw coins to determine their sequence of performance. With a shock she realized that the phrases she constructed were precisely the types of things that she might have worked out ordinarily by other methods. She decided then that, since she moved and worked so easily and naturally to jazz music, jazz would become her compositional mainstay.

The musical piece that she works with, however, hardly ever turns up as the accompaniment for the dance but instead serves to get her across difficult stretches of composition. When a dance is finished, she then places a sympathetic musical structure alongside it. One of the most successful pieces that she has done in this manner is "Poison Variations" (1970), a work for two couples.

"Poison Variations" began as an idle speculation after Keen had worked on a production of Hamlet—the play, not a dance version. The position of the play, of course, is that the queen does not know that her husband was murdered, and it intrigued Keen to construct a situation in which the opposite was true, that the queen was actually an accomplice to the plot. As an idea, it presented an immediate interest to her but did not offer her enough developmental possibilities, and it appears buried in the dance as only one episode of six "poison" variations. Three of the dancers turn on the fourth, pour something in his ear, and he tumbles off. For the rest of the dance, Keen enlarged the idea to include a more general speculation on the ways that people are unreliable to one another in less-charged situations than murder. The work is one of her finest pieces.

The four people in the dance enact various ambiguous situations that might or might not have serious import. In one section, they display a plastique body petulance holding the configurations that result from stamping a foot on the ground. Keen choreographed a warm, sexy solo for herself, during which the other three make hostile chops and thrusts at her without her being aware of what is going on. A man furtively strings an imaginary bow and another raises an arm as if to strike her, as she moves blithely on. The last variations of the dance contain some of her most felicitous movement inventions. A trio of two men and a woman perform a series of involved supports and lifts for one another that suggest beautiful shapes rather than individuals dancing. The dancers assist one another, and the center of their attention is on what they are doing, with scarcely a thought as to why they are doing it. In the final segment, the two men assume the positions they had in a variation at the start of the piece, which involved a series of falls and catches. This time, as one man launches into a forward fall, the "catcher" steps casually aside to do something else and the man slams down prone. It was a sharp and witty conclusion to "poison" variations.

Concurrent with her concert dance concerns, Keen has a strong interest in the theater and in musical comedy. Almost from the start of her career, she has felt the pull of stage presentations, which is the reason she seriously studied mime at one time. She appeared in a mime production off-Broadway in the early 1960's and more recently has choreographed a series

Elizabeth Keen in *Bird Poem*, Judson Memorial Church, June 24, 1963. Photo by Al Giese

of dramas and musicals for neighborhood groups in Brooklyn. Despite the fact that the performers are not of professional caliber, Keen has drawn a great deal of pleasure from working with them. These productions represent the largest casts for which she has choreographed. Ordinarily Keen has not choreographed for more than six people, but in a recreation of *West Side Story* she worked with forty-two performers.

One of the most interesting aspects of this work has been the opportunity for Keen to use theater in the round. During her concert work, Keen has ordinarily kept a frontal orientation in the pieces, even at Judson Church, which does not have a proscenium arch. The productions for the neighborhood groups are ordinarily given in the street, with the performing areas delimited with a chalk line. The performers are drawn from the neighborhood and the viewing distance can be from as far away as a nearby rooftop or as close as one inch across the chalk line.

Her current teaching career in the drama division of the Juilliard School of Music further reflects her interest in theater. As one who is not interested in abstract theory but in the instant communication of the dramatic idea, Keen fits comfortably into the situational world of the theater.

What most distinguishes her approach to dance from the traditional one is its non-linear fragmentation of ideas into little emotional epiphanies. The variety of means she employs to achieve her effects is staggering. One of the greatest defects of the academic world of historic modern dance was its rigidity in demanding dramatic characterization. One simply had to conform to naturalistic narrative in order to be seriously considered. Freed from stories, Keen happily employs an anthology of choreographic attacks, some of which work and some of which do not. Her basic interest is in movement and the throb of human gesture. She will approach dance from any angle that she chooses with a non-doctrinaire insouciance. She has trained herself in ballet almost as much as she has in modern dance, and in addition to involving herself in the mime world of dumb show, has studied the forms of European court dancing. The movement styles of any or all of them are liable to show up in her work. She refuses to adhere to theory of any one sort, not even to the most advanced. The effect of all this, the rapid shifts of her intellectual and emotional focus, is to lead her constantly to inspect the ordinary with fresh eyes.

In "Recipe"(1967), she placed herself at a piano and in her movements "speculated" over the fleeting impressions that dart across the attention of one taking piano instruction. In the center of the dance—which developed away from the piano bench—she had a recipe read out ("take one dream, stir in—"), a deft if unorthodox use of words to make precise the speculative nature of the dance. On occasion, she also has used film to express the moods of a dance and appended it to the movement almost as one might attach a sound score. In "Rushes" (1967), a quartet for girls in white leotards, the dancers had a film of themselves in black leotards doing related movements. It was one of Keen's most successful design pieces. From time to time, she has also created formal movement patterns to classical scores as in "Suite in C Minor" (Bach, 1965) or "Formalities" (Stravinsky, 1963).

Jazz has continued to interest her, and one of her finest solos, "Scanning" (1967), was the most recent piece in which she used a jazz score as a direct accompaniment to movement. "Scanning" is a dance about the shape of movement and a study of movement from various sides. In the piece, Keen moved with beautiful vigor, taking off again and again in leaps only to topple and rise once more. It was a virtuoso display piece and one that showed her clear involvement with the physical joy of being a trained dancer. The work rendered a sense of straining and reaching and never quite attaining that which was being striven for.

Other dances created in the same year showed a similar interest in the theme of frustration but none with the spectacular technical display of "Scanning." In "Short Circuit," Keen littered her stage area with a variety of properties, including ladders and volleyballs, and showed the movement difficulties of moving around these intrusive physical objects as the young boys and girls of the dance showed a similar difficulty in forming couples with one another. In a solo, "Stop Gap," done just prior to this piece, she had set herself up in a domestic situation in which she dithered and tarried with various props which continually prevented her from accomplishing anything concrete. She would move in one direction only to discover, say, a clothespin in the pocket of her housecoat and have to attach something to a line with it, or, as she was about to do something else, she was distracted by the sound of a tea kettle whistle, which took her attention to another task. It was a multi-media study of distraction, incorporating slides and carefully timed incidents to make clear the dissipation of energy. At the end of the dance, she had accomplished virtually nothing, but had expended a maximum of effort, and was exhausted.

One of Keen's most self-instructive pieces has been "Sub-Sun" (1968). From an audience standpoint it was nearly incomprehensible, combining as it did all sorts of film with varieties of movement, some of which were interesting but none of which dominated and gave coherence to the piece. For Keen, this variety was an attempt to get at the different energy levels of movement in various physical locales. Films were used in the dance, and among them were long passages showing pilings on the city dockside, or, contrastingly, tangles of branches from a country area, or the view of sunlight on water. The lighting design by Beverly Emmons imaginatively threw slots and speckles of light on the stage for the performers to dance upon, but the work refused to take wing. It could not really draw from the film representations of the physical spaces but only on its own theatrical actuality.

The question of movement outdoors and indoors, however, continues to plague Keen. The basic issue for her is: Do you move the same outdoors as you do indoors? Her experience with outdoor theater will certainly contribute some answers to the problem, and one of her projects—the use of a city rooftop—will no doubt offer others. The discovery of a large and available commercial building rooftop in Manhattan which has a view of water from three sides began the project. She found the building by accident and reacted to it by conceiving of a dance for it.

In a small way, this interchange of discovery and response is typical of Keen's methodology. She does not reason about the necessity of doing a particular dance but lets her pieces grow out of the flow of experience. She is a strong, forceful dancer with an equally strong intuition to put her skill to imaginative choreographic use. Her treatment of theory is cavalier, although she can give reasons for her actions after their occurrence. Her unpredictability is part of the charm of her career and of her body of work, which reveals her as an eclectic with solid instincts for movement.

Art Bauman

Sifting for the Right
Combination of Elements

Arthur Bauman is not so much a creator of choreography as a fastidious editor of movements, sound, and light. He works at his own deliberate pace, selecting and reevaluating all of the elements of a dance, and discarding any that he considers unsatisfactory until he has arrived at a version that pleases him. He develops his works out of an idea and then spends the choreographic time assembling and choosing those combinations of materials that best suit the conception of the dance. He once came across a remark that Robert Frost made about writing one of his poems that described the process accurately. The poem came to Frost in a rush one afternoon, and then after he had written it down he spent the next six months editing it. So, in effect, with Bauman.

Because of his extreme care with all of the materials that go into a piece, each of which receives the attention it would get from an individual specialist, his small-scale dances have the polish of a full-scale stage production. Bauman does not take chances with anything in his productions, although he does use chance as a compositional technique. He is his own strongest critic and most rigorous analyzer, to the point of taping personal monologues in which to look for thought and speech patterns.

He was born and raised in Washington, D.C., and attended George Washington University. There, he was involved in both the dance and drama groups and choreographed several pieces for each of them. During his college years, he also studied at the Washington School of Ballet (run by Frederic Franklin). When he was graduated from college in 1959, he came to New York and enrolled at the Juilliard School of Music, where he came to the attention of Louis Horst, who was giving his composition course. Bauman was one of his aptest pupils at the time, and Horst encouraged him to develop himself as a choreographer. Bauman stayed enrolled at Juilliard as a full-time student for a year and then continued as a composition student after dropping most of his other courses. He also studied at the Martha Graham school and the Metropolitan Opera School of Ballet. In addition to ballet and modern dance classes, he maintained an interest in dramatic and Broadway musical work and studied at the June Taylor and the Herbert Berghof schools. He also managed to find time for a course in film production at New York University, as well as appearing with the Weidman, Hoving, and Sanasardo companies.

But Bauman's special combination of painstaking choreographic skill and modest performing ability placed him in a position where he could not easily assemble entire evenings of his own work in rapid enough fashion, nor could he aspire to a performing career to support himself. He elected to follow a middle course of part-time choreography and part-time unconnected day work.

Bauman, like most new choreographers, was faced with the problem of where to perform. Hall rental was too expensive. The Kaufmann Concert Hall at the "Y," which had seen the growth of a modern dance generation in the 1930's, found itself continually bypassed by the generation of the 1960's, which favored churches and other free halls that had shown themselves to be accommodating to dance. In addition to being free, they possessed most importantly an enthusiastic and open attitude toward experimentation. One of the places which attempted to provide space for young choreographers was the Clark Center for the Performing Arts, housed in the Young Women's Christian Association on 50th Street and Eighth Avenue. Bauman went for an audition and was invited to include his work in a program with three other choreographers. The piece was "Journal" (1962), for five girls in practice clothes.

"Journal" began with the five girls kneeling and looking upward and then launching into movement in response to the "Go" signal of a flickering green light from the wings. The piece consisted of a series of classically clean patterns enlivened by humorous asides in the movement. Bauman used newspaper titles such as "Editorial," "Classified," and so forth to separate the episodic sections of the dance. Its production values were well thought out, and Bauman demonstrated a skilled theatrical sense of timing in the manner in which he brought his dancers on stage and took them off and created images of photographic intensity and explicitness with them. The difficulty with the piece was that it lacked strong developmental impetus. A clear image would be created with the beginning of each section and would then be removed to be followed by another strong "picture." It gave the piece wit, but at the price of a certain disconnected jerkiness.

In 1962, he and several other students at Juilliard had wanted to give a performance of their pieces. Riverside Church, which had a suitable auditorium, offered them the space and asked that the dances be directed to Biblical themes. It was not an especially congenial type of subject matter, but the hall would be given to them freely if they could put together a suitable program. They decided to agree to the stipulation, and Bauman prepared a solo for himself on the figure of "Job." The evening was encouraging enough for the group to establish itself as a performing unit. Calling itself "Contrasts," the group played a half dozen dates in colleges and community centers in the northeastern United States in the following months. Bauman was the chief choreographer, as well as the co-director.

The group needed to have a large-scale closing dance for the end of the program, and it was decided that Robert Starer's "Ariel," a large choral work, was a suitable score for such a dance. Bauman listened to the music and elected to use the third movement. One of the pleasantest aspects of the Morningside Heights institution-heavy atmosphere is revealed in the relative ease with which Bauman was able, first, to contact Starer at Juilliard, which was then just across the street from Riverside Church, and, later, to do some research at the Union Theological Seminary, which was equidistant from them both. Among the other pieces that Bauman prepared for "Contrasts" in 1963 were "Desert Prayer," a female solo, and "Now is the Time of Singing," a duet for himself and a girl.

The "Contrasts" group had a moderate success, but not enough to sustain year-round activity. For Bauman the experience was an opportunity to work and to perform in professional surroundings and conditions. He had to prepare a certain number of pieces on thematic material, which was not particularly interesting to him, and he had to put together a finale piece, which no one else was inclined to do. It was the start of a professional attitude toward work.

None of the pieces that he choreographed were of any particular distinction, with the exception of an abstract work for three girls and himself called "Nocturne" (1963). It was commissioned by George Washington University and was set to a suite by Gunther Schuller. Bauman assembled the music by editing it on tape in the way he thought it ought to sound. (He became so adept at sound editing that he was able to remove a single note if he had to and place it in another place in the score.) He also interpolated some live guitar music into the piece at spots that he thought appropriate. The dance itself was an abstract work, and the costuming had a suggestion of Near-Eastern exoticism, with the girls clothed in wispy harem pants. It was not a piece he was interested in keeping in his active repertory, but it was one in which he gave an indication of his future working method. Bauman is interested in juxtaposition rather than straight developmental unwinding of material. He produces the particular tensions and choreographic surprises in his work from the interesting ways in which he places bits of movement alongside one another so that they benefit from an associational relationship rather than a sequential one. Bauman choreographs individual units of his dances, each of which is complete in and of itself. He does not develop his choreographic idea in a flowing manner, having each part build upon the one preceding the way that a play might flow. The process is more like the filming of a motion picture in which scenes are shot out of sequence to make the most economical use of time or energy and then are edited into a meaningful whole.

At the same time that Bauman continued working on his own choreography, he had also held a number of jobs in the theater as a production assistant or stage manager. He took the Juilliard Dance Ensemble on tour and worked with the Fifth Avenue Opera on a series of operas as production assistant. He was production stage manager at the Louisiana Pavilion (which presented *The Magic Flute*) at the New York World's Fair in 1964–1965 and assistant in four productions of the New York City Opera. During the summer months, he did choreographic work for summerstock productions of musicals and operettas. He operated in this way for two years. It was an indecisive time, during which his energies were divided by a variety of concerns, none of which had to do with concert dance choreography. Dance Theater Workshop, which was established for presenting experimental choreography, was to provide him with a means for returning to the dance world as a choreographer, and later he was to become one of its directors.

Dance Theater Workshop, founded in 1965, was and is a producing unit that invites the work of new choreographers. It provides them with rehearsal and performing space, along with some necessary publicity information so that their work may be seen and reviewed. It is run as a non-profit foundation and its programs are ordinarily held in a loft-studio, although performances have been given on larger stages such as that of the Manhattan School of Music. The loft space is small and intimate, and in this small space Bauman was to sharpen many of those elements that existed in his choreography into a series of successively more accomplished pieces. The immediate proximity of the audience and the restricted performing area were turned to advantage by Bauman, who realized the photographic possibility of the area. He began to tailor his works exactly to suit the loft space. In progressive seasons, he premiered "Errands," "Headquarters" (both 1966), "Burlesque/Black and White," and "Dialog" (both 1967). Each of the pieces, all "photographic" in aim, progressed logically out of the preceding one.

The first, "Errands," is a trio for three men who are costumed like long-distance runners. The backs of their pullovers carry numbers. The three engage in a series of competitive and mime situations which have a keenly honed sense of unimportance. Nothing of what they do has any consequence, and yet they work very hard at doing it. They have a foot race in a circle, or a man adjusts his tie in an imaginary mirror only to discover that he has meticulously straightened his tie on a collar that is blatantly too large for him. The movements are purposeful and abrupt in the mime sequences and efficiently workmanlike in the runs. It was an imaginative use of the modular structure that he had begun to experiment with in "Nocturne," the abstract piece he had done for the "Contrasts" group.

The next piece in the series that Bauman created for Dance Theater Workshop was "Headquarters," in which he prepared an imaginative tape collage of sounds combining elements of machine-gun fire as well as lush, aggressively romantic film music. The sounds formed a series of aural images over which Bauman laid appropriate movement for a couple. They were dressed in pajamas, and the set consisted of a clothesline with clothes hung upon it—and, at the opening of the piece, the two dancers draped across it. They moved away from the line and back to it in a series of combative duets. The piece was a further exploration by Bauman of his modular use of dance and sound.

In "Burlesque/Black and White," he prepared a quartet for himself and for three girls who were presented with a mannequin exactness. It was a piece that drew little on movement invention to make its points, relying instead on the dancers' abilities to strike sharp-edged poses and create situational incidents. As the work begins, the three girls are under a plastic sheet beneath which they struggle a bit. They then emerge to look at one another. They are all wearing slips. A blackout ends the section. In the next section, the girls walk around to an aural background of street noises and look at one another, striking attitudes. A mirror crash is heard and they frantically begin, in gestures, to make themselves up. They then begin to take clothes from a large container on stage and each dresses herself in a different style. In the next section, a man (Bauman) is seated in a chair, his back to the audience, and he reads a newspaper while a girl dances to a Beatles' song and tries unsuccessfully to interest him. The man puts down his newspaper, takes out a cigarette, holds a drink in his hand; a girl swivels his chair around to the position she wants, revealing that the man is wearing a blindfold. The three girls join again at the end, wearing black, and the sounds of commercials are heard.

In all, the piece is a capsule resumé of frustration carried out in a well-chosen series of pictures, almost as if they had been taken from the pages of a group of magazines. The piece was well received, and Bauman was subsequently invited to "The Place," the center for modern dance activity in London, where it was presented with considerable success. It was danced there by three girls of precisely the right stylistic types, who contrasted strikingly with one another.

The final work from this series of "photographic" pieces contained the least amount of active dance movement and was prepared almost in the way that one would edit a film. When he was working on "Dialog," Bauman made a series of cards that contained the most interesting of the situations that he had developed from among a number of solo rehearsals. He spread all of the cards out and began to shuffle them until an interesting

Art Bauman (seated) in *Burlesque/Black and White,* Dance Theater Workshop, 1967. Photo by Edward Effron (Courtesy of Dance Theater Workshop)

pattern began to develop. Since he wanted to include a series of films in the piece, he began to edit the cards almost as one might edit a film, only he did it before the film was made. When he came to the actual shooting of the film, he found that most of the work had already been done in the "editing" of the cards.

The piece begins with the sound of a businessman's voice on the telephone asking for some report figures. Bauman is dressed in an everyday suit and carries an attaché case. The films, projected behind him, show the escalators and long, deserted marble corridors of an office building. On stage, he begins to run in place in front of the frightening empty interiors. The film of him shows him wearing the same clothes in which he appears in the actual performance. The voice makes demands of him (the stage Bauman), and the large word "stop" flashes on the screen, but he finds that he cannot and continues his activities, which include running in circles and measuring things. The voice finally demands "Resubmit it," and a large picture of Bauman, now reduced to a flat photographic image, topples over and falls forward, bringing the piece to an end. "Dialog" was the most successfully achieved of Bauman's stop-and-start choreographic pieces and shows the progressive refining of his image-making dance style into a lean and highly technological presentation. It was to represent the end of this vein of choreography for him.

The next piece he made (also for Dance Theater Workshop) was "Relay" (1968), with which he remains dissatisfied. The work took place in two studios. In the first, he danced inside an enclosure with the audience around him; in the second, he placed the audience in the enclosure and danced around them. The piece was conceived in relation to two differing performance areas and audience positionings, and designed in opposition to the strictly frontal orientation of his former work. It was an attempt to reshape and freshen previously developed materials but it remained becalmed, though Bauman had obviously begun to alter his "photographic" approach.

Bauman found himself in this situation—delving into his past works to develop a new choreographic approach—for the next year and a half. The impasse resolved itself through applying the compositional methodology of improvisation that he had used privately in developing "Dialog." He had always been personally fond of improvisation but had not used it as a method of working directly with dancers. Until he prepared "Chances" in 1968, it had always been for him a private source of movement invention, but now he began to rehearse in a series of improvisational sessions with a large group of people. Slowly one or another dropped out until a core group that was sympathetic to this method of composition remained. Bauman then created a piece out of their work together and called it "Approximately 20 Minutes" (1970). Like "Relay," it was not frontally oriented, and he designed it to be presented with the audience surrounding the dance area.

He developed a series of cues for the dancers to take from one another, and they reacted to the music and in turn affected the musicians. Bauman also asked his lighting designer, Gary Harris, to develop a variable light design. The design was interestingly conceived, and the stage was alternately flushed with full light or darkened so that the dancers appeared in silhouette. Bauman, who had been studying "effort-shape" conceptions of dance movement, attempted to find and react to the sources of movement in and of themselves and not for any narrative or dramatic sense.

As in all of his previous work, he was concerned in this "improvisation" with organizing systems for movement, but now he had moved on to the game situation. The rules were laid out ahead of time, and he then allowed the dance to develop within their framework. Put another way, having taken the proscenium orientation of dance as far as he could with all the technical means at his disposal, he returned to examine the motive energy of sheer movement. The effort served to reintroduce a kinetic impetus that had been missing from his work of the previous year and a half, and kept the intellectual precision which had been one of his primary concerns. In the piece, he combined natural gestures with the more stylized passages of dancing.

"Approximately 20 Minutes" represents a new departure for his dynamic energy level, which is now considerably heightened but, at the same time, a logical extension of his choreographic premises. It is undoubtedly the start of a new series of projects in which he will continually refine his starting position. If Bauman maintains his ordinary cycle of creative activity, two years on and two years off, he will have developed his new "Project" or "Event" series significantly by 1972.

Artists

Activity As Art

Of all the choreographers associated with the explosion that toppled the conventions of historic modern dance, no group was more uninhibited in presenting new material in unusual ways than were painters and sculptors. Their inclusion in the dance world was only possible because of a confluence of exploratory movements among both dancers and artists, each of whom were testing the limits of their own medium. Art confined to an easel is comparable to dance confined to a proscenium stage and to a defined technique of telling stories. At the end of the forties and the beginning of the fifties, the only choreographer whose work had any interest for many artists was Merce Cunningham. Cunningham had cut loose from stories in favor of movement materials in the way that a contemporary generation of abstract expressionist artists jettisoned representational pictures in favor of painting. Cunningham admired the work of advanced artists and often asked them to create decors for his dances. The freedom he gave them was almost unlimited. Cunningham did not force ideas on his collaborators; he encouraged them to be independent. Having himself reordered movement into an all-over field where no predetermined locale established degrees of importance, he was not hesitant about using mixed lighting and decor to enhance his effects. Cunningham had all of the requisites of a good collaborator but the collaborators could only go so far: It would have been patently impossible for any non-technically trained person to attempt to dance with Cunningham's company. Cunningham's movement at its core was disciplined and required a high order of skill. Painters could be uninhibited painters and designers with Cunningham but could not become "dancers" until the post-Cunningham generation questioned the necessity of technique.

One of the first artists associated with active performing was Robert Rauschenberg. During the summer of 1952, while Rauschenberg was at Black Mountain College, Cunningham and John Cage played a concert there. The following year, Rauschenberg collaborated with them on what has come to be considered the first "happening." When Rauschenberg

Left to right: Deborah Hay, Robert Rauschenberg, Lucinda Childs, Robert Morris, Alex Hay, Jill Johnston, and Yvonne Rainer in Rauschenberg's studio, March 12, 1963. Photo by Al Giese

settled in New York in 1954, he associated himself with the Cunningham company as a costume, set, and lighting designer. In his painting at this time he was interested in all white and all black canvases that also in one or another way received the shadows of those persons and things that approached them. It was an attempt to produce some interaction between viewer and object, an effort to introduce the changes of time activity into "timeless" art. He was attracted to the world of dance in the way that other painters were attracted to film. It was an art of both space and time.

Rauschenberg's efforts in the theater continued to be decorative for several years. Shortly after he began to work with the Cunningham company, he also began to work with Paul Taylor. Taylor had danced with Cunningham for one season and then began to follow his own choreographic career. Rauschenberg became Taylor's designer and worked with him on a number of productions, designing props and costumes. One of his most successful collaborations with Taylor was "Four Epitaphs" (1956) (later, in 1960, changed to "Three Epitaphs"), for which he created a set of costumes that made the dancers look like carbonized lumps. He also created the original light design for the piece. He worked with Taylor for about five years and continued with Cunningham until the middle of the 1960's. Toward the end of his collaboration with Cunningham, he devised an imaginative and variable design for "Story" (1963) which allowed him to get on stage performing various tasks. In London, for example, he painted a picture.

In 1961 and 1962, he created his first dance events, "Collaboration with David Tudor" and "The Construction of Boston." At that time he also visited the composition course being given by Robert Dunn but did not become a regular member of it. In mid-1963 he created one of his most successful pieces, "Pelican," for the "Popular Image" show sponsored by the Washington Gallery of Modern Art, in which a group of dancers from Judson participated. "Pelican" was a pas de trois for two men on roller skates and a trained dancer on point. In Washington, it was given in a skating rink (when it was repeated in New York, it was given in a television studio). Rauschenberg contrasted two means of movement in the work. He and the other man entered the performing area kneeling on wheeled axles and worked their way to the center of the area. There they were joined by a dancer who approached them on point, and they partnered her. She then picked her way off, and the men began to skate around smoothly. It was a striking contrast in different modes of moving: the smooth flow of the wheeled performers and the elegant, articulated flow of the dancer.

One of the most interesting aspects of Rauschenberg's dance pieces is their concern with the thrust of gesture and the ways in which he draws attention to the act of handicapped moving. There is a drive in his works that always keeps one aware of a forward surge, even when the choreographer putters around in an interesting byway of movement. Another characteristic of Rauschenberg's pieces is an extensive use of stage properties. Rauschenberg has an imaginative reach that gathers in all sorts of objects to draw some sort of associational sense from them. In this regard, he puts his dances together in a way that is similar to his object-and-painting combines.

While with the Cunningham company during its world tour in 1964, Rauschenberg presented "Elgin Tie" in the Moderna Museet in Stockholm. Although the piece included a cow, it was basically a solo in which he descended from a rope hung from the ceiling and lowered himself into a drum of water. On his way down the rope, he performed various activities, including squirting some water from a waterbag into the drum. He had intended to ride the cow out of the performing space at the end, but contented himself with leading it away. During the tour he also created "Shotput," in which he performed athletic activities on a darkened stage with lights attached to his leg.

In 1965, Steve Paxton, with the late Alan Solomon, organized the "1st New York Theater Rally," which was intended as a showcase for the various new means of movement and new presentational approaches to theater that had developed since 1960. It was to bring artists and dancers together in a series of twenty-two performances. For the occasion, Rauschenberg created "Spring Training," a conglomerate of motion and frustrations that might express the surgings and mild amorous disappointments of a typical spring. The piece combined contrasting locomotive styles such as the wanderings of ponderous turtles and, subsequently, the light and percussive movements of a tap dancer. Rauschenberg himself strode around on stilts during the turtle ramble. Tableaux were created as three girls did dance variations in wedding veils, and at another point Rauschenberg mopped up splattered eggs. Finally he appeared in a white formal jacket and mimed a strumming motion while a Hawaiian guitar plucked out "Taps."

Rauschenberg went on to create three further pieces during the remainder of 1965 and 1966, including his most lavishly scaled work "Open Score," but has not interested himself strongly in performance since that time. His dance concerns seem to have been subsumed in the body of his other artistic concerns, as in a sculptural panel of large boxes that remains a blank row of mirrors unless activated by audience noises, at which point they flicker intermittently to reveal photographed arrangements of chairs. Technology in the form of lights and servo-motors now supplies much of the kinetic energy that he previously worked with in terms of people.

Sculptor Robert Morris, like Rauschenberg, interested himself intensely in dance at one point in his career. He never had had any formal dance training nor did he aspire to a dance career. Movement, however, always played a part in his work, whether the movement was suggested by sounds of physical labor or directly portrayed by a person performing a motion task. He is interested in action, in the act of creating anything. He once made a box that had a tape recording of its own construction playing endlessly inside of it. His own performances are sculptural constructions that are precise and economical. Morris has a natural performing skill, and he presents clearly the weighty force of moving, through concision and economy.

Before coming to New York, he was involved in theater projects and film-making in San Francisco. During his marriage to dancer Simone Whitman, he was influenced by her task- and play-oriented approach to movement. Before he began to choreograph any of his own pieces, he collaborated on several. One was done with Robert Huot, a work performed at Judson Church called "War." It was a brief work in which two men (Morris and Huot) garbed in outrageous helmets and armored vests swung and slashed at each other with swords to the sound of a gong. In Washington, D.C., he collaborated with critic Jill Johnston on "New Poses Plastiques." In addition to these co-choreographed pieces, he performed in the dances of a number of choreographers from among those who belonged to the Judson group.

In early 1963, he felt he was ready to present his own first piece, "Arizona." It was divided up into various "demonstrations," one of which consisted only of lights swinging in diminishing circles. In another section, he kept altering his position almost imperceptibly as he transcribed an arc of attention of about 180 degrees. In another, he moved a bar balanced on top of a pole and looked at the bar from different sections of the room. As is characteristic of Morris' work, all of the actions were concise and purposeful. Morris deplores waste material or motion.

None of Morris' pieces contain what could be called a music score, yet he very carefully selects the sounds to accompany the motions he is performing. In "Arizona," he had a description of corralling cattle, and in "21.3," he accompanied himself with a taped reading from an art history book, while he stood at a lectern and silently made appropriate gestures.

One of his most successful pieces was "Site," which consisted of a large open area with a series of white painted panels. Morris himself was dressed in white, wearing workman's gloves, as he shifted the panels around. The sound of sawing and hammering was heard from a small white box standing on stage. The whole atmosphere was efficiently antiseptic, when suddenly one panel was removed and a nearly nude girl was seen against another white panel in the pose of Manet's "Olympia." Morris' sturdy workman, however, took no notice of the girl, dealing with her fleshly presence as if it were just another object in his task.

This was one of the earliest dance uses of near nudity in a public theater, and it in fact created a certain amount of anxiety among the sponsors of the program over possible police interference. None materialized. But Morris was not done with nudity. In 1965, he used total nudity for a man and a woman (himself and Yvonne Rainer), in one of his finest dances, "Water-

man Switch," which was also his most attention-getting work. The piece
was a series of male and female solos, clothed or partly unclothed, accompanied at times by slides of a man throwing rocks. The score was splashing
noises, a Verdi aria, and a lecture by Morris on the properties of an agitated
body of water. An androgynous figure, a girl dressed in man's clothing,
held various objects such as a string on which the boy and girl sent
messages to each other via tugs. At the conclusion of the piece, the couple,
who were now totally nude and clasped tightly together, shuffled off stage
on a set of gray, parallel railroad tracks. As they were going off, Morris
released a gush of mercury from a small pouch in his hand that flowed
down his partner's back.

Because of the nudity of "Waterman Switch," little attention was paid to
the sound construction of the work in its alteration of male and female roles
and the internal reversal of various sequences. A photograph of the nude
couple ran in *Life* magazine and criticism of the piece was offered in *Time*.
Morris, with tongue in cheek, wrote *Time* a corrective letter in which he
explained that he and Rainer had not been "wearing nothing" but were in
fact covered with a light coating of oil. The merits of the piece, however,
were scarcely discussed, given the furor over the nude passages.

And no attention at all was paid to "Check," another Morris piece on the
same program. It was first produced in Sweden in the Moderna Museet and
then shown in New York at Judson. Morris complained that the piece was
not seen to best advantage in the smaller church, but for many it was one of
his best works. Like most of his dance pieces, "Check" did not have a
feeling of flow. It was a work made up of situations that were almost
complete in and of themselves. The movement, as always, was purposeful
and direct despite the fact that the piece was the largest-scaled work that
Morris had attempted. Previous works had been designed for one to three
persons at most; "Check" required a cast of about forty, divided equally
into two teams. Each team wore an identifying ribbon, either red or blue,
and the performers mingled with the audience, which was seated in the
center of the church in a roughly rectangular shape. At selected times, the
performers reacted to the blast of a whistle and marched to opposite sides of
the performing area, where they then went through movement drills at the
direction of the team leader. When the drills were over, the performers
infiltrated back among the members of the audience until they were again
called out by a blast on the whistle.

There was a blatant contrast between the casual movements of the
performers moving among the audience and the braced purposefulness
induced by the commanding whistle. When the bulk of the performers
were in the audience, various other "checks" were applied to individual
performers who stepped out from the mass. A slatted light divided a girl up
into neat venetian-blind strips, while along another wall a running man was
immobilized in the flickering beam of a stroboscopic light. And, again and

again, the crowd in the center of the performance area was brought into struggling life as performers attempted to rally around opposite banners when the whistle was heard. At the end, the performers flowed into the audience again; the whistle did not sound and the piece was over.

Morris has not created any public performance pieces since 1965, although he has begun to examine the performance qualities of materials in his sculpting. He has always had a sensitivity for the natural tendency of material, whether it be human or inanimate. Currently he is working with substances that demonstrate the law of gravity—felt, cotton batting, or solid beams that tumble into interesting configurations. During his career, Morris has created self-monitoring devices, such as the box already mentioned containing the sounds of its creation and a light attached to a meter that registers the amount of electricity needed to make the light operate. One of his most daring performance efforts in such works as "Check" was to create self-aware people structures with all of the waywardness that one must allow for in performance. For Morris, the step up to a large group that began in "Check" was a daring jump from the controlled situation he earlier favored, the solo or the intimate trio. It is a pity that he has not so far explored further the natural movements of a larger group.

Carolee Schneemann, the "Olympia" in Morris' work "Site," is in her work as untidy as Morris is methodically neat. Schneemann is a collagist, and she has a striking figure which she allows to be seen as much as is admissible under the law. Her dances are, in effect, a series of mob pieces dedicated to the celebration of the fleshly and the sensual. Schneemann does not concern herself with the finer details of choreography so much as with the broad outlines of the effects she wants to achieve. Her most famous piece is "Meat Joy," a passionate and manipulative evocation of the similarities between limp flesh and flesh quickened by the vital fluids of life. It was performed first at an avant-garde festival in Paris (sponsored by Jean-Jacques Lebel) and necessitated that Schneemann leave the country one step ahead of the police. She settled for a short while in London, where she came upon a church that seemed willing to take a chance, and she proceeded to stage her epic of epicene delight there. Things were going well until the vicar's wife entered the dressing room, where most of the cast was changing (without the benefit of separated dressing rooms). They had to scrub dye off one another and found that a communal changing situation was the quickest way to do it. In the face of the total incomprehension of the vicar's wife, the performers locked her into an elevator and sent her screaming up to another floor. The performances were concluded before the arrival of the police, and Schneemann returned home to stage "Meat Joy" at Judson Church. It is a piece in which program credits are handed out to the local butcher as often as they are dispensed to the usual technical staff. Fish, fowl, and frankfurters are hurled about in the piece with careless abandon as are the bodies of the protagonists.

The work develops slowly through a series of casual encounters between males and females turned loose in a large central area littered with plucked chickens, frankfurters, and fish (unfilleted). The performers embrace, walk, roll, slither, tumble, and carry one another around. At times they pause and daub each other with paints that are placed nearby. People are piled upon one another and then strewn with the fish and fowl carcasses. By the end of the piece all have been pulled, tugged, and painted so that the entire group is reduced to the same limp state as the "meat." It was a sensually physical piece that cumulated slowly but with great effect.

Schneemann always starts her pieces from drawings and then proceeds to animate them. At one time she conceived of a dance that would feature performers inside burlap sacks slowly tolling cowbells, but never worked out the sequence of motion required to produce the look she was after. In most of her pieces, not a great deal of technical skill is required other than a certain loss of inhibition. Performers are expected to throw themselves into the pieces and not to hold back. The choreography provides a great deal of interpretive room for the energetic. But unless the cast of performers really has the proper brio, Schneemann's work has a pallid look.

For Schneemann, the important thing is to wallow in the material. She is not inclined to tell anyone the specifics of a role but only to turn performers loose in an environmental situation in which they can exercise their natural tendencies. During an early session of the Judson workshop that was held in the gymnasium of the church, Schneemann showed up and demanded that the entire space be utilized. Someone pointed out that there were heating elements and so forth involved in the intimate architecture of the room. Schneemann's doctrinaire reply was the elements should be incorporated or covered. There was no middle ground. If anything existed in the performance space, then it was to be used.

Schneemann seems almost indifferent as to where she works. The one constant running through all of her performances is that the space be utilized. She has performed in the regular proscenium stage, in the open-bay situation of Judson, and in the music room of St. Marks-in-the-Bowery. In each case, Schneemann has attempted to make the most use of the space which was available to her. It was at St. Marks that she presented her quiet, mysterious piece "Water Light Water Needle." As was customary with her, she covered the area with shreds, in this case newspapers, which she referred to as "nesting" materials. The audience was invited to settle down into a comfortable bed of crumpled newsprint in order to enjoy the performance. What Schneemann had done for the piece was to take the cupboards of the room in which it was being presented and turn them into ad hoc incubators. Periodically during the dance, people would burst out of a cupboard with the same urgency that chicks peck their ways out of the restraining shells that contain and protect them. Meanwhile, outside of the room, mysterious lights shone fitfully behind the windows.

Another of her works, done in a different space, was "Snows," performed at the Martinique Theater in New York on a thrust stage. As the audience entered, the performers were clustered like a group of homeless natives in the center of the performing area. The piece was a multi-media mixture of lighting effects, movement, and film. The films had to do with natural and man-made disasters—avalanches, earthquakes, crashes—and the performers had to work their way through the combination of both. It was a piece of vintage Schneemann full of the fallout of civilized activity and pregnant with portents of the future.

Although she does not possess any discernible formal technique, Schneemann is a performer of special talents. She is concerned with movement. It is difficult, critically speaking, to tell exactly why her pieces differ from "happenings," but they do in their flow of energy. The movement element in them is of such an order that one cannot ignore it in favor of other more dramatic bits of action. She herself refers to her pieces as kinetic theater. Her use of music is eclectic and seems more to rely on mood setting than on any rhythmic considerations. Sound for her is an element of theater which has to have some place in production, but it does not distinguish any of her pieces. Her lighting is casually arranged. She does not depend on lighting effects nor does she seem overly concerned with the effects of costuming. (In "Meat Joy," she specified that her performers wear bathing suits and all showed up in the briefest ones possible.) For most pieces, she simply asks that performers present themselves in street clothes.

Schneemann is a child of nature and her choreography is of a casual order; her special contribution is that of uninhibited gusto. She has drive and an organizing sense that allow her to frame situations in which persons are able to create a viable dance work without having any special dance skill except for a strong enthusiasm. With Schneemann, offense is all. There is no provision in her work for meditative reflection; she is continually on the attack. She wants to engulf her audience in a bath of sensual experience. Of all the artists who have involved themselves in dance productions, Schneemann is probably the one who has come closest to the ecstatic feeling of moving in space. She has approached dance from its bodily rather than its conceptual component.

As different from Carolee Schneemann as tap water is from the Ganges is painter Alex Hay. Hay was introduced to dancing through his wife, Deborah Hay, and later went on to create a modest but fascinating body of work on his own. Hay is tidy. Neatness is a habit with him, so that he does not have to think about leaving loose threads in his pieces. They simply do not exist. Everything is accounted for. During his military service, he was a control-tower operator in the Air Force, and many of his pieces show an inclination to control activity from the directing stance of a command voice. Hay has tended to work on an intimate scale and has not allowed his pieces to move beyond the range of six performers. He has never shown any particular concern for music or any other rhythmical structure and has relied on the precise *apercu* rather than an enveloping web of motion to carry his kinetic ideas.

In "Colorado Plateau," he moved a half dozen male and female bodies around a designated area through the directions of a tape-recorded voice. The variations of the piece were characteristically slight: He would place a vertical person on the horizontal or vice versa at the direction of the voice or move them to a different location. In "Prairie," he prepared a lovely solo that was performed around the various parts of a tubular pipe construction. Hay ascended the scaffolding with a number of pillows attached to his body. An unctuous voice continuously inquired if he were comfortable or not as he struggled around the construction. Eventually he was driven off by the solicitous concern. Like most of his successful pieces, it was a solo.

Probably the most accomplished dance that he put together, and the one with the most impact, was "Leadville." In it he was first seen perched on top of a pole, covered in silver body paint in a silver costume—in effect, a robot. The pole was also colored silver. Slowly he began to descend the pole and to approach the ground. A measured countdown of intoned numbers was heard as he approached the audience's level. When he had planted his feet on the ground, he began to walk slowly forward toward the audience. He groped and tested the ground tentatively as a voice on a tape intoned the deliberately spaced words: "I . . . wish . . . I . . . were . . . a . . . ." The space between the words was filled with the sound of rushing feet. Hay, as the silver man, advanced slowly toward the audience with little jumps, and suddenly the sound of a popular song was heard, "Red Roses for a Blue Lady," and the man in silver broke into a cumbersome social step. He extended his arms in the approved ballroom style but had no partner to share his dance with. It became apparent that the taped sound that was accompanying the dance was coming from a recorder strapped to Hay's back. About this point, it also became obvious that the tape was running out upon the floor and was not being taken up on a pickup reel. The silver-plated robot man bled sound before the audience's eyes. As he approached the front of the audience, he dropped to his knees and, with a fierce pride, aimed an imaginary traversing machine gun toward the spectators of his agony. He slipped closer and closer to the floor, and with the last bit of expelled tape was prone. None of Hay's other works have had the impact of "Leadville."

One of his largest-scaled works, not entirely successful, was designed for the "Nine Evenings: Theater and Engineering" and was called "Grass Field." In it he sat with a large amount of electronic equipment strapped to his body and stared into a television camera. Prior to sitting down, he had placed a hundred squares of cloth around the performing area, and as he sat two other persons picked them up and stacked them in two piles with long sticks. During the picking up, Hay sat immobile in front of the closed-circuit television camera, which recorded all of his facial motions and projected them onto a towering screen placed behind him. Despite the fact that Hay is a concentrated and intense performer, the broad scale of the piece worked against it. It was overly amplified and enlarged for the modest movements that had been devised to occupy the area. At their best, Hay's pieces are like enamels—compact, smooth, brilliant-hued, and precisely delineated.

Painter Robert Huot has some of the clean intellectuality of Alex Hay, but he possesses a belligerent forcefulness that removes his work from the fastidious. Hout has done relatively few pieces, and with one exception has not interested himself in actual performance outside of collaborative efforts, among them "War" with Robert Morris and "Tank Dive" with his wife, Twyla Tharp. The exception came with an "Angry Arts Festival," when he decided to do a work called "Wall," a composition that shows a clean, sensitive feeling for motion overcoming obstruction. Having placed a white wall on stage, he demonstrated its strength by having a performer fling a hard rubber ball against it. After it had rebounded a number of times, the solidity of the wall was established. Suddenly a burly figure (Huot) burst through the wall in a physical demonstration of the power of determination. The wall was soundly constructed but the "dancer," moving with the requisite force, was able to break through the barrier it constituted. Like Rauschenberg, Morris, and Hay, he has created decor and costume designs for a regular dance company but now seems to have discontinued his own interest in choreography.

During the decade of the 1960's, members of the art world interested themselves extensively in the performing arts. The "happening," for one, was a form of dramatic theater, and it was logical that the expanded borders of artists' interests should include dance. At the "1st New York Theater Rally," the high point of the collaboration between artists and dancers, a large variety of movement approaches were shown side by side, affording the audience an anthology of the newer theatrical approaches. A number of fine works were shown in the twenty-two performances. Among the artists, Jim Dine, Claes Oldenberg, and Robert Whitman offered "happenings." Oldenberg also offered a "dance" event which consisted of a telephone in a spotlight which rang several times. Rauschenberg, Hay, and Morris presented dances. Kinetic art was represented by Whitman's "Shower," a film of remarkable reality. In it, a girl took a shower and it was projected on a screen in a shower stall with a curtain of real water running down the clear glass door. Judith Dunn, Deborah Hay, Steve Paxton, David Gordon, Trisha Brown, Lucinda Childs, Yvonne Rainer, and Carolyn Brown offered dances. The difference between the dances and the "happenings" was that the dancers all had movement as their propellent force, while the "happenings," though they contained movement, did not depend on it for impetus as much as they depended on the spurts of surprise from the events they contained. Whether the collaboration between the world of dance and art represented by the "1st New York Theater Rally" will continue is an open question. The rally was held in 1965; it remains to be seen whether there will be a second one.

Some Others

A Round-Up

John Herbert McDowell, essentially a composer, was associated with the Judson Dance Theater from its inception. He has written over a hundred scores for dance, ranging from short two- or three-minute collages of sound to full-length scores for Paul Taylor. McDowell has composed for film, for regular concert performance, and for casual "musicians" playing dime-store toy instruments. Before the development of Judson, McDowell worked extensively off-Broadway with drama groups. He also attended Robert Dunn's composition course and contributed a special wit and enthusiastic élan to the group. In the special performing flux that was the Judson Dance Theater, he found that he was drawn into creating dances as well as providing accompaniment for them. A trained dancer once told him that he had managed to do a series of impossible things in one of his pieces—which McDowell explained to himself as the accomplishment of someone who did not know any better.

McDowell did not have any strong technical skill but he did study movement in a class (conducted by Alec Rubin) that was primarily designed for actors. For the class, he prepared a series of short studies of some interest. In one, "Auguries," he explored the use of hands. At a certain point he concentrated on looking into his hand as he spun rapidly around until he collapsed. With wobbly legs, he teetered on to the next section of the dance, in which he had to climb a platform.

There is a wild streak of exhibitionism in McDowell, and in "Eight Pas de Deux, Pas de Trois and Finale" he gave it full rein. The first section of the dance began with an empty stage appointed with a moth-eaten pillar and wilted flowers as a taped selection of Strauss waltzes surged and flowed into one another. Suddenly McDowell was hurled out from the wings onto the stage in a flying split and totally demolished the set. The next section began with a stage full of litter; McDowell performed duets with eight different girls in a row, while a ninth tried to pick up bits and pieces of the demolished set, unobtrusively. Later he was carried across the stage on the heads of eight other girls while rose petals were strewn on him. The music

John Herbert McDowell (center) in *Eight Pas de Deux, Pas de Trois, and Finale,* Judson Memorial Church, June 23, 1963. Photo by Al Giese

built to a towering climax. Suddenly the curtains closed and opened, the dance ran out of energy, and the tape slithered to a halt. When the curtain opened for the curtain calls, the stage was covered with the entire cast of seventeen lying down. Like many of McDowell's pieces, this one has a worm within its apple charm, a surface glitter and showiness presiding over faded glamour.

The ironic comment is never far from McDowell, even in his titling. "First Act Finale" he prepared to music from *Fledermaus* which is actually the finale from the second act. "February Fun at Bucharest" of course had nothing to do with the time of year or the locale named. There is a rococo efflorescence in his pieces, sometimes enhanced with touches of the florid personal stylistic quirks of others. In "Dance for Two Rows," he had a double line of people slowly move from one side of the performing area to the other, singing in a mournful tone "You've got to hide your love away," and from time to time one or another would step out to do an intensely personal variation that McDowell had constructed, using the characteristics of the performer. The performer would then retreat back into the moving and moaning mass.

Though in many of his pieces McDowell has used contrapuntal movements, as might be expected of a musician, he also has been acutely aware of space, and once constructed a dance designed to fill the entire performing space at Judson. It was a four-minute work performed by seventy people divided into two teams, the "whites" and the "reds." The white team moved back and forth across the balcony with long banners as the red group and two soloists, James Waring and Remy Charlip, filled the performing area at audience level in the church. It was an extravaganza—set to the length of a popular song performed by the Righteous Brothers. (Curiously, McDowell has tended to use the music of others rather than his own for his dance pieces.)

During the summer of 1963, the second year of its existence, Judson Dance Theater was offered free use of the Gramercy Arts Theater for a week. As was usual for Judson productions, the audience was admitted without charge. It was not the first time that the group had performed outside of the church, but the week at the Gramercy Arts was the most intensive barrage of new work they had put together anywhere but at Judson. Previously, small groups had performed at Woodstock or at the "American Wheels" skating rink in Washington, D.C., or in the city at the small Pocket Theater, but these were single concerts. At the Gramercy Arts, three individual programs were presented in seven days, with virtually no overlapping material in the programs.

Two of the most outstanding pieces were Elaine Summers' "Country Houses" and Beverly Schmidt's "Blossom." Summers was one of the original Judson group (she had organized the first trip to Woodstock), and in "Country Houses" she decided to utilize the entire auditorium in the production. Accordingly, performers were scattered throughout the theater, including the balcony. Ruth Emerson hung upside down from the proscenium and read texts from Oscar Wilde selected by Robert Dunn. The piece was a miniature recreation of a patio party in the country. On stage, beautiful visual tableaux were created by the performers who were in white. Other performers moved in the aisles and across the edge of the balcony, and disembodied snatches of conversation kept drifting up from various parts of the theater. The sound accompaniment of these isolated conversational phrases drifted in the air with non-sequential but highly provocative charm.

In "Blossom," Schmidt presented one of the most successful combinations of film and live performance that had been made up to that time. Schmidt was the soloist and she was also the figure in the film. The film sequences were taken in slow motion black and white in a dance studio where Schmidt did a series of technically accomplished dances. On stage she appeared three separate times in three different costumes that the film also projected behind her. The first time she had a child's play hoop and performed in a somewhat halting fashion. The second time she wore a flowing young girl's gown and showed a more accomplished presentation of the dance material. Her third entrance was made against a gaudily colored flower slide projection. Suddenly, she emerged directly from the screen, where she had been standing invisibly in a cotton shift of exactly the same pattern as was shown on the screen. She slipped out of the shift and began to dance in the same accomplished fashion as the performer on the film, which was again projected. She had progressed in visible stages into the skill of the film image. (She was later to present this piece under the title of "Duet for One.")

It was on the last of the three Gramercy Arts programs that Deborah Hay and the late Fred Herko collaborated on "Elephant Footprints in the Cheesecake-Walk"; the assemblage was of individual sections that each wanted to do and those that they decided to do together. Herko was one of the most technically accomplished dancers to appear at Judson and possessed an infectious enthusiasm for performance that few could match. He had worked in television and had appeared with John Butler's company uptown but found the atmosphere of Judson to be especially congenial to his temperament. He was flamboyant and inclined to spread his energies thinly over a broad range of activities, but when he decided to dance, his performance had a special savor. His best dance was probably "Little Gym Dance before the Wall for Dorothy" (1963). It was a short solo in which he entered the performing area in street clothes and performed a rapid, brilliant variation and exited out of the door through which he entered.

At exactly the opposite pole of technical competence from Herko was Al Kurchin, another member of the Judson group. Kurchin had little formal training but had an athletically alert body. Because of the freedom of the

Judson situation, he was able to dance well in a variety of pieces. He even had the opportunity to choreograph his own. On one of the early Judson programs, he offered "Garlands for Gladys." A series of chairs were set in an arc. Kurchin sauntered out and came to a foot-hopping halt to stare at them. This was repeated a few times until the last entrance, when wearing a naturalistic mask, he assaulted one of the more "feminine" and delicate looking chairs. The piece was a small and well-realized study of an open-faced ogler turned into a masked, anonymous assailant. His humanity only returned when he took off his mask.

One of the most enjoyable of the "camp" productions presented at Judson was "Black and White and Sparkle Plenty," created by Deborah Lee and Charles Stanley. Lee had danced with the Paul Sanasardo company and Stanley was an actor and costume designer. The piece was done in three movements, the first to a spoken text by Paul Eluard, the second to music of Fauré and Strauss, and the last to selections of popular music sung by the performers and to a taped collage of fragments of other popular tunes. The dance opened with Stanley, formally dressed in tails, walking over to a spotlight. Lee entered in a flowing, formal dress, and Stanley recited poetical sentiments while following her around with the spotlight. She danced a short series of lyrical passages and he changed the colors of the light to reflect the tone of the texts he was reciting. In the second movement, a man seething and bounding with excitement (not Stanley) ran from side to side, gathering up beads and ornaments which he draped over himself, finally slipping on a flowing Indian headdress. Completely covered with ornamentation, he ran down into the audience to distribute eucharistic wafers to its members to share his joy. The third section of the piece again had Lee and Stanley. She wore the same formal dress as in the first section, but Stanley had slipped into a sequined sheath. Both danced around the area, and a collage of sounds accompanied them. At one point, while Kate Smith was heard singing "God Bless America," Stanley broke into a frantically disciplined series of calisthenics. At the end of the piece they both slowly ascended a tall ladder from opposite sides, singing. As they reached the top, the spotlight which had been following them drew in tightly to focus on their faces and then went out. The piece was full of warmth and nervous vitality, and it offered these qualities with elaborate performing brio. It had humor and was able to spoof itself as easily as it spoofed the pretentions of film spectacle. Despite its size, it had some of the production values of large musical presentations. The lighting was clever and effective, and the costuming was chosen with a keen eye to reflect the varying moods of the dance. All in all, it was suave, hectic, and jangly, and finally outrageous *en travesti*.

At times, so simple a stage device as a shielded flashlight was used by one of the younger choreographers as the basis for a dance. Significantly, the person who used this device was William Meyer, who had assisted at

Judson in various technical capacities. Meyer decided to create a small galaxy consisting of girls carrying the flashlights in the dark. They glided around in "Star Piece" with an indifferent coolness to one another, and from time to time the darkened but not totally blacked-out stage area was lit by the fitful glow of a red flash. Considering the relatively limited space that was available to the dance, the feeling of spaciousness that it created was simply amazing. The piece conveyed a sense of the loneliness of the void.

Phoebe Neville, a miniaturist in movement conceptions, has also directed her attention to the use of stage properties. In "Termination," she wore a gas mask and a long Renaissance style robe and quietly expired. Across a darkened stage in "Terrible," she and three other hooded figures moved slowly and heavily, barely illuminated in pencil-thin shafts of light, accompanied by Tibetan monks' chanting. In another dance, Neville painted large staring eyes on the surface of her drooped eyelids and performed a variation that led her trembling to the threshold of a doorway that suggested a passage to another world. In a fit of humor in "Mandolin Dance," she and two other dancers leapt up and down repeatedly in place to the mandolin music in Prokofiev's *Romeo and Juliet*. Neville has a somewhat Oriental approach to dance, relying on long pauses and small-scaled movement to make her effects rather than on an extravagance of motion. Her dances grow in interest after the initial strangeness of their settings are accepted.

Humor was one of the ways in which the newer choreographers came to terms with the conventions of the past. It was a way of pointing out the inadequacies of the tenets of historic modern dance, held by a previous generation. David Gordon and Valda Setterfield were two of the most amiable saboteurs. Gordon choreographed a string of works for Setterfield and himself in which they showed the stylistic skill of old music-hall comedians. Both had worked with James Waring prior to the emergence of the Judson Dance Theater. They had been exposed to the bizarre ambivalences that Waring combines in his work, and the shifts in it between performance posture and "civilian" relaxation. After the early years of Judson, Gordon ceased choreographing and Setterfield went on to become a member of the Merce Cunningham company. Gordon appears infrequently as a performer and only with the Yvonne Rainer company. Both he and Setterfield are strong technical dancers and have a wickedly perceptive wit.

During the early years of Judson (1962–1964), they provided some of the most consistently pointed comments on other styles of dancing and behavior. "Fragments" was a choreographic look at the ruins of humanity in some horribly projected future. A husband and wife behaved like fitfully friendly automata. They were covered in silver makeup and costume, and lived their lives, such as they were, in front of a television set which was constantly on. The set was the focus of their living room, and they retired to another section of the performing area away from it only to rest. The characters expressed themselves in unconnected spasms of movement and gesture that transpired in front of the television set. They engaged in skits of movement that included a ventriloquist and dummy, a bit of elegant erotic movement, some tumbling, and a staged wrestling match (which included a three count to insure a secure "pin"). All was bathed in the effluence of sound and image being discharged from the television set. After each brief engagement, the couple appealed to the audience with gestures like those of performers after a particularly successful acrobatic turn. The piece was a hilarious tragedy.

In "Random Breakfast," Gordon and Setterfield again assembled the shards of situations into a mosaic of mimicry. The work contained six sections, one of which was a flamboyant striptease by Setterfield which ended with her flouncing off, attempting to maintain dignity in a fringed G-string. In another section, Gordon spoke earnestly to the audience about how to construct a dance that would please audiences while he performed the movements he was explaining. He was solicitous in his discourse and did not want to leave out anything that might be expected by an audience, including a repeated variation for familiarity, a bit of anxiety, and connecting runs between thematic treatments. The presentation was caustically witty and did not miss any of historic modern dance's cherished clichés. Setterfield did a section in which she portrayed a nun happily doing little tasks with a light heart and a trippingly spritely run. After she had done all of her chores dutifully, she exploded in a torrent of four-letter words and smashed herself in the face with a cake. For the finale, Gordon wore a top hat and did a mime section of the late Judy Garland as Garland's voice was heard singing "Over the Rainbow." The contrasts between sound, the spoken word, and silence, and between the different characters of the nun and the stripper, were carefully placed to draw the maximum effect. It was one of Gordon's most successful pieces.

Other performers who had previously worked with James Waring displayed a similar sense of the ridiculous, and each displayed it with individual accents. David Vaughan portrayed the touring balletic has-been in "Chrysanthemum Waltz: Secrets." In the piece he partnered Marian Sarach with great presentational esprit and little technical flair, as would befit the slightly gone-to-seed dancer. Arlene Rothlein, another associate of Waring, presented several accomplished solos at Judson, one of which, "Morning Raga with Yellow Chair," had a special charm. Rothlein was gifted in her titling as well, offering such intriguing fare as "Enceinte for Isadora" and "It Seemed to Me There Was Dust in My Garden and Grass in My Room."

Of all the dancers who offered works that partook of a combination of the humorous and the serious, none seemed so closely in tune with the spirit of James Waring as did Aileen Passloff. She had worked steadily with Waring before Judson existed, and in the course of her career has produced a substantial body of dances. Yvonne Rainer mentioned that Passloff was an

David Gordon and Valda Setterfeld in *Fragments*, Judson Memorial Church, April 28, 1964. Photo by Al Giese

influence on her dancing career and others appear to have drawn from her combinations of period styles.

As a performer, Passloff has great presentational skill and a wonderfully noble face which she often uses to show aloof detachment, only to slip into a grin or a leer to turn the spell around entirely. Passloff is in love with the past but aware of her life in the present, and her synthesis of the two provides much of the motive drive for her dances. She has a fondness for ballet and a keen appreciation of current dance, and often combines elements of them both in a work. She has included danced passages in her pieces that have been performed in high heels, tap shoes, or on roller skates. Her finest works always seem to be those in which she examined the behavior of two or three people at a balance point in decision.

Passloff delights in such things as doing six different style dances to music drawn from as many composers. She had explored the dual aspects of woman as lady and wanton with special vigor in "Bench Dance," which subtly combined two dancers and two benches. Lucinda Childs was the slightly removed and dignified female with a sedate bench and Yvonne Rainer flipped and slipped around her flame-red bench with lusty vigor. In "Strelitzia," Passloff set two dancers going in a forest scene, showing the relations between dumb creatures acting in the zone between molecular randomness and purposeful drive. Occasionally a dance with a large number of elements will slip out of her creative control and dissolve into its component parts, some of which nonetheless remain of extreme interest.

Some of the more unusual presentations of dance material were pieces prepared by Joseph Schlichter, who sometimes chose to work with plastic sheeting. The dominant impression of his pieces is a weighty intensity. During one dance, Schlichter appeared nude in a hollow plastic sheeting cube roughly as large as the stage area. The variation of the dance consisted of Schlichter throwing himself into puddles of red, white, and blue paint on the stage until he resembled a patriotically daubed primate. In "From 1 to 10 to 7" he placed himself behind a transparent plastic sheet which isolated him from the audience. He was wrapped all over with various colored rubber strips. He extended his arms and flattened himself against the sheet of clear plastic facing the audience. A dark-clothed anonymous figure traced his outline on the plastic. When the tracing was finished, Schlichter moved off to perform a series of variations with his outline left facing the audience. The dark figure padded around after Schlichter and picked off bits and pieces of the rubber stripping. At one point, he pounced unexpectedly and knocked Schlichter to the floor, but then released him. Schlichter commenced his lonely variation again, and the shadowy destructive figure began his slow picking again. In watching the process, it was obvious that all of the discretion was in the latter's hands and that the figure in rubber just had to endure until there is nothing left to pick, after which there will be only the hollow outline. Schlichter has not been a prolific choreographer and in recent years has not presented any new work.

As the creative ripples expanded outward from Judson, many other novel presentations of dances were tried. Carolyn Brown in "Balloon" created a duet for a boy and a girl in front of a large weather balloon on which there was projected a series of films. The balloon was tethered to occupy the space slightly above and behind the dancers, creating a cloud of film images over them. Don Redlich made interesting use of his own filmed image in "Dance for One Figure, Four Objects and Film Sequences." In it, Redlich contrasted the actual performing space on stage for himself with the vistas afforded to him in the portions that were filmed down long corridors.

Barbara Roan, a graduate of the Erick Hawkins company, began choreographing her own works using props in an enigmatic but potent manner, taking such everyday actions as throwing darts into a board and blending such actions in with the flow of the dance. Toby Armour, after working at Judson for a number of years, moved to Boston and continued to choreograph in the mood of amiable incongruity which she had made distinctly her own. Dan Wagoner, a featured dancer with the Paul Taylor company, left the latter's company to pursue his own career, and while he retained the basic movement vocabulary of the company, he manipulated it to his own special needs. One of his most effective works was "Brambles," in which he did a series of fluid variations against a "'background" of imaginary posts, musical tones, and "pictures" (all of which were verbally described by poet George Montgomery in pauses between the sections). Murray Louis, who has worked closely with Alwin Nikolais, created a substantial body of work, among which his imaginative "Junk Dances" occupies a prominent place. It is set amidst the scraps of city living— tattered posters and tenement vistas. The couple who occupy this urban scrap heap claw intriguingly at each other's psychic barriers, and the man finally ends up covered with blinking lights and decorated with empty cartons in a travesty of a Christmas tree.

Laura Foreman has eased into the area of experimentation carefully rather than thrusting herself willy-nilly into its heady atmosphere, but once arrived she has been imaginative in mixing her media. In addition to preparing her own work, she has devoted more than equal time to creating a working atmosphere for other choreographers in "Choreoconcerts." If for nothing else, she could be commended for bringing modern dance back to The New School for Social Research in New York, an early bastion of the historic generation, that tended to ignore dance in recent years. But it is as her own choreographer rather than as another's advocate that she commands interest. Foreman has steadily increased her use of multi-media elements, handling such diverse elements as singers, film projections, and slides in almost any conceivable space she encounters, from a gymnasium to a church. The message is usually a form of baffled nostalgia in which the present is harshly contrasted with the past—remote or immediate. For Foreman, the times are out of joint, and the way it is best demonstrated is through the instant replay of society's electronic spoor of video and sound tape contrasted with live performers in works like "A Time," "Study," or "glass and shadows." She refrains from any firm conclusions, but through disharmonious contrasts asks interesting and disturbing questions about the relevance and pertinence of day-to-day events in the trajectory of ordinary life.

A charming child of nature is James Cunningham, who resembles a figure out of an infant's nursery book: bizarre, colorful, and, at the same time, unexpectedly effective in his naïve unorthodoxy. Cunningham has a formidable performing élan and possesses an acrobatically commanding skill. It hardly matters what type of solo material he prepares for himself, since his special combination of insouciance and elastic resilience usually suffices to make the piece workable. He delights in mixing together as many elements as possible, incorporating film, slides, music of the widest diversity, props of incredible variety, and passages of conversational monologue, not to mention ballroom dance and simple running. He has worked with as few as two people, as in his duet "Lauren's Dream: October 1969," and as many as nearly a hundred in "The Junior Birdsmen." Cunningham's appeal is immediate and bubbly; he uses instant silliness to make long-term sense. Some of his pieces fail to coalesce because of their incompatible mix of elements, but one has the feeling that, like fairy-tale personages, he conceals a home truth beneath the glittering frivolity and fantasy.

It would be impossible to mention all of the experimental work carried out by dancers freed from the chain of naturalistic incident and narrative continuity, but adaptations of their work permeate nearly all of the theatrical world. What was somewhat outlandish has become somewhat voguish in its eager assimilation by popular producers. The suitability of the novel forms to conventional uses only confirms the basic accuracy and responsiveness to contemporary needs of the original impulse.

Some Thoughts
After the Revolution

It is somewhat ironic that every major university in the country now has a theater in which modern dancers can appear but that these now are theaters in which a substantial number of modern dancers do not want to be seen. The historic modern dance generation—the generation of Martha Graham—which had fought to escape from the gymnasium setting in which it had been forced to appear, won its battle. It escaped from the gymnasiums, redolent with the atmosphere of physical culture, to the theaters, with their non-muscular appeal of high culture. The historic modern dance generation was socially minded, concerned with questions of respectability, and intent on proving that it was as worthy of recognition as was ballet. If, by definition, it could not have the balletic pedigree of nobility then at least it could demonstrate the breeding of the mind that is conveyed by being located in the houses of the intellect, the universities. Modern dance achieved respectability in an amazingly short time and, even more, became the most exciting form of theater ever created out of the American experience. It was obvious to anyone who attended theater that in modern dance a form of performing electricity was operative in the United States that was young, dynamic, questing, and communicative. Historic modern dance was alert to the social movements that were taking place in the society—America of the 1930's—into which it had matured. Modern dance was monumental, modern dance was concerned with "good music," modern dance had no patience with the dregs and fripperies of romanticism, modern dance was earnest, modern dance had little time for play, modern dance was serious. Modern dance was brilliantly adapted to the aspirations of an ideological age. And modern dance was dead on its feet somewhere in the early 1940's.

After the early 1940's, Martha Graham, who virtually invented historic modern dance singlehandedly, worked on, being intermittently fruitful, in the vein that she had developed. She continued to explore the ways of epic theater far beyond the appropriateness of such theater and the social premises to which it related. Those of lesser talent fell by the wayside and produced work that was old upon its birth. Graham endured in the way that original talents have always endured: by instinct, not by rules. But in the early 1940's, it had become increasingly obvious that modern dance needed a radical transformation—it needed to be personalized, to accommodate to the interests of the individual as broadly as possible and not restrict him in a formal system. The old battles had been won, but the generation that won the fruits of the victory was shackled by the victory. The generation that followed wanted to move naturally and not to posture.

It no longer seemed attractive to make up dances that were about things other than themselves. To do so was a manner of falsification and, additionally, was liable to be misunderstood as poetic metaphor often is. Ideology was the handmaiden of stories, and, to the new generation, the ideology of the 1930's was remote whereas movement was compellingly immediate. It saw story-telling as a form of illusionism that was about narrative flow rather than the fact of moving. To this generation, moving itself had a great many interesting characteristics that had not been examined choreographically. The art of dancing was in fact a closely held family secret among those who were involved in taking dance class or appearing professionally. The newer choreographers wanted audiences to see that the physical act of moving could be beautiful without having to represent anything other than its own precise trajectory, weight, modulation, and duration. Telling stories was a subtle form of pretense which attempted to turn the simple motor mechanics of the body into dramatic mime. For a generation that had not been involved in the roil of ideology, straightforward dance relationships were the more central interest.

Drama, in the sense of narrative continuity, was first dropped by Merce Cunningham to free the dancer for a more methodical and searching examination of the craft of dancing. It was the start of a period of self-analysis that was pursued by modern dance in a myriad of ways after Cunningham's breakthrough. Everything was questioned and broken into its component parts, and many parts, once thought essential, were discarded.

In an effort to determine whether dance was restricted only to those who had submitted themselves to a special discipline, dances were made with people who did not have any formal training. As dancers well knew, the very act of going to a dance class brought with it a built-in philosophical attitude. Anyone who perseveres in the study of dance has drummed into the muscles an attitude toward himself through the carriage of the body that is an implicit reflection of how the society imagines itself. Just as ballet preserved and elaborated the carriage of nobility, historic modern dance

Yvonne Rainer in Carolee Schneeman's *Newspaper Event*, Judson Memorial Church,
January 29, 1963

imposed emotional tensions on the body of the dancer. To be freed of technique then became for some contemporary modern dance choreographers a positive good rather than a capricious or lazy whim, for to be free of technique meant to be free of certain imposed tensions. The freedom from technique made possible the creation of dance structures that did not incorporate a preordained emotional set for the performers.

Traditionally, movement in dance had been generated from the trained dancer in action. Some choreographers began to look outside the classroom at the trained bodies of athletes as a possible source of movement invention. Others looked at people walking and performing ordinary tasks. It became interesting for the new choreographers to examine the mechanics of the body engaged in work or play to create dances in a "found" way rather than to determine all of the movements all of the time. All of these new compositional devices were designed to allow the maximum amount of freedom to the dance and not to impose schools of movement upon performers. It was a direct counter-action to the structured formalism that had been the main thrust of modern dance in the 1930's.

The newer choreographers rejected the logic of the intellect in favor of a more instinctive handling of materials. Chance, play, and random activity were the expressions of a freer but less controllable form of determination. The result was a strong "personalization" of dance which was not directed to social or political ends but, in essence, to a celebration of existence from moment to moment.

Other experiments were made to test the qualities of movement and even to test whether movement was necessary at all. For audiences habituated to a powerful stream of dance energy being poured at them from the performer, the sight of a man sitting on a chair doing little and calling it "dance" was difficult to comprehend. It was even more difficult to comprehend exactly how much work was required on the part of the dancer to get himself to stand still. But the fact is that being immobilized by circumstance is a vastly different thing from attempting to maintain tranquil stillness facing an audience.

It became clear that stillness was important. The act of calming one's own body serves to diminish the dynamics of the audience expectations if the audience is at all receptive. The physical quietness produces an attention to detail that might ordinarily have been missed. The experience for the viewer is like looking at the contours of a starkly simple Chinese vase as compared to a baroque urn. In many of the dances that have been made based on minute body alterations, there is also a heightened awareness of the moment-to-moment sense of time as well as a changed spatial focus. That which might have been overlooked is regarded attentively for its own sake. Such presentations reflect a concern with isolating component elements which is better known in Eastern societies than in Western theater. This concentration of attention serves at times, when well used, to create a semi-hypnotic fascination which gradually induces a sense of quietude and contemplation of things for themselves. Dances of minute movement create a form of theater that calls for a type of patience that has to be cultivated and is not normally indigenous to the United States, where the expression of raw energy tends to obscure the parts in favor of the overall flow.

Various technical devices were used at times to show the activity of the apparently still body to the audience. In a simple but effective lighting design, the shadows of the dancers were thrown upon a cyclorama so that the small movements could be seen quite clearly (Rudy Perez, "Loading Zone"). In a more elaborate manner, the face of a performer was shown on a magnified television screen as he sat and stared into the closed-circuit camera (Alex Hay, "Grass Field"). Attention was drawn to facial expression in a variety of ways, including the creation of a movement score for the facial muscles quite independent of any other body functioning (Steve Paxton, "Jag Ville Gorna Telefonera"). This invention was an extreme expression of the movement-questioning in which modern dance was engaged.

The entire exploration of movement stemmed from the basic question of why any movement has to follow from or lead into another. Traditional technique is based on the idea that a movement in any part of the body produces a counter movement in another part of the body, and that the harmonious blending of these is dancing. Dancers of the most recent dance school wondered what would happen if they did not automatically perform the counter movement but instead attempted to bypass it and conventional wisdom and perform another movement. The results in some cases were startling, were somewhat conventional in others, and were impossible to sustain in yet others. In these efforts, much of the change took place in the body of the dancer, and it was not apparent to the observer exactly how difficult it was to maintain balance and energy output in some of the simplest-appearing postures. The dancers, in any case, learned much about the basics of the craft that were not included in the dance courses they had taken. Many concluded that simple awareness and concern with the body's natural movements was the basic requirement for dancing, that the enjoyment of and respect for the body were the keystones of dancing, and not any rigidly imposed formula of training. It was a radical shift in thinking for a technique-conscious art, but it was choreographic thinking, and the essence of modern dance is choreography and not technique.

Ballet is defined in terms of technique and would not exist without it. It manages to exist quite happily for long periods of time, performing technical combinations that have little but virtuosity to commend them. In contrast, the theater dance form known as modern dance would disappear into music visualization or mass gymnastics without a steady infusion of choreographic intelligence. There is no technique to modern dance in the sense that ballet has technique. Modern dance consists of intelligent approaches to movement, the approaches designed to create significant form. It is theatrical if it wishes to appear in a theater or not theatrical if it wishes to appear in a gymnasium, but it is always involved with formal considerations. The design of the dance is what modern dance is about, and the physicality of the dancers is the means it chooses to achieve its ends. Thus, the newer choreographers created a blizzard of dance forms, none of which seemed to have anything to do with the concerns of their elders.

Music and its component elements came under the same scrutiny as the act of moving. It was questioned as the "natural" accompaniment to dance. The function of music for most dancers had been a rhythmic ordering of time, to which the dancers accommodated movement more or less well. Trained dancers, even those in the ballet world, had questioned the necessity of music in the 1930's. Martha Graham made one attempt to choreograph in silence, but was displeased with the result and never bothered further with the experiment. Serge Lifar of the Paris Opéra Ballet worked with the concept of choreography as being the controlling part of dance and created several ballets in silence, to which he appended a rhythmic drum accompaniment. He even went so far as to designate his function as being a "choreauteur" rather than choreographer—in the sense of an arranger of dances to music. Central European expressionist dance had explored the idea of the self-accompanied dance using a variety of percussive instruments, but most of the experimenters wanted the sound and the dance to mesh ultimately in a rhythmic fashion. One has to go back to the Italian futurist writers and painters of the World War One era to encounter the conception of sound being used non-rhythmically as aural decor for a dance. None of the productions that the futurist dance manifesto described were ever publicly realized, but the descriptions of the pieces included mechanical noises whose varying intensities would have an emotional impact on the audience and were to coexist but not influence the movements of the dancer. (The description also cited elements of non-dance trained movement.) The one actual piece that resulted from the flow of such ideas was a musical theater spectacle arranged by Serge Diaghilev, then resident in Italy. It consisted of a dance without dancers in which decor, movement, and light play were the dynamic elements, and to which the "Fireworks" music of Stravinsky was played as an accompaniment. The ideas were to wait for another three decades before being taken up as a serious part of dance.

Music for the newer choreographer was considered along non-dependent lines and anything aural that happened while a person was dancing was accepted. Music did not need to be prepared especially in order to be performed during a dance, nor did it even have to be reproducible in exactly the same way from one performance of a dance to another. Music thus conceived could be the normal sounds that would occur in any space occupied by several hundred or several dozen people—and in some instances it was. Dancers invited audiences to make sounds that were as simple as rustling a program or clearing their throats at certain sections of a dance. Gus Solomons, Jr.'s, work is an example.

On one occasion, Solomons invited the audience to ask questions during the course of a solo. These questions were not answered by the performer, but their nature made the dance take on various emotional colorations. One person asked about the carriage of the torso, and the entire audience, it seemed, immediately focused on the physicality of the dancer. Another asked a question about what the dance meant, and attention focused on the choreographic patterns in the work. The unanswered questions were a subtle way of demonstrating how, though the movement remains the same, the accompanying sound has a great deal to do with the way the movement is perceived. In another concert in which there were a series of concurrent films shown in adjoining rooms, the sounds of the dancers laughing or breathing hard, or the snatches of popular music used as the score, served the same function of changing the perception of the dance and, in this case, the film. The result is akin to that achieved by turning down the television volume and switching on another sound source to replace the program's sound track. The combination produces incongruities, sometimes dramatic and sometimes humorous, but in either instance it changes in a most imaginative way the image being perceived.

The old concept of the self-accompanied dance, which previous dancers had accomplished by means of handheld percussive instruments, was applied in modern dance electronically with the use of contact microphones taped to the body of the dancer (Alex Hay is one example, Yvonne Rainer another). The amplified sounds of the body's own articulations then became the music that accompanied it. Other dancers spoke about what they were doing as they did it and that became the "music" of the dance. At other times, dancers simply made noises, such as a shout or even a scream, to accompany the movement that they were engaged in. Every one of these sounds, whether an intelligible spoken word or an inarticulate scream, colored the movement—which was one of the functions that traditional music had always carried out.

The rhythm of music was no longer used exclusively by dancers as a base upon which to move. Counting became its substitute. The remarkable memory of the ordinary dancer is demonstrated by the amount and complexity of the counting that is done during the course of a dance. (A member of the Merce Cunningham company literally has the equivalent of a dozen symphonies committed to memory during a season of repertory. It would be the rare musician who could make the same claim.) Many choreographers decided not to use music or sound in any form at all. It did not contribute anything to the quality of movement as far as they were concerned but rather detracted from it by competing with the movement for the audience's attention. These dancers and choreographers rehearse in silence and perform in silence. A perfect example of the independence of choreography from its parallel music score was shown at a performance in 1969 of the Merce Cunningham piece "Canfield." Because of union conflicts, a strike prevented the musicians from performing the score, but the company went on and danced the piece with no hesitancy or diminution of dance impulse. It is known that Cunningham never uses musical accompaniment in creating a new work and choreographs in silence, but it sometimes takes a public incident, such as the musicians' strike, to convince a somewhat skeptical public, which has been nurtured in the idea of music and dance being inseparable.

Independence of the contributing elements was chosen as the basic operating procedure of modern dance in order to discover just how closely and in what ways the various elements of a dance were linked together. If dance could do without music and technique, could it also do without rehearsal? If it could do without elaborate lighting designs, could it do without visible light of any kind? If it could do without decor, could it do without costume? If it could do without any of these, could it do without dancers? The answer to the latter was the only "No!" Some attempts were made to create dances verbally or by printed suggestions so that audiences would conjure up their own movement sequences. But although these "concept" choreographies were interesting, they were exceedingly frail in the physical world of dance.

While the scope of dance had been vitally enlarged by the rigorous pruning of elements, dance as such had acquired a certain rag-tag air. The revolution of the newer choreographers was created outside of the theatrical system and outside any source of standard funding. There was simply no place for the younger contemporary dancer or choreographer to go for money. Technique-oriented schools could not in conscience meet their requests and theatrically oriented foundations were unable to justify to themselves expenditures to assist modern dance. The form of patronage that became most common for the dancers was the patronage supplied by artists and art patrons, with a strong assist from various churches that were community-minded and wished to present community projects.

The ecclesiastical performing areas were tax free and so prohibited from charging an admission fee. Thus the dancers for the most part became dependent on voluntary contributions from their audiences, which rarely met the rudimentary costs of production. Dancers, of course, were not paid, a fact that contributed to a camaraderie of poverty and solidified the looseness of the movement. Patronage on a personal basis or from art museums became the only regular source of income for many.

The art world, which was in the throes of a series of continuing artistic revolutions, was particularly sympathetic to the experimentation of the dancers and choreographers who were working in other than traditional ways. Many artists, as we have seen, were themselves interested in performance. At first, the interest was concentrated in dramatic incidents such as the "happenings," but they later concentrated on the movement and manipulative aspects of dance forms more closely. The high point of such artistic interest culminated in the "1st New York Theater Rally," jointly assembled by a dancer (Steve Paxton) and an art historian and scholar (the late Alan Solomon).

Given the lack of funds, the maintenance of a company was an economic burden that most of the choreographers could not afford, and so they devised various ways of working without much money. A form of "services" barter was developed in which dancers danced in each other's works on a reasonably reciprocal basis. Another means of cutting costs was the development of a group of performers who were not technically trained and who would work with a choreographer for the pleasure of participating in the dance-stage experience. Performances were generally held in non-fee-paying locales, such as the half-dozen churches in New York that were sympathetic to dance, or in outdoor locations for which only municipal permission was necessary. Community centers would often permit performances in a gymnasium without a fee, and artists, along with gallery owners, were willing to allow loft performances without a fee. Since costuming was often rehearsal clothes or casual street wear, the expenses for these items were kept at a minimum. Since music in the copyright, and therefore fee-paying state, was not often used, this expense was virtually eliminated. Once the money requirements were reduced to the lowest level, it became apparent that work could proceed in the face of general critical hostility from the dance world. What money there was originated mainly from patrons in the art world, and they liked what they saw.

After the dancers had rigorously examined all of the tenets of the artistic discipline in which they had grown up, they turned their attention to the audience which provided the sounding board for their work. The dancers attempted to change the traditional behavioral habits of the audience. Some of the most rigorous performance strictures were dictated by the physical construction of the theaters in which dancers had to appear. Professional theaters, like professional performing disciplines, embody certain philosophical attitudes in their very construction. One has only to think of the illusional expectations aroused in an audience by the knowledge that sets can be lifted directly off the stage and disappear in the "flies" above, or of the anticipation that wings arouse for subtly timed entrances and exits onto the performing area, to understand what these attitudes are. The challenge presented by the audience arose both from the physical plant and from the viewing habits that the traditional plant had supported.

The first change made by modern dance was in the physical environment of the dance. The audience found itself closely associated with the performers and not separated from them by the gulf of the orchestra pit. Within theaters where the pit existed, dancers attempted with varying success to come out to the audience in unorthodox ways. They staged parts of the dance in portions of the house that were ordinarily considered nonperformance areas or, conversely, invited the audience to sit on stage as might be done for a musical recital. The change in focus caused anxiety among some members of the audience, but many found it pleasant to see the dancers from a more intimate distance. To still others, the assault that was being made on convention was interpreted as a personal attack and was resisted vocally and, sometimes, physically by shoving or blocking performers.

When appearing in locations that were not bounded by the convention of the proscenium arch, dancers simply allowed the audience members to flow around the performance area and find their own desired location for viewing. Performances were sometimes structured so that the dance proceeded at several locations at the same time, and the audience was free to remain in one place or stroll to the various areas and see what other parts of the dance looked like. At times the audience was free to remain at any one spot for as long as it desired. At other times, the audience discovered that some of the performers were seated among them and that at some point the performers would leave the audience sector to join the other dancers. In other performances, especially those held in art museums, the audience would be viewing the dancers across long vistas and turn to discover another group quietly dancing only a few feet away. Dancers would often split up into small groups, each performing a discrete unit of the entire dance structure, the whole of which the audiences could collect and assemble for themselves.

A great deal of responsibility was placed on the interest of the audience. The dance was not simply presented to the members of an audience nor were they compelled to view it all in any sequential way. The emphasis was on a participational association with the performers. Audiences on occasion were allowed to suggest movements to the dancers, which they in turn would perform as well as they could. In some dances of this sort, after a short period of observation, many members of the audience could sense the drift of a variation and request interesting developments of it in terms of direction or complexity. The audience was allowed to see exactly how a dance developed and sometimes was even invited to participate if its members were so inclined.

But nothing was compulsory. Some of these experimental dances in public places enjoyed a great success, while others were swallowed unflatteringly by the crowds that came to see them. In every case, however, the audience had an opportunity to enjoy an uncustomary freedom.

If anything has characterized the dance revolution of the 1960's, it has been freedom—the freedom to move in new and unaccustomed ways in places that have been excluded from conventional theater dance. The newer choreographers have reached out to establish contact with audiences by any means that they thought would succeed. The dance world into which they were born had been rigidly structured to preserve a gulf between performer and spectator, each proceeding, it seemed to the younger choreographers, on a private, insulated course that did not allow for the freedom of exchange that they considered a characteristic of theater. In their opinion, the dance experience of audiences was beginning to be removed from the world of reality. An audience that needed the satisfactions of intellectual social consciousness in another generation now needed a direct physical proximity to satisfy its hunger for reality.

The older conventions of the theater were the conventions of an enlightened elite. The newer ones were more egalitarian and a bit less tidy. The difference was like the difference between the stylized amphitheater productions of the ancient Greeks, with their fundamental unities, and the roisterous Elizabethan theater.

The progenitor of the revolution that produced contemporary modern dance, Merce Cunningham, straddles the world of the traditional and the world of the new with surpassing ease. The generation that followed him, bursting forth in the summer of 1962 with a series of concerts at Judson Church, has not attempted to. Many of those who participated briefly in early experimental programs have discontinued performing careers or have entered other forms of theater life. A dedicated nucleus has continued working wherever it was possible, attracting vigorous new talents to the stream of dancing that is now the main current of modern dance.

Modern dance has entered a new phase of self-conscious exploration. The stories of a socially conscious age have been preserved now only in the work of some black choreographers who find the passionately stressed lines of the historic modern dance movement congenial. These choreographers are as aware of social inequities as was the second modern dance generation, and the strain and the anguish-stressed lines of this generation's choreographic movement are highly useful to artists attempting to create political action. But the dance generation that succeeded historic modern dance finds that it is more involved with the processes of producing an effect than with the effect itself. It is involved with the values of personal, concrete experience rather than with the pieties of traditional theatrical "frissons." Historic modern dance won the battles of the theater, and contemporary modern dance is directing its energies to what can be called the motional problems of life.

Index

NOTE: Titles of dances are indexed alphabetically (not by choreographer) and italicized so they may be easily differentiated from other entries. *A Space Ruckus* is indexed as *Space Ruckus, A*.